THIS
BRIGHT
DAY

THIS BRIGHT DAY

AN AUTOBIOGRAPHY

by LEHMAN ENGEL

Sleep not, dream not; this bright day
Will not, cannot, last for aye.

—Emily Brontë

MACMILLAN PUBLISHING CO., INC.
NEW YORK

Copyright © 1974 by Lehman Engel

Macmillan Publishing Co., Inc.
866 Third Avenue, New York, N.Y. 10022
Collier-Macmillan Canada Ltd.

LIBRARY OF CONGRESS CATALOGING IN PUBLICATION DATA

Engel, Lehman, 1910-
   This bright day.

   Autobiographical.
   1. Musicians—Correspondence, reminiscences,
      etc.
I. Title.
ML410.E56A3   782.8′1′0924 [B]   73-8352
ISBN 0-02-536110-4

FIRST PRINTING 1974

Printed in the United States of America

To Celeste, Phyllis, and Beatrice
and
My Loving Friends

IN THE PREFACE to Robert Craft's *Stravinsky*, the author makes an important point which I would like to paraphrase here. "Didn't Stravinsky know any ordinary people?" one critic has asked, and perhaps these pages do contain an overdose of celebrities. (They do *not* contain the ——s, the Stravinsky's closest friends.) However that may be, I lack the novelist's talent that can make "ordinary" people interesting; whereas the extraordinary ones take care of themselves, with little help from me.

Contents

Contents

Acknowledgments

I would like to acknowledge valuable suggestions offered by Eudora Welty, the late S. N. Behrman and the late Margaret Webster, who read this manuscript totally or in part. Also family information provided by Frances Loeb. I am further indebted to George Tyler and Vivian Perlis for permission to reproduce two letters from Charles Ives, to Fred Plaut and Arnold Weissberger for the use of photographs, and to Mrs. Sean O'Casey for allowing me to quote from a letter written by her husband. Also Ray Roberts, my editor. I also want to acknowledge the invaluable help of Robert Bishop, James Quinlivan, and scores of others who, over a period of thirty years, have helped to prepare this manuscript.

Preface

A DOOR AT THE REAR of the house led out on a flagstone terrace. The trunks of the high old trees that defined the limits of the terrace were largely concealed by enormous azalea bushes that were almost solid masses of purple, red, pink, and white blossoms. Like Mississippi, I thought. I walked left and down a few steps where, spread out before me, there was an immense formal garden. At its far end, a row of nearly black cypress trees framed the multicolored flowers and flowering vines that lay before it in immaculate designs. The odors of each kind of blossom assailed and defined: roses, peonies, wisteria, daisies, and many more—just as in Mississippi. The intense heat of noon was another, though less gentle, reminder.

I was at Villa I Tatti—the celebrated home of Bernard Berenson —because Sam Behrman and Eudora Welty had written letters introducing me to the old man and asking him to receive me when I reached Florence. I had telephoned the day before and Miss Nicky (Mariano) had said that Berenson was in bed with a painful back ailment that would prevent his seeing me, but I was nevertheless cordially invited to visit Villa I Tatti and be shown the art, the library, and the garden.

As we stood in the midst of the garden, enveloped in colors and fragrances, an excited Italian maid invaded the quiet orderliness with out-of-breath phrases, meaningless to me. The young secretary, who until then had remained discreetly silent, was suddenly propelled into motion: Mr. Berenson was feeling better and would like me brought to him.

Why had it so often happened in the garden?

The fragrances, the colors, the heat, nostalgia, disquietude, strangely surrounded by peace.

For had there not been the garden in my childhood, where at sunset I had listened to the brittle song of crickets, felt the intimacy of a quiet world protected by the aura of love left me there so long ago by my grandmother . . . ?

THIS
BRIGHT
DAY

1: Genesis

Tʜᴇ sᴜᴍᴍᴇʀ ᴅᴀʏs were beautiful and hot; the winter, penetrating and damp. I can remember almost every minute since I was two, everyone we said "Good Morning!" to. (This was everybody.)

Grandpa Lehman—a small, sensitive man, with a rolling black moustache and tight curly hair—had left Alsace in his early twenties to escape military service and had come to Madison Station in Mississippi. He had arrived alone and close on the devastating heels of General Sherman.

Although the South was poor, Grandpa saw in it a certain promise. He had not been there long when he made the acquaintance of Celestine Wolff, who had come from Paris to visit her brother in Jackson, about fifteen miles away. She was little and aristocratic, drank essence of orange water for indigestion, and boiled easily into a temper. She brought with her across the ocean a large volume of *Roses* by Redouté filled with exquisitely colored lithographs, and a pale-green square sugar bowl with matching cream pitcher made by Josiah Wedgwood. Although she was ten years older than Grandpa, they were married and were always in love.

The day Grandpa arrived at Madison Station with his bride was long remembered by Aaron and Celestine Lehman, although it was probably forgotten by their neighbors who became their friends. For that day marked the first sight anyone had ever had of a female Jew. When Grandma stepped down from the train into Grandpa's arms, the single dusty road, Madison Station's main street, was deserted. All doors were closed, all window blinds drawn. Suspicious eyes peered out between the slats of shutters as Aaron led his bride home to a single room behind his general store.

They did not remain in Madison long but moved to Jackson, the state's capital, on the bluff of the muddy, willow-draped Pearl. There Aaron opened a general store with living quarters behind. In eight years, there were five children. Lee was the first, Isadore next. Then came the three girls—Beatrice (called "Trixie" or "Tatsie"), Juliette (my mother), and Flo.

Aaron never accumulated any money; yet in a short and transplanted life, speaking English with a French accent, representing Judaism—but without orthodoxy—in a Christian world, he was elected to the city school board, founded a home for old ladies, was president of Beth Israel Synagogue, and was respected as one of the first citizens of the capital city.

For many years the Lehman family continued to live in back of the store, which sold everything: vegetables, calico, nails, feed, patent medicines, penny candy, shoes, and licorice, jewelry, and plows. Stores like Grandpa's had a cool spicy odor in summer and retained their pleasantness when warmed against the winter damp.

More than selling went on in that store—the customers (black and white) were friends. Most of them, from farms in the usually impoverished countryside, came into town on Saturday, making it a busy day for Grandpa and his family. Everyone helped: Lee and Isy carried bags of feed and flour to the waiting wagons. Juliette sold imitation jewelry at a small table on the sidewalk. (She herself wore tiny gold earrings that dangled from pierced earlobes.) Grandma waited on shoppers, but also discussed personal things. Trixie cooked the meals. Flo played as children will—under the feet of everyone.

Ethel, a colored woman, brought butter and milk from the country and bouquets of flowers wrapped loosely in wads of wet newspaper. In its time, honeysuckle fell out of the corners of the news pages and later roses, gardenias (which we called "cape jessamine"), yellow tiger lilies, and wild violets. Although Ethel knew that Mrs. Lehman loved flowers, she didn't know that the heavy scent of gardenia and narcissus nauseated her. For the butter and

The five Lehman children. *Rear, left to right*: Lee, Beatrice (Tatsie), and Isy; *front*: Juliette (Mama) and Flo (*seated*).

The Lehman family, circa 1900, with Grandma's cousin Maurice ("C'n Mo")
Wolff. *Standing, left to right*: Cousin Mo and Uncle Isy; *seated, left to right*:
Beatrice (Tatsie), Grandpa, Grandma, and Uncle Lee; *on floor, left to right*:
Aunt Flo and Juliette (Mama).

milk, my grandfather gave Ethel equivalent trade-value in his store.

There were others, too: Old Man Volunteer brought collards and
tomatoes, string beans, peas, potatoes, corn, lettuce, and parsley. In
return, he took feed for his cattle and farm implements. And there
was Lizzy, who sold live chickens, their legs tied together, their
heads held in haughty disdain. Grandma would pinch them in the
right places and know their worth. But none of these farm people
ever merely traded; they spoke of their families and illnesses, weddings and crops, sewing and debts. In the wintertime they were
welcomed with hot soup, and in the summer, with cold lemonade. If
they could not pay, my grandfather did not make them feel unwel-
come. He knew that crops were undependable and that the people
would be there as long as the land.

As soon as they were old enough, the children had jobs after
school. Lee, who was handsome and something of a dandy, clerked

in a store until he was a little more than twenty; then he had a better offer in Meridian, and he left home.

Isy became the agent for a laundry in Memphis. With a colt named Ida and a wagon, he collected soiled clothes, dispatched them daily to Memphis on the afternoon train, and delivered them a few days later. His business grew so quickly that in a few years he secured backing for the establishment of a local steam laundry.

As things became better, Grandpa built a wooden two-story house next to the public school. It was white, had Doric columns along the veranda, was more comfortable than handsome, and had plenty of space for everyone. Juliette worked as a stenographer for a coal concern until Isy's business grew so large that she became his "office force." She also found time to take piano lessons and was thought to have become "accomplished" when she crossed her hands while playing selections from *Il Trovatore*. (Later she insisted that had she had *my* opportunities, she would have been a concert pianist.) Kinky-haired Flo, who worked at a switchboard for the telephone company, cultivated her voice, which she used trillingly at the small synagogue. Trixie continued to help at home.

My grandfather drank a jigger of bourbon each morning before breakfast but nothing more unless there was special company. Grandma made a powerful wine called "cherry bounce" in a large earthen crock, and a strong brandy utilizing the plentiful peaches from her garden.

The friends who came to call paid court to a queen. Often she received her guests in her garden, beautifully laid out in squares. Along the side bordering the schoolyard there was a hedge of purple artichokes, rows of yellow squash alternating with shiny purple eggplants, borders of small red tomatoes, and "multiplying" onions mixed in with a running vine of tiny pink roses. Parallel to the artichoke hedge and running the length of the garden there was a sturdy grape arbor whose leaves found their way into many a pickle jar. Among flowers and vegetables arranged meticulously there were spices and herbs seldom to be found in other gardens: mint, parsley, dill, thyme, rose geranium, pepper, onion, garlic, and many others. Only recently when I toured the châteaus of the Loire did I understand that the mixing of vegetables with flowers was called the "French style."

This garden was the pride of my grandmother's life, and she was so devoted to it that years later, when it had declined and bore no resemblance to its once glorious state, she continued to visit it as an old and cherished friend.

In summertime there were family picnics in the country or "socials" at which Trixie was the belle. Occasionally, there was an excursion by horse and buggy to Vicksburg, and when Grandpa went to New Orleans on business he took one of his family with him. On these trips they usually heard a performance of the French Opera. Once Grandpa saw Booth. It was in 1888. Among our books there was a complete Shakespeare inscribed to him by the eminent actor. I do not know how Grandpa came by it, or how or if he had ever known Booth.

But even in Jackson there were sometimes great events. Once Sarah Bernhardt appeared at the Century Theatre. Grandma attended the performance and afterward she and the Divine Sarah embraced and wept and spoke French, which Mama, standing by, could not understand. Mama never found out whether or not they had ever been friends.

Juliette, who was small like her mother and voluble, met Ellis Engel, who traveled out of St. Louis as a clothing salesman. He was one of a family of nine who had migrated from Poland to Raymond, Illinois. Ellis had had no education beyond high school; he was sensitive and handsome, and when he married Juliette he brought from his home a thirty-two-volume set of English and American poetry that he had bought at a great sacrifice but had never read.

During their five years of married life before I was born, my father, in partnership with my grandmother's cousin Mo (Maurice), opened a dry-goods store. This went into bankruptcy very shortly. He, Cousin Mo, and my mother spent many years of their lives paying off all the debts. As a result, my parents abandoned their own home and moved into upstairs rooms in the Lehman house.

Cousin Mo—always unmarried—went to live in Alligator, Mississippi, where he spent the rest of his life clerking in a dry-goods store. Although he spoke English brokenly, he had long before forgotten his native French.

My father once again became a traveling salesman, selling shoes,

Mama, about the time of her marriage to Papa.

Papa (Ellis Engel), in 1905, at about twenty-five.

Mama and Papa on a trip to St. Louis shortly after their wedding.

then shirts, always in the poor South. He traveled for five or six weeks at a time during certain seasons and then for several weeks did not leave home at all.

Papa, quiet, warm, and seldom talkative, loved gambling next to good food. Everybody knew it, and Papa did nothing to conceal it; but knowing Mama's fears (anything was a fear and poverty was anything), he avoided telling her the results of his games. Sometimes he would buy her an expensive gift. Only then did she know.

Everybody respected Papa's knowledge of gambling, and he basked in the reputation of being lucky. During one of his trips he found himself with a Lehman family cousin, Sylvan Loeb (who was also a drummer), in the tiny Mississippi town of Sunflower. Both young men had very little money. Papa, asking Sylvan to lend him all the money he had, took their total resources (ten dollars), and got into a crap game which continued all night. Next morning Papa split the profits with Sylvan, who, in spite of being nervous, was not without some faith in Papa's know-how.

On another occasion Papa somehow won a baseball team but lost everything trying to operate it. Still later he was shooting craps in a "joint" on the outskirts of Memphis when several masked men held up the place. Croupiers and customers alike were ordered to stand against one wall, hands in the air, while they were relieved of money and jewelry. The story is told that when they came to Papa, they passed him by without taking anything. Unlike Willy Loman, Papa had real friends everywhere.

Papa's first cousin Gussie Engel came south from St. Louis, and her visit resulted in her eventual marriage to Isy. At first they also lived on the second floor of the Lehman house. Trixie and Flo were then forced to share a single room, and their lives were inseparable from that time on. They had beaus and they often went out to parties, but they never married.

On a Sunday morning in 1910—earlier in the year that I was born—while Isy and Gussie were on their honeymoon, my grandfather went to collect rentals for shacks that he owned. My family always sat down to breakfast when he returned at ten. Trixie, sleeping fitfully, had been dreaming that she saw her father killed by a train. She awoke unable to shake off the horror of her dream. Grandpa was late in returning. They waited. The telephone rang

Grandma and Mama put me
on display.

and Trixie fainted. Nightmare joined hands with reality. Grandma
could never cry and she never adjusted to Grandpa's death. She
simply never alluded to it.

When I was born, I was named A. Lehman Engel. The initial was
for my two grandfathers Aaron and Abraham, and I was called
"A. Lehman"—an attempt, I believe, at achieving a kind of nineteenth-century elegance (as in "J. P. Morgan," "Francis X. Bush-
man," "J. Montague Glass") and my mother's need not to offend
anyone. That name persisted until nearly sixteen years later, when
in Cincinnati my new friends unceremoniously discarded the initial
and forever after relieved me of one of my several embarrassments.

The day before my fifth birthday I entered Lee School next door
to our house. Mrs. Dalrymple, who taught the first grade, was a tall,
charming lady who wore purple and carried an enormous alligator
bag. She often came to lunch at our house, and it was she who
suggested that I start school a year earlier than usual; if I failed to
advance it would not matter.

At three or four, and well-dressed.

At five—not so dressed up—riding the only kind of 'cycle I was ever permitted to ride.

Left to right: Celeste, Phyllis, a traveling photographer's donkey, and me.

I have only pleasant impressions of grammar school. I disliked none of my teachers, and I remember them all. The fact of school seemed a good one to me, and I went through it without scholastic mishap or any particular distinction.

I do recall the first time the tough Kane brothers, who lived on the "back" street, chased me home after school shouting, "Sheeny!" I didn't know then what the word meant but my instincts warned me to outrun them and to avoid them and their kind ever afterward.

The Kane brothers chased me throughout grammar school always shouting their war cry. They never caught me. When they moved to another town, others came along to take their place. I was afraid of them because I was not nearly their physical equal. I would have to run faster and to stay at home when possible.

Celeste ("Sister") and Phyllis Lehman (Beatrice came much later), the daughters of Uncle Isy and Aunt Gussie, were my constant playmates. Sister was my age, Phyllis two years younger. While the girls were quite young, Uncle Isy built a yellow brick bungalow topped with a red tiled roof across the street from the Lehman house. When he took his family to live in it, Aunt Flo said she would never forgive him, but all of us continued to be close together.

Uncle Isy's business boomed. Aunt Flo had replaced Mama in the office at about the time I was born. Her life was dedicated to the laundry from then until, in self-defense, she broke away twenty-five years later. She usually worked until seven each night except Saturday, when she stayed until eleven. When she came home to dinner, she was frequently called to the telephone to hear customer complaints. Mama "kept" the general books on Sunday and helped in the office when the monthly bills were sent out. Even at home the laundry became the background for conversation at nearly every meal: who had failed to pay bills, who had borrowed money, and so on. I learned to have respect for people of means—even if their characters were unsavory. I learned to have disrespect for wastrels and for people who got married without having assured their financial futures. Money was always the topic.

Having the laundry to absorb her energy and a good income from it to support her and Tatsie unquestionably drained from Aunt Flo the interest, courage, and physical freshness to plunge into marriage. She postponed making a positive decision until the passage of twenty years made it for her. She had gone out driving almost nightly with an insurance salesman ten years her junior. This—whatever it was—went on for twenty years. He asked her repeatedly to marry him, but she could never bring herself to consent. One night he failed to show up. His wedding to a widow was announced in the newspaper a few days later.

When I was twelve, during Aunt Flo's career at the laundry, my mother returned there to a regular position, which she occupied for another twenty years, remaining long after Flo became an insurance saleswoman.

Since both Mama and Aunt Flo were deeply involved in Uncle Isy's business, our mealtimes occurred when work permitted. On Saturday nights, when they worked late, Celeste, Phyllis, and I hung around the office until closing time playing with the delivery men, whom we had always known, and when they were too busy, we amused ourselves with adding machines and typewriters.

Mama, with her nervous energy and even her constant tensions, undoubtedly was the backbone of Uncle Isy's business. Her efficiency when she worked was beyond question. But her "working" was constantly peppered with talking and most of this was *not* business. She telephoned her friends. Her friends telephoned her. Conversations were never brief, and even in those days Mama never wanted to let anybody go. When she saw customers leave or pick up laundry (all customers were friends or became so quickly), Mama would rush from her desk behind a glass partition to hold them like the Ancient Mariner's wedding guest.

Early in the summer mornings, before the sun was hot enough to drive her back into the cool, dark house, my tiny, bent-over, gray-haired grandmother used to sit in her rocking chair on the front porch concealed from the street and the sun by a sturdy vine of white Marachel Neil roses. The roses were deteriorating, and the vine was ragged, but the luxurious odor and the soft velvety texture of the petals gave Grandma much pleasure. Each day I brought her reading glasses and the morning paper, which caused her to boil over at news of the German army on the outskirts of Paris. It was then that she taught me "La Marseillaise" in French, and together we would sing as if we were an army. Then I would lead her into

Grandma in front of the house on South State Street about 1910. Note the white columns unabashedly surrounded by plants growing in buckets and tin cans; such containers were not uncommon in the South, especially at that time.

the house through the dark summer-shuttered dining room, the narrow pantry, and the kitchen, into the breakfast room where we ate grapefruit that Grandma herself had segmented meticulously and sugared the night before, so that the halves could "draw juice."

After breakfast, eaten off a red and white checkered cloth, Grandma—against doctor's orders and the helpless pleas of her family—would wander down the back stairs, through a wooden gate as rickety as herself, into her dream-world garden. Later, when I grew a little older, it became mine. In her garden, there was no longer anything conventionally beautiful or anything special. The artichoke hedge had long since disappeared. The grapevine—no longer an arbor—was propped up untidily against the fence on one side of the garden. Onion plants near the gate were so old that their tall seed-flower rosettes made them seem to have been intended only for decoration. Small peanut plants bobbed up here and there at random. Crawling vines of squash, cucumber, cantaloupe and watermelon became hopelessly entangled along the ground; string-bean vines clung to the wire schoolhouse fence. Tall sunflowers made a background for an infant peach tree, but there were still dill for pickles, and parsley and mint among scattered flowers. Two high pecan trees sheltered it all.

Amidst the disorder which was the remnant of her once meticulously kept garden, Grandma pecked about like an old hen. She pulled out a weed, gathered some radishes and a squash, picked a few impoverished flowers or brushed away damp soil from the growing parsley.

The nurse (also cook, housemaid, and everything else except gardener) I had for the longest time was named Gertie. She had begun working for my family as a teenage girl some fifteen years before I was born. She was short, black, and wore her hair in short plaits that stuck straight up at unexpected intervals. She was generally good-natured and, considering the magnitude of her job, she deserved canonization. She earned four dollars per week, which was more than most other people paid their servants at that time. Her extra benefits were also unusual, but she *worked* for them.

Her day began in the kitchen at 6:45 A.M. If she were occasionally a few minutes late, everyone knew it, and Gertie came to know they knew it. She had to start a fire in the kitchen range with wood she had to bring in from a shed. In winter she laid and lit coal fires in several other rooms in the large house (the coal also had to be hauled indoors). Breakfast for five or six had to be cooked, the table laid, and the meal served. This usually consisted of fruit, cereal, eggs with bacon or ham, biscuits or pancakes, meat or fish (calves liver, fried chicken, or mackerel), cottage cheese, preserves, and coffee!

Later Gertie would clean the house and prepare and serve dinner, the large midday meal. Her cleaning was subject to the kind of scrutiny that would make an admiral's white-glove inspection look superficial. She also rinsed the ladies' silk undergarments and stockings. She killed and plucked the chickens (which had a yard of their own behind our house), fed and watered the unmolested ones, cleaned and dressed the victims for cooking.

Daily midday dinner in our house was absurd. Typically, it ran:

Fresh soup
Boiled beef (used in the soup) with boiled potatoes
Fried chicken (three or four)
Four or five fresh vegetables (for example, fried tomatoes, mashed
  turnips, peas, string beans, and fried potatoes)
Corn bread
Salad
A platter of cold meats and cheese
Pie and ice cream
Iced tea

Gertie usually took care of me in the afternoon and then went home at about five o'clock, staying to serve supper only on rare "company" occasions. But daily she prepared supper dishes and left them so that later they had merely to be heated.

Despite the quantity of food, the members of my family always drank a "Co-cola" in midmorning ("to make us belch," they said), had lemonade and cookies, or ice cream in the midafternoon, and never retired without first having a slice of watermelon, a cold chicken leg with bread and butter, or a sandwich. Yet none of them was stout.

Gertie worked seven days every week and an infrequent request for a day off for an annual church picnic or the funeral of a friend resulted in a bewildered family conclave that never refused the request (made, at most, two or three times a year) but always considered it an expression of ingratitude.

Gertie was usually told she could have the day off provided she would first come in, fix breakfast, and "brush around" the house.

Gertie lived with her mother in a two-room house (the rent was fifty cents per week) and she was permitted to take home all the food she wanted. Medical bills were paid by my family. They also gave her clothing for work and social events (sometimes new, some-times castoffs). At Christmas she received twenty-five dollars, a new dress, coat, purse, perfume, candy, shoes, undergarments, etc.— everything she needed to wear, and other, smaller gifts of money from our relatives and friends.

When we were quite small, Sister, Phyllis, and I took naps after lunch, then were bathed, dressed handsomely, and taken for a walk. Our nurses, their stiff white aprons contrasting with their pure black faces, laughing happily, lolled behind as we skipped ahead. Early in spring we went to watch the swirling, muddy yellow water of the Pearl River. We would stand high above it on the bluff and then venture across the planked bridge. Standing by the iron railing that vibrated with the slowly jogging wagon traffic, we gazed at the weeping willows on the sandbar opposite, their long branches dipping langorously into the river, stirred dreamily by the muddy yellow current. I used to stand staring silently, lonely and alone, somehow assured of a wonderful world far away behind the trees and the sandbar and the river.

Sometimes our walks took us to Old Confederate Park—a small

green square in the center of which stood a modest obelisk dedicated to the Army of the Confederacy. Sister, Phyllis, and I delighted in rolling down the cool grassy hill behind the obelisk until we were stopped by a broken wire fence. Dizzied, we would stand looking far ahead and below—over a railroad track rusty with disuse that lost itself in high grass and weeds—at the limitless green valley beyond. Out in the silence, there was again the friendly promise of a bright world away from the aloneness. Grass-stained and tired, we were dragged home to supper.

This was fall. And it was the time of goldenrod bright in parched fields. Goldenrod announced school, which was preceded by shopping trips and the pulling out of last winter's clothes, long laid away in camphor balls, the odor of which continued to permeate them for months. I dreaded the shopping because it was Mama who had to be pleased. She never asked me if I liked something because she alone knew best.

Pecans fell in the back yard; crisp leaves crunched noisily underfoot. Odor of chrysanthemums rose out of the damp dead leaves and the smoking leaf piles. Summertime barefoot boys and girls covered their feet. The school bell rang.

Even when the temperature is well above freezing, Mississippi in winter is damp and cold. It is even cold when narcissus, jonquil, and hyacinth bloom in the yard. Our large white house was heated by coal-burning gratefires, but many rooms were closed in winter except for sleeping because they were not heated. It was usual to get up out of a warm bed and race into the next room to dress by a sputtering fire. The coal crackled and banged. Facing the fire, our fronts burned while our backs froze. In winter I used to dress by the light and heat of the fire in Tatsie and Aunt Flo's room, which had once belonged to Grandma.

I accepted school without question. At noon recess, as I ate dinner (my mother sitting with me), Tatsie would cross into the schoolyard carrying a large pot of freshly made soup. The cook would follow her with bowls and spoons and a large basket of crackers. Tatsie sold the soup to the children, most of whom were poor, for five cents, and many of them came to depend on it. Just as often, the soup was given without charge.

Often during the winter afternoons, Mama sat at home in the half-light of the fire, sewing or reading a book—always compulsively occupied. She would urge me to do my homework or (later) practice the piano. She discouraged me from going out to play with other children, partly because she felt that they were "roughnecks" and I might get hurt. They were also "beneath" me—the leftovers in a rapidly deteriorating neighborhood. But mostly it was Mama's fear. I could not ride a bicycle or a pony because I might break my neck. (She had a repertoire of broken-neck incidents she could recite in the rare event of an argument.) And the fears were not limited to bicycles and ponies but included "taking colds," upsetting my stomach, not dressing warmly enough, getting blood poisoning from a scratched knee, contracting fevers, being killed crossing the street, offending an aunt, failing to remember a birthday, not visiting an old lady, being impolite, soiling my clothes. The fears, easily communicated, were incessantly fed and cataloged.

Being younger, less robust, and conspicuously cleaner than the boys I went to school with, I found coming home a lonely if welcome escape from what particular horror I never thought to ask. After all, I seldom knew any of these boys. Arrival at school coincided with the ringing of the morning bell. Lunch recess was spent at home. The dismissal bell propelled me once again through the dividing hedge into our own yard—two feet ahead of the Kanes.

I remember standing before a frosty window, my nose pressed against the glass, looking out at nothing, hearing faintly the distant jagged sounds of children's high voices, designless in play. In the house everything was silence and waiting.

Many of these afternoons were spent in making "scene boxes," for which I used large cardboard cartons. With a knife I would gouge out one end of a box, which thus became the proscenium of a stage. Across the box top, I carved out narrow slits for letting in scenery consisting of pictures cut from magazines and pasted on cardboard. There was always a curtain (usually a handkerchief pinned around a stick) and sometimes a flashlight to provide illumination. I never meant to give a "show." These scene boxes were made only for myself.

During these days, I also began to play the piano "by ear" but was not given lessons until I was ten because my parents thought my interest was merely a whim that they could ill afford.

I saw whatever shows came to town. Al G. Field's Minstrels was an annual event. Fritz Leiber brought us tattered grandeur in Shakespearean repertoire. There were Walker Whiteside, *Maytime*, *Blossom Time*, *The Student Prince*, *Chu Chin Chow*, the St. Louis Symphony Orchestra, Paderewski, John McCormack, Galli-Curci, and Sousa's Band, and the Redpath Chautauqua, which brought smiling culture in a large tent for five full days each spring.

But my most profound experiences were in the Majestic Theatre, the local moviehouse: the Griffith pictures, Gish, Nazimova, and Chaplin. A small orchestra presided over by Sara B. McLean at an upright piano accompanied the pictures. Mrs. McLean would lean far back in her swivel chair peering at the screen over the top of her nose-glasses. The "score" consisted of bits and pieces taken from movie-music albums: "hurries," romantic melodies, marches— primitive music whose dramatic intentions were clear to all. The music changed as abruptly as the film frames, and Mrs. McLean would indicate these changes with a sudden jerk of the head, cutting off the orchestra often after she had already plunged ahead. (The music always warned of approaching danger.)

When I was ten, I began to take piano lessons with an aristocratic southern lady who had her pupils do a variety of things: we played duets and trios, learned rudimentary harmony and history of music, and had "scrapbook parties," at which we pasted pictures of musical artists, composers, and operatic scenes, from phonograph record catalogs and music journals, in blank books.

Almost immediately after my lessons commenced, I began to compose. There were several short scraps of things, then *The Scotch Highlander* for piano, my first complete "piece." Charles Wakefield Cadman came to Jackson to give a recital of his compositions, and I was able to meet him. He was gentle and enthusiastic and the only composer I had ever met: indeed, the only one (I thought) who was not dead. He heard me play, saw my single composition, and was encouraging. We began a correspondence that continued until his death more than twenty years later. And years before his death, his letters ironically became pleas for me to arrange New York performances of his compositions!

Soon after this meeting with Cadman, I decided to write an opera. I had never heard one, but I was fascinated by photographs in the *Victor Book of the Opera*. I began by drawing and coloring a title page: *Alfred*. An Opera in One Act by A. Lehman Engel. The characters were A Lady; Her Suitor, a Knight; The Lady's Maid; and The Lady's Father; and the scene, a castle tower during the Middle Ages. I wrote words and music for a solo, a duet, and a recitative, then abandoned the project only (!) because the words were too much trouble to write.

My second piano teacher, Miss Emma Manning, scheduled my lessons at 8:00 A.M. in the summer nonschool months. I would ring her doorbell, then see her through glass panels sleepily descending the stairs while fastening her corset. After lessons—half an hour later—I went next door to the beautifully kept house of my cousins, the Loebs, for breakfast.

Saturday was, especially in summer, farm-folk day in town: the day for greeting friends, exchanging news, selling produce, buying supplies. I would wander out on our front porch in my pajamas in the early morning and see the caravans of wagons already crawling slowly by. I always found Mama sitting there as Grandma had done; Tatsie was often with her. They sat partially shielded from view and the rising summer sun by a thin vine of large purple morning glories that had replaced Grandma's long-dead Marachel Neil. They sat in their "wrappers" rocking, their hair piled unsteadily on the tops of their heads.

The caravan had to pass our house between the Pearl River Bridge and the business section, which was rapidly encroaching upon us. Most of the farm-folk rode in long unpainted wagons drawn by a pair of horses. Others squatted on the wagon's floor with the farm produce, while sometimes women sat with extraordinary dignity on straight rush-bottom chairs placed without anchorage on the wagon's floor. A few men rode on horseback. From dawn until noon this caravan plodded slowly in; from noon until sunset it passed in return. All of the people (seeing us on the front porch) nodded their heads in greeting whether they knew us or not, and they never seemed to be talking among themselves.

Some stopped their wagons. Little barefoot boys, women with small girls, men in fraying sombreros peddled produce from door to door: eggs, cantaloupes, blackberries, figs, squash, beans, tomatoes, chickens. Tatsie or Mama bought while planning meals, and often a vegetable woman had to hear creation, revision, and re-creation of an entire week's menus before knowing whether or not she had sold ten cents worth of snap beans.

On summer Sundays I rode with Mama and Aunt Flo to collect their rents, for each of them had borrowed money to build a row of two-room shacks for colored occupancy similar to the ones Grandpa had owned. Each rented for fifty cents weekly, and although the collections from twelve houses in two districts could have been accomplished in half an hour, it took half a day by the time Mama and Aunt Flo heard each family's personal history and in turn dispensed lengthy, and often merely tolerated, advice.

Poor as these shacks were, most had been transformed by their occupants into homes. Brilliant red cockscomb grew tall out of the parched earth before nearly every house and vegetables filled the yards in the rear.

The side yards of flowers at our house, and the garden of weeds behind, more and more tended to separate us from our neighbors. Our friends increasingly moved to the north end of town. Uncle Isy sold his beautiful bungalow at a loss in order to rear his children in a "better" environment. In our old neighborhood, filling stations replaced corner homes. A hamburger stand pushed one house half a block behind it. Two houses gave way to an overall factory; another was demolished to make room for a tombstone display yard. The remaining homes, vacated by their original tenants who had once been our friends, were now operated as cheap rooming houses. We no longer had any life in our neighborhood outside the borders of our property. Mama wanted us to move away also, but Aunt Flo, for sentimental and financial reasons, steadfastly refused, and she continued to refuse for nearly fifteen years after I left home.

When we had visitors during the summer evenings, my mother used to entertain the women on the wide front porch, where, in spite of the mosquitoes, they sat talking and gossiping in shrill voices. Every bull's-eye they scored produced resounding laughter. The husbands, led by my father, would go indoors to play cards. The children who had been brought along and I would play out on the infrequently night-traveled street under an overhanging arc light. An almost solid mass of flying insects attracted to the lamp made a frantic perpetual circle-tour of it, somewhat resembling the rings around Saturn.

When visitors left—always many hours later—my mother kept them standing, talking, never *seeming* to want them to go. Often nearly half an hour passed in drawn-out leave-taking and at last when the visitors had resolved to break away, my mother's almost pathetic question came:

"Well, you all call that gone?"

In spite of her many and obvious faults, which included gar-rulousness, she was attentive to everyone. It can easily be argued that she was generous because she hoped her generosity would be reciprocated. Nevertheless, no one of even her most distant friends ever left Jackson on a trip without her sending a "going-away" present. This was of necessity inexpensive, but I was embarrassed to hear her extol its pathetic virtues:

"You know this bath-powder is *very* fine, although you may never have heard of it."

Well, no one ever *had* heard of it because it was Liggett's forty-four-cent "special" for the week, but this advertised fact never fazed her.

When relatives of friends died, she was the first to send mountains of superb food on decorated silver trays to the mourners. This was also, of course, a general custom, and the result was that a house of mourning suddenly became a banquet hall. However, it will always be a mystery to me and to my then-remaining Aunt Gussie that when Mama herself died, only her doctor and his wife sent a platter of food. There was so little in the house that Sister, Phyllis, and Beatrice were forced to go shopping on the morning of my mother's funeral.

One summer evening when my family and I were sitting on the front porch and speaking quietly among ourselves, an incident oc-curred which at the time I could only feel but did not understand. About ten o'clock a young colored girl on her way home from work neared our house as a flivver occupied by two stalwart young white men drove up quickly and squealed to a sudden stop. One man hopped out and blocked the path of the girl. He spoke to her. She refused. He became insistent. She tried to run away. The other young man joined his friend. The two of them carried her, screaming, into their car and drove quickly away across the river bridge into the night. I was emotionally upset, not understanding anything except that the girl was being forced to do something against her will. I yelled at my uncle and my father, who did nothing. They said simply that I did not understand. Then I peered up and down the dimly lit street, and as far as I could see, other men sat on other front porches. All were rocking peacefully, some fanning themselves.

During the afternoons of the late summer, not many hours before sunset, from the days of my earliest recollections until I left home when I was fifteen, I often found myself behind our house in the wilderness that had been my grandmother's garden. There was wild, crawling, lush ruin everywhere: green, heavy, pathless. I would stand in the midst of it for hours, facing the sun, inhaling the warm, heavy jungle fragrance of the high grasses and weeds. Overhead and behind me the branches of the now overwhelmingly high pecan trees spread immovable. Before me, tall sunflowers oozed thick honey for swarms of bees. Wild vines curled sturdily, clutching, jealously squeezing tall flowering weeds. Lazy sounds coming from distant chickens going to roost and slow, far-off train whistles alternated with one another. Sometimes the faint yells of another little boy, bringing his cow home from a nearby pasture, drifted into the garden and mingled with the other sounds. Then as the setting sun filled my staring eyes, I would be roused out of my real, though solitary, world by the clanging of supper bells.

This was my garden—not that anyone else wanted it or that anyone had ever given it to me, but it was my one place of refuge and mine alone. Only my grandmother, of all the others, had ever stood silently with me in its high damp grasses. Now I was alone with the garden and the aroma of her love, which would continue for me to pour out of every flowering weed. For it was now more than a garden: a shrine, a temple, the only true place of mystery and worship I would ever comprehend. The undulating *Sanctus* of the crickets sang the praises of heaven and earth, and I was continually renewed in faith and spirit, given fresh promise again and again (as when I gazed down the slope in the park or dreamed through the willow branches at the river), fresh promise of a world in which I would shed my loneliness and become completely and only myself, and it would be all right. More than the crickets sang it. The mystery in the pathless temple would continue for me not merely for as long as I could attend but when in the future I would go away forever and when the house would be demolished and the garden-temple smothered under concrete, I would be able to summon it again intact wherever I was. The promise, the song, the distilled dream have never failed me even in the roar of the life I never envisioned there in the garden.

During these years at home, I outgrew music teacher after music teacher. My entrance into high school at twelve in another end of town was fraught with increasing terrors. The old and by now deeply embedded fears were hard at work. I was projected into a class of strangers who seemed hostile. Now—far from home—I was obliged to mingle, for I no longer enjoyed the protection of the nearby family house. I was still the youngest in my class and still the smallest, the only one to continue (at my mother's insistence) wearing short pants and long black stockings. In my mind's eye, I was still an infant. The other boys were bigger and rougher—or so they seemed. I was a Jew and still frightened of the old battle cry. I also played the piano, a thing which boys simply did not do.

At twelve. In high school, but still a midget.

Inside the cafeteria, I ate alone. I felt that all eyes watched me and I was fearful of blunders, of dropping things, or of any slight fault. If I finished lunch quickly, I returned to the study hall in order to avoid playground encounters.

In class I was tense and self-conscious and could do nothing well: I merely got by. I made two friends, and in my final year I was invited to a few parties by the girls and boys who came (probably) to know that we had things in common. But to me, these parties—given by boys and girls who lived in the best part of town in fine, aristocratic houses, non-Jews, people with a lifetime of growing up together—held their own terrors. I was unused to them, their houses, their ways of life. I felt merely tolerated, a visitor on probation, one who must behave better than the rest, not merely as well. The end of the party was a blessed relief. I had again gotten by, but there was never any pleasure, and there would surely be another party and more terror.

At my mother's insistence, I had become a member of the Boy Scouts but had, of course, failed miserably at being transformed suddenly through it into a different kind of boy. I was the compulsory member of some unfortunate sports team at each weekly Scout meeting. That team always lost the game, and the reasons were not mysterious. When attendance at summer camp was proposed, I violently opposed it. I had never slept away from home except on trips with my parents, because I was still plagued with nightly bedwetting. The thought of the helpless days at sports and the even more helpless nights after which I would suffer the pain of being laughed at struck me with new horror. My mother insisted that I go to camp. The first night there, I deserted—a full pack on my back—and walked home in the friendlier dark, alone.

I graduated from Central High School, wrote an alma mater song, led the school orchestra at the graduation exercises in Schubert's "Marche Militaire" and the *Aïda* "Triumphal March" and did not otherwise distinguish myself.

Once during that last summer I went swimming in the municipal lake at Livingstone Park, where I ran into Frank Lyell. I had known him slightly in school (he was in the class with Celeste, a year behind mine) and he also had studied with my first piano teacher. We swam out to an anchored raft where I was introduced to a girl in the class ahead of mine. I knew her by sight as the daughter of the owner of Jackson's first skyscraper, an eleven-story insurance-company building, and gradually we became lifelong friends, with more in common than I could have ever dreamed anyone might have had. She was Eudora Welty.

During that final year, I gave a solo piano recital in the Episcopal Parish House. It must have been a grim affair, but all the friends of my family came, sent expected baskets of flowers, and applauded loudly. No one there knew how really badly I played. But I did.

In spite of my piano playing—and playing did seem to be what I was to do—I easily persuaded my parents to allow me to go all the way to the Cincinnati Conservatory the following fall. (All music students in the South went to Cincinnati.) As I look back on my leaving, I recognize the utter flimsiness of the line that led me to do the most important thing in my life. My piano playing certainly did not warrant my being sent to a conservatory in a distant city. My parents made financial sacrifices to accomplish it and in turn expected that music must become my profession. Once they had accepted the idea, a great responsibility fell on me. If I had been taught by a discriminating teacher, he would have argued against a musical career. As it was, nobody knew better, and I left home.

2: Exodus

In the fall, both of my parents accompanied me to Cincinnati.

Across from the vine-covered conservatory, at Mrs. (or "Mother") Haacke's recommended boardinghouse, most of the residents were musicians or music students. It was a rambling place without distinction, but as we ate an ample meal, Mama was content that I would not starve.

My tiny room in the attic with its dormer window contained a gas heater, a wash basin, an iron bed, and a floor covered with worn linoleum. I had never slept in any place so poor, yet I was able to accept it without question because it was mine. At Haacke's there would be no arguments about which necktie I would wear or how much sleep I needed. There was no key to my door, but no one would invade my privacy. It was the first time I had ever had a door on any room.

It was the first time I had no need to run away from people my own age, when I could make friends of my own, know people who shared my interests and tastes without having them certified. I became so much a part of the Haacke household that I could even laugh at the years of pursuit by the Kane brothers, for Agnes Haacke, the older daughter, used to chase me up and down staircases yelling, "Persecution of the Jews! Persecution of the Jews!" Her mother would embrace me and say quite lyrically, "He has hair like our Savior."

That was not all. I still wet my bed. Mama had spelled this out to Mrs. Haacke, who made no fuss about it but dutifully changed my bedding each morning. After only a couple of months this life-custom suddenly stopped altogether and forever. I was at last also free of that.

How?

Had I not been the most tractable young man imaginable? Had I not worn laughably outmoded clothes because Mama had decreed it? Had I not gone calling on all the ladies of her generation and even those from her previous generation when I was about to return to school? (Not only did no other boy ever do this, but not even a single girl.) Did I not docilely, unquestioningly, go on countless rounds of preposterous social errands because Mama would burden me with guilt if I demurred? And, too, she had (she said) nearly died when I was born, and she was working at the laundry to help provide my education and various other advantages. Well, within this submissive, languishing organism that was me there had to have been some hostility, but it was not until many years later that I was to learn from my psychiatrist Dr. Schaffner that its expression took the form of bed-wetting. Ah—*that* was what all the medical doctors I was exposed to never fathomed. And that accounted for the miracle that happened in Cincinnati when I no longer needed to express my unconscious hostility: Mama was not there and the bed-wetting that had prevented my living a more normal childhood, spending nights with friends and holidays away from home, and enjoying all the other taken-for-granted pleasures that belong to nearly everyone's growing up and that painlessly prepare most boys for manhood—all of these denied me because of uncontrollable physical imperfection now mysteriously vanished. It was as simple as that.

In the late mornings at Haacke's, individual practicing gradually commenced: one man fluted over the groaning of his roommate's double bass; another appeared to be having sexual intercourse with a cello; a fat jovial man played congenially on the tuba (he was Bill Bell, who married Mrs. Haacke's daughter and became Toscanini's prized tuba player); and others practiced wildly as only violinists will. In Mrs. Haacke's music-ridden house, I was learning (and without study) the colors of the orchestral mosaics. In time I began to know the entire orchestral family intimately without tuition. This was, of course, an accident, but life-producing as few lessons were ever going to be.

My parents had been advised that a certain concert pianist would be the best teacher for me. Although the fee was high and they were told that I would need two lessons weekly, my parents signed contracts for my tuition without mentioning their financial problems.

I met the other pupils of my teacher (who had not yet returned from Europe) and their facile playing terrified me. It was instantly clear to me that I didn't belong in their class. Day by day, as I thought about my lessons, my courage began to slip farther away. It began to seem impossible even to audition for my teacher.

Finally, he arrived. I played timidly for him. (I suspect the fully paid tuition was responsible for his self-control.) During lessons he paced the floor offbeat and occasionally lunged at a second piano (literally taking matters in his own hands) to play a passage. Because of the exorbitant tuition my parents were paying and because people of my home town were eyeing my progress, I felt I had made an awful mistake in trying to succeed at piano playing. This awareness only intensified my nervousness at lessons and (as in high school) sharply decreased my receptivity. Always the fears.

Probably as an escape from theory lessons that I did not understand, class lessons that were superficial, and piano lessons that terrified me, I began to write music. There were minute piano pieces and filmy songs, and then without any self-consciousness I began writing music to Ernest Dowson's two-character verse-playlet *The Pierrot of the Minute*. I wrote only to satisfy a feeling that demanded work. The demand became so intense that if I failed to work for a single day, I suffered guilt. The importance of my conservatory work faded as the year went by, but I had no idea of abandoning it.

I attended some performance almost every evening. At first, symphony concerts proved difficult for me. All symphonies seemed overlong and tedious. Two years passed before I approached them with any joy.

The program notes for the symphony concerts were written by Rabbi James Heller, to whom I had earlier presented a letter of introduction. "Jimmy" and his young and vivacious wife were opposite to almost anyone's idea of a typical rabbinical couple. They were socialites in Cincinnati and lived lavishly; the rabbi seemed to me as interested in music as in problems of a purely Jewish nature.

My mother was happy to find in my daily letter home that Mrs. Heller had invited me to sit with her at the Yom Kippur morning service where no one without a ticket could have gained admittance. Yom Kippur (the Day of Atonement) is the most sacred of Jewish holidays, and Jews who seldom observe any holiday rituals will at least be present on Yom Kippur and will fast from sundown to sundown. My family was religiously strict only on this latter point.

After the morning service, there is an intermission of an hour or so between the morning and afternoon one. I followed Mrs. Heller out of the temple as she admonished: "Hurry along. We haven't much time."

We had hardly reached the outside when we were joined by Jimmy, who had quickly discarded his synagogue robes and the three of us sped to their home where we enjoyed a splendid lunch!

I could hardly wait to write about this to my mother, who could not possibly have complained about it, since I had eaten under the most distinguished and sacred auspices. And this was, of course, forever the end of my Yom Kippur fasting.

I found theater and opera immediately compelling. In that first year, I saw Ibsen and Sheridan, Barrie and O'Neill, Gilbert and Sullivan, Connelly and Kaufman for the first time. I saw Mary Garden and understood something about great performers.

I was engaged as accompanist to an amateur light opera company that was preparing Victor Herbert's *Mlle. Modiste*. I was an abominable pianist, had had no experience accompanying, and could not read music fluently at sight. The conductor was a nervous man, and with my assistance he almost failed to survive the production. In an effort to play correct notes I was invariably behind his beat. I would stumble, then stop to go back and right a wrong. In my timidity I played so softly that the chorus was always off pitch. After rehearsal pauses everyone knew where we were resuming except myself. On each of these occasions the conductor trembled with rage, while I sat helpless with fear. But I liked working on a

show, and I suffered through it to the very end. Not long afterward
the conductor died.

Throughout that first year in Cincinnati, it was impossible for me
to reconcile my curriculum with anything in the living world. Harmony lessons advanced according to schedule, not growth. History
of music was an endless exercise in the memorization of complicated
names, dates, and ancient nomenclature. I learned that Guillaume
de Machaut was born circa 1300 and died in 1377, but I had not the
vaguest idea of how his music sounded. What little I learned was
not only dead in itself but appeared never to have lived at all. That
most of it still goes on living was a fact that only came to my
attention ten years later and through my own efforts in the world of
the Madrigal Singers and because of our financially bankrupt era. I
understood nothing then, attended classes, did everything I was assigned to do. But I understood no connection between rules and
living music.

Composition of my little opera *The Pierrot of the Minute* advanced rapidly because, being uncritical and unselfconscious, I
made no revisions, was troubled by nothing that I wrote, and wrote
everything that occurred to me. I brought the score-in-progress to
my theory teacher, who was so astonished that he made no criticism. He liked what I had written, which in no way conformed to
the rules (which I had never, in any case, comprehended), and he
was therefore at a loss to offer help. Even I knew that what I had
written was an excess of foolishness.

When I went home for the summer, my family thought I had
grown up and that I "talked like a Yankee." It was true that I had
gained a certain amount of independence and preferred working or
reading to talking endlessly with my family. I even dared to repri-
mand my mother for opening my mail and created a schism that
caused her to refuse for a long time even to read the letters that I
offered her. I had added final g's to words and reintroduced r's
where they belonged.

Returning to Cincinnati in the fall, I intended to continue where I
had left off. But I had learned accidentally during the first year that
only *my* parents were paying the full price for piano lessons, that
everyone else had either full or part-payment scholarships. When I
complained to the registrar, she appeared to consult my record

(which I knew would not warrant any special consideration), and she concluded that she could offer me a special "part-rate scholarship." Realizing how much money my poor parents had paid out unnecessarily, I became angry and quit the conservatory.* This action could not have been more surprising to me.

The next day, on my own, I entered the College of Music in downtown Cincinnati—miles away from Haacke's—a school without campus or glamor. This unadvised action thrust an even greater responsibility upon me. My new teacher was a patient old man who gave me lessons in composition and orchestration under terms of a partial scholarship.

I also spent parts of two days each week at the University of Cincinnati studying English and psychology. And for the first time —with Negro students in my classes—the question of racial discrimination became important to me.

My little opera was completed, and my new teacher decided to have it produced the following spring at the college. No one could say who would conduct it, but I was to start rehearsals. At the first orchestra rehearsal, I lifted my arms and brought them down, but no one played. This happened again and again. Filled with embarrassment, I explained the opening to my student friends. The next time I raised my arms they played. Once they had started, I hesitated to stop lest I should fail to get them going again. During the months of rehearsal I learned something about conducting, something about the orchestra, about rehearsals, and eventually I recovered my speaking voice, which I had lost in the terror of that first rehearsal.

By spring it became obvious that I was to conduct *The Pierrot of the Minute* myself, and my family drove to Cincinnati to attend the performance. The newspapers liked it, and although I was happy, I was not misled. I enjoyed the sounds that my orchestration had made. They were not new sounds (as I was to learn only later on), but they were new to me. At the time, I was moved by the romance

---

* The College-Conservatory today—a merger of my two alma maters and now a part of the University of Cincinnati—long ago became a highly reputable institution with high standards and forward-looking curriculum. The period to which I refer here was nearly a half century ago and there is no similarity between today's school and the one I attended.

and the drama and what seemed to be my personal way with a musical phrase. For the first time I felt that I had some definite musical talent: I was no longer a fraud.

At the end of this, my third year, my composition teacher wanted me to continue with him and offered to put me on the school faculty. I rejected this offer in favor of going on to New York. I knew that I still needed to learn many fundamentals, and I made definite plans to leave Cincinnati, with or without blessings, at the close of the year.

For three years I had lived alone through the terror of the pianistic competition that I discovered at the outset was far beyond me. I lacked the facility for it, the talent, even the nervous system that helps to propel young players fleetly over the keyboard. Had I acknowledged this to myself at the time, I think I would not have been able to go on living. For it was not for myself alone that I had to succeed: there were the members of my undiscerning family, the expenditure of the hard-to-get money of my parents, the expectant and wrongly proud community of former teachers and family friends whose scandalized disappointment I could not have faced.

But when I found that I could actually create music of my own (this almost nobody else then living could do!), that I could make an opera, that I was—in the eyes of my teachers and those swift-fingered students who long ago assumed they had left me far behind —unique, I could now face a falsehood no longer painful to me and replace it with a truth at once more important and, for the very first time, real. I knew that I had not even begun, but at last I was on my way.

I had made some special friends who in various ways reached out into my future life. There was Walter Levin (later Lawrence) of San Francisco who studied piano, then voice at the conservatory. Shortly after my own arrival he was to come to New York to go on with his studies. Through him I met the elderly, elegant Mrs. David Workum, who was to provide me the following year with New York introductions. A spinster, Miss Leah Rosenthal, who was a great provincial bore, sent me to her sister in New York, Elsa Moses, a would-be actress who, with her husband Harry, produced *Grand Hotel*, *The Warrior's Husband* with Katharine Hepburn, and *The Old Maid* with Judith Anderson and Helen Menken. The Moseses,

Walter, and I became close friends. Through them I met their intern protégé, Dr. Irving Graef, who later, and for life, became my physician and a dear friend.

Another and more important seed was planted in Cincinnati. Having "realized" *The Pierrot of the Minute*, I began looking for another verse-play appropriate for musical treatment. In the public library I found one called *Yniard*, by John Martin. I began setting it and finished sketching out a first act. As I was planning to go to New York, I became a regular reader of the Sunday *New York Times*, where I saw the dance criticism by a John Martin. I wrote a letter inquiring as to the possibility that he was "my" author, and I received an immediate affirmative reply, with the request that I call him when I reached New York. John Martin was also to become a lifelong friend and was to introduce me to the contemporary dance, which was to involve the earliest part of my creative life.

One thing leading to another—a vast network of proximity, chance, time, and chemistry. This (and much more) was all to happen in New York, but it had its genesis in Cincinnati.

There it was that I learned that people could like me for myself, that many likable people shared my tastes and enthusiasms, that I was not a strange creature alone and isolated in a hostile desert. It began to seem even possible that I was far from being the grotesque little boy I had appeared to myself to be as I ran from the "Sheeny!" cry of the Kane brothers, as I cringed at recess time in the mighty presences of the husky boys in high school, friendless, will-less, physically outlandish in my long black stockings, impotent as in the Boy Scout games, solitary in the interests and tastes that impelled my every waking moment and sleepless dream—it now began to seem even possible that this new world of mine was the only real one, that in it I was not grotesque and I was not alone. I had finally awakened from a nightmare. It was as permissible to admire a sunset or write a song, I had found, as it was to raise a chicken or compute a bill. My world was not made of only rainbows: it also had substance. For love was no longer solitary and outgoing and intangible like the feeling in the garden behind our house: it could also be given back to me.

3: New York, New York

My MOTHER CONVERTED New York into a city of terror. I was not to talk with strangers, my money was to be kept in an inside pocket, street crossings were dangerous, I was to regard everyone with suspicion.

Nevertheless, on a warm afternoon early in September my train slid through the tube under the Hudson River and emerged safely in the heart of the city. Bert Blaw, who had married a friend of my mother's, met me and delivered me to my uptown hotel. After hurriedly unpacking, I proceeded downtown immediately to the theater district via subway.

That first descent into the drafty, humid, subway underworld was unforgettable. The many small electric bulbs dotting the tile walls flickered slightly, imparting a subtly diabolical air. The man in the change booth to whom I offered a dime seemed to throw the two nickels at me. Glowering from his cage, his eyes were almost invisible under a green shade. Strong, quick gusts of musty, grit-filled wind whirled around from every direction. Along a bench a drunk lay snoring, a fresh puddle of vomit on the dark pavement beneath. Rows of innumerable steel posts divided two sets of tracks and supported the street above.

Amid a wild confusion of sudden smelly, gritty, whirling drafts, a train roared along the track and squealed to a stop. I was quick to rush aboard. Once in motion again, the train raced furiously past station after station. I thought it would never again stop, but the people around me read their newspapers without concern.

With the sudden stop of the train at Times Square, the people snapped into life and hurried out. I followed quickly, stumbling up the stairs in an effort to keep up with them. The men found their girls waiting for them under a drugstore sign. When several other girls reached the street, they slowed their walk and sauntered away with little apparent purpose.

Reborn out of the dim purgatory of the subway, I was awed by the running, leaping, diving, climbing appearance and disappearance of magical lights. They assailed with messages, offers, announcements, warnings. They spelled out words; shot luminous arrows into space, told time and temperature, materialized into jiggling comic figures that disintegrated with equal speed.

I lost myself in the slow turgid crowd of hand-holders and night strollers who seemed content simply with the excitement of watching the pleasures of others. There was noise, too, under the flickering lights. Impatient taxi drivers honked and bellowed profanely at traffic. Corner newsboys shouted unintelligibly. Police whistles screamed. But people began to come into focus, and I discovered that they were not a race apart—New Yorkers—but people such as I had always known. They were white and black and yellow and brown and red, but that did not seem to bother them or (for the first time in my life) anybody else. Many couples spoke together loudly in strange languages, but other heads—on other wavelengths—did not turn to stare. The poorly dressed were as much at home as the stylish.

I saw a sign: "*Street Scene* by Elmer Rice." I was thrilled at being in the same city with this play, which I had read about, and I leaped at the opportunity to buy a ticket. The show would not begin for nearly an hour, but lest I be unable to find my way back again I remained on the sidewalk to watch the passing crowds. Happily assured that no one took the slightest notice of me, I melted into the crowd.

The audience began to arrive. First came the holders of cheaper seats, mostly small groups of women. They were dressed more simply, I thought, than the female members of my family. Large cars driven by liveried chauffeurs began to drive up, and a colored doorman assisted the passengers to the curb. These men and women were dressed formally, and the men wore dark red carnations in their lapels.

The inside of the theater was surprisingly small, and the performance, like everything else I saw that night, seemed miraculous. The scenery was solid and realistically detailed. The performers seemed vital. Here at last—and at first for me—were the theatrical ingredients that for so long I had had to accept on faith.

I lived in a series of hotels in rapid, filthy succession. I had seldom before been disquieted by trash-laden streets or drunks sleeping in doorways, but not to have a congenial place of refuge to retire to was a serious lack I had never before encountered. My room at Haacke's in Cincinnati had been unluxurious but clean. In my various hotels, the rugs were grimy. The bathrooms wore the rings of many earlier marriages. An accidentally pulled-out sheet revealed bloodstains on the mattress. Roaches staged haughty quadrilles in just any place. Curtains hung lifeless with the weight of dust. Outside in the corridors brassy life lunged by at all hours.

For two weeks I took refuge in the apartment of distant cousins, the Wrights. At last I found a room on 111th Street that was clean though also dark. The landlady, a tall, friendly, angular maiden-lady, sublet all the rooms in her apartment except her own. Her curiosity was not infrequently manifested by her right eye at the keyhole of my door—a phenomenon that led to my hanging my hat on the doorknob.

When I first arrived in New York I had a steel cashbox of letters of introduction. The people these were to lead me to were representative of every kind of life in New York and I presented every letter, except one to Toscanini from a teacher in Cincinnati. I could never bring myself to take up one second of the great maestro's time. He could gain nothing from me. I could not have asked anything of him. What could I have asked? Years later I was to meet him, but then it was to be because of his interest in what I was doing.

My family's friends sent letters introducing me to their New York relatives, and there were some I had already met. These included Leota Blaw from Jackson and her husband, who had met me on arrival in New York, and Leon Cohen and his wife Von, and others. All of these people lived on the Upper West Side and resembled my own family. Their apartments were comfortable and conventionally attractive with "matching" furniture and the "right" decorator-type accessories. All of them had a single servant, ate quantitatively, were generous with their invitations, and wanted to be helpful in any possible way. They were simple, more-or-less well-off members of the middle class (like my family), and they welcomed me. Because of the limited experience of entertaining "company," the nervousness of the cook (who also served) was apparent, just as it was obvious that the linens, silver, and china I was honored with were seldom used. I understood all of this from home.

I also had letters from friends of my own making in Cincinnati. Most of these people were wealthy world-travelers and were—in varying degrees—art-, theater-, and music-conscious. They lived on the East Side in elegance, surrounded by "unmatching" objets d'art and opulence.

Through Mrs. David Workum in Cincinnati I met her wealthy, very deaf sister, Mrs. Gustav Blumenthal, and their cousin, Miss Evelyn Leo (Rubin Goldmark's friend), about whom I will have much to say later. These women were as dissimilar in their respective ways of life and interests as it was possible for people to be. They were about forty years my senior. I felt at home at Mrs. Blumenthal's teas and dinners, was indulged in New York's finest restaurants, and was limousined to theater and opera. No one would have believed that my tails (obligatory in those days) had cost only twenty-five dollars.

Mrs. Blumenthal and others like her lived graciously. They introduced me to a way of life that was new and truly glamorous. Although I was charmed by them, they were by no means realistic. Mrs. Blumenthal suggested that I might enjoy Sherry's on Park Avenue for breakfast, which would cost me only $1.75 for *everything*! And this was in 1929, when I had no difficulty having the same *everything*! at a drugstore counter for 20¢.

I knew her throughout the rest of her life (as I have nearly everybody else I ever knew), and when she died a few years later, she left me a pair of eighteenth-century Roman bronzes set on marble Directoire bases. When I collected them I found labels pasted on each base and in her strong handwriting, reminding me of her equally positive voice, she had written, "GIVE THESE TO LEHMAN ENGEL, 350 East 54th St." This was a command.

Many years after my introduction to Mrs. Blumenthal, Mr. Gold-mark, and later to Mrs. W. Murray Crane and many others, I was greatly impressed by their "free" surroundings, which included furniture, pictures, and bric-a-brac from all periods and places. Now, long-settled in a double apartment (two small ones made to connect), I have during the past twenty-seven years collected and surrounded myself with what, to many people, would spell clutter. But I love every item of it. The walls are literally covered with (mostly) signed and numbered lithographs, etchings, and posters. There are many Picassos (including a small drawing), Miros, Chagalls, Dufys, Cocteaus, Toulouse-Lautrecs (one given me by Montgomery Clift), Buffets, a Laurencin, two Klees, two Blakes, two Rouaults (given me by Morris Stonzek), a Dali, and many others. I have three Robert Edmond Jones set designs (one given me by Jones himself, the other two given me by Dr. Bertram Shaffner), one Oliver Smith design, a James Reynolds, a Boris Aronson, an Eckart, and two Eugene Bermans. I bought most of the pictures from, or through, Jim Wise. A single Piranesi from the *Imaginary Prisons* series was the first picture I ever bought.

There are also a number of Picasso ceramics, a reproduction of Renoir's *Head of a Little Girl* given me by David Merrick, and two other museum copies.

There is a painting of me by Harold Rome and a bronze head sculpted by Matilda Parrish.

But these are by no means all. There are Steuben bowls and vases given me by orchestras, a tall, square hand-painted Japanese vase given me by the *Scarlett* (the musical version of *Gone with the Wind*) company in Tokyo, two Tony Awards, a gold medal from the Jackson Opera Guild, a silver one from Sigma Alpha Mu fraternity, three Greek icons, two Sicilian (Carthaginian) heads for plants, two old Turkish puppets framed in a lighted shadow box, costume designs by Rouben Ter-Arutunian and David Ffolkes, Mexican bric-a-brac, a candelabrum from Bayreuth, a tall vase from Vienna, a large white porcelain hand (given me by Thomas and Ellen Royal) from the Space Center at Houston, my grandmother's Wedgwood sugar and cream pitcher, a clock from Evelyn Leo and one from Tokyo, a pair of lamps from New Delhi, three large glass shelves of colognes and scents in my bedroom, and many many more things.

I love all of them, and do not see them as clutter but as an extension of myself. I use a scent on my handkerchief, smoke rich dark cigars, have many green plants and always fresh flowers. But this present narrative excursion is forty-three years ahead of itself.

Clarence Adler, the pianist and teacher, had himself been a Cincinnatian, and so I was inevitably sent to him. As a successful professional man he fit squarely between the two groups, Eastsiders and Westsiders. He knew them socially and drew his pupils from both. It was Clarence who introduced me to Aaron Copland.

Copland always had a genuine interest in new composers. He brought me into contact with others of my age, and we became the Young Composers' Group. During a couple of years we met weekly, played, and discussed and fought about music. Aaron listened, giggled, was interested, never interfered.

The Young Composers' Group included Bernard (Benny) Hermann,* Jerome (Jerry) Morross, Vivian Fine, Israel Citkowitz, and three or four others.

Vivian and I went to movies frequently. She was particularly fond of Ruth Chatterton's soapy tragedies because they made her laugh.

Benny was the most colorful, persistent, loquacious, argumentative, and opinionated. As he spoke (which was always), he would continually twirl a short lock of hair around his right index finger. As soon as anyone else tried to talk, his face automatically took on a vague, faraway look, and indeed, for that moment he seemed to be transported to another planet. It was he who precipitated most of the fights. He attacked everyone else's music brutally and impatiently. He pushed his way into the Juilliard Graduate School the following year and was tossed out at the end of the season. Jerry was his friend and Benny-and-Jerry became a single word.

It's strange how people in a small town know each other, speak in passing and not really know one another at all. Although I had met Eudora Welty in Jackson before either of us went away to school, it was not until several years later in New York, when a group of Jacksonians were there each simultaneously pursuing various schoolings, that we had first real contacts.

---

* Hermann composed the music for many of Orson Welles's films, including *Citizen Kane*.

Top row: Lehman Engel, Israel Citkowitz, Jerome Moross, Marc Blitzstein, and Bernard Herrmann; *second row*: Henry Brant, Harrison Kerr, Herbert Elwell, Walter Piston, and Aaron Copland; *seated*: Wallingford Riegger, Randall Thompson, Robert Russell Bennett, Wesley La Violette, Vivian Fine, and Richard Donovan. *Photo by Settle*

Eudora was at Columbia along with Dolly Wells and Frank Lyell, who had first introduced me to Eudora in the Livingstone Park lake. I was at Juilliard. We chanced to meet here and there. I think it was at Norma and Herschell Brickell's (also from Jackson) where all of us, including Nash Burger, whose father used to play cards with my father, often went.

Each summer all of us went home to swelter, and there the threads grew stronger. There were about five such summers before I began staying on in New York with work to occupy and to pay me. But at home Frank, Eudora, Hubert Creekmore, and I used to meet at Eudora's, and we formed what we called the Night-Blooming Cereus Club, the total membership of which sat up to see the glorious white flower with the yellow feathery center bloom. The morning after, it looked like a swan with a broken neck.

Those summers are jumbled together in my memory. During one

of them Eudora did some letter-writing for me. Perhaps it was at another time that she took many snapshots. Several of them are among the best any photographer ever took of me. I have one of Eudora, who really invented "camp," sitting in a tree, a Spanish shawl around her shoulders and on her face an uncharacteristic expression of would-be disdain.

With the passing of time, many things happened to us separately, and we seized every opportunity to communicate and to be together. On my visits to see my family perhaps twice a year—and more often in my parents' failing days—Eudora was, as she is today, always available whenever it is possible for me to get away from family and family friends. To insure our being together to talk without interruption, she usually picks me up in her car—never a fancy one—and takes me for a ride just anywhere away from everybody else.

LEFT: I snapped this picture of Eudora Welty with her camera. Frank Lyell was the Señor; Eudora, the unwitting inventor of camp, was herself above it all. RIGHT: Taken on a summer vacation in Jackson by Eudora Welty. I was about twenty.

At her house or mine while my mother was still alive, or at any of my cousins', Eudora always enjoyed her bourbon and I my scotch.

She has endured a great deal. Her father died many years ago, but her mother lingered in poor health for some years. When finally it became necessary for Eudora to put her in a nursing home in Yazoo City, more than an hour's drive from Jackson, Eudora drove to see her nearly every day.

During those days she developed the habit of starting her work at 5:00 A.M. so that she could spend several hours of writing without interruption. She still retains that habit.

Very shortly before her mother died, Eudora's two brothers—both married and each living in his own house—died within days of each other.

I have seldom heard her refer to any of this, and what suffering she experienced she kept as her very own.

She is selfless, simple, timid, unworldly, and dedicated to her work. She has had every possible honor and success heaped on her, but nothing has ever changed her life style or her nature. She lives in Jackson—the only place where she feels comfortable—travels when it is necessary only on trains (if possible), and speaks so quietly as to be often inaudible.

She lives in her parents' house, which is very nice and devoid of any fanciness. It has two stories made of dark-red-to-purple bricks, and Eudora lives as she prefers—alone. The front yard has large pine trees, and the house is surrounded by japonicas (camelias) of all kinds and colors. Behind the house there is a lovely garden containing more camelias and gardenias. The garden is no longer as well manicured as it once was, but I imagine Eudora prefers it that way.

Now devoid of family responsibilities, she works consistently and hard. As she prefers never to discuss her work-in-progress, I seldom ask her what she is doing.

If I have given any notion that, like Emily Dickinson, Eudora is a recluse, let me assure you that she is not. She has many old friends, all of whom respect her privacy, and everyone in Jackson is deeply proud of her distinguished achievements.

By the time fall of that first year had set in, Rubin Goldmark, with whom I hoped to study composition, had returned from Europe. (He had taught Gershwin, Copland, and many others.)

On a late-September afternoon I was summoned by a handwritten letter to an interview with the old man at the brownstone house in the West Eighties, where he lived with a brother and his family. A manservant ushered me into a cluttered second-floor studio where Mr. Goldmark awaited me. He was immaculately dressed in a black suit and had long soft white hair and a thick white handlebar moustache. He wore a hearing aid and every so often had difficulty hearing. He smelled of cologne, although the room was hazy with stale cigar smoke.

The walls were covered with dark-red damask paper, which was only intermittently visible behind the immense mass of autographed photographs, pictures of composers, framed awards, trophies, and such. Everywhere there was too much, but in some strange way it all bore an air of belonging.

Mr. Goldmark felt that I should spend a year with private teachers "brushing up" on my theoretical knowledge, which I knew was incomplete, and then I would be able to get a fellowship in composition with him the following season at the Juilliard Graduate School.

The year passed rapidly. I worked hard, saw and heard much, and was dazzled by New York.

I was nineteen, enthusiastic, and full of hope for my future, but the year was 1929. In the newspapers I read of disaster and the end of everything for many people. On the streets mature men dressed like remaindered bank presidents, hotel managers, or headwaiters would ask me to buy them a bowl of soup. This cost five cents at that time, crackers included. I could afford to help. My parents supported me. Mama was back as the head of Uncle Isy's office at the laundry, and Papa was still selling shirts in the always-poor South, but 1929 to them was no different from any other time.

Walter Lawrence, my closest friend, and another vocal student, a friend of his and also from San Francisco, Stanley Lichtenstein, and I became a theater- and opera-going triumvirate. The three of us were often together. Stanley, who had no visible financial problems, would buy expensive clothes and accessories at Fortnum and Mason, invite Walter or me or any other friend to try on this and that, and then insist on our taking it because he thought it suited us better!

Next season, after a hot summer in Jackson, I returned to New York to the Juilliard and to a one-room apartment in the Village. Fellow students came and brought their friends because most of these boys and girls lived with their families in Brooklyn or the Bronx and had little opportunity of receiving their friends at home. The pyramid of people grew rapidly, eventually including not only composers but actors, painters, poets, playwrights, and dancers; it was not unusual to find far too large a crowd there in my single room.

Nearly all of us beginning then together about 1930 did have one thing in common: the need to work around the theater. Perhaps all along that was what we really did want to do. Perhaps we were enticed by the idea that through the theater we could find an audience and earn a livelihood. It was certainly clear to us that composers of abstract music—symphonies, quartets, and so on—had neither of these opportunities. The many small special concerts that we attended regularly in those days (the League of Composers, the International Society for Contemporary Music, the New School) attracted only a scant group of listeners—mostly those of us, so to speak, "in the family"—and certainly nobody earned a penny from such performances. Even the prestige gained from such programs was *en famille* prestige, about which the general public could not have cared less. This factor, I think, also accounted for the cultish quality of the music itself.

I was twenty and the radio sang "Life Is Just a Bowl of Cherries." But it was 1930, and in the cold crisp light of winter I saw grown men standing on Fifth Avenue corners stepping from foot to foot (going nowhere) to keep from freezing. They marked time, selling apples. There were many corners and many men. And many men standing in line on Times Square awaiting free soup and bread. There were bitter cherries in those bowls.

Walter and I went to everything: concerts, opera, dance, and theater, although it was toward the theater that we leaned most strongly. We bought season tickets for the Family Circle (the fifth floor) at the Metropolitan Opera—where we were horrified by many of the ruined voices we heard and the old-fashioned, shabby productions. We went to everything our season tickets offered *except* the operas of Verdi and Donizetti, which we were as yet too unwashed to appreciate. (We thought of ourselves as snobs.) At these, we stood in front of the opera house's filthy facade and peddled our seats.

Wagner, however, was a different story. Frank Lyell reminds me that there were eight *Walküre* performances that season and that I attended all of them as a standee!

It was during the 1931 season when a group of us unwashed young avant-garde "composers" attended the matinee premiere of Deems Taylor's (we referred to him privately as Damn Stealer) opera *Peter Ibbetson* (renamed by us *Peter Rabbitson*), overseeing everything from our standing-room vantage point.

Of course we hated the opera. It was too conventional, too "vanilla" and dull; everything was beneath our youthful contempt, but we kept our places to the bitter end.

Then—when all the music was finished, the work was entirely concluded—something happened: we found ourselves caught up in the *occasion*. There was enormous applause. The singers bowed again and again. They were then joined on stage by the conductor and stage director. There was cheering for the composer, and at last he was brought out—a tiny man outsized in every way by all the others around him. The audience's demonstration was deafening, and by this time, we neophytes—undoubtedly seeing ourselves in Mr. Taylor's place—joined in the excitement.

At length it became mandatory that Taylor make a speech. (What honest thing could he say? Could he assume that the noisy demonstration indicated the public's enthusiasm for his work? Or was it simply the occasion?)

Taylor extended his arms, palms outward, and there was instantaneous breathless silence. After a very long pause, he spoke, simply and tastefully, and we with our snobbishness, were annihilated because we were deeply moved.

"When you go to your homes this evening, please remember that you have just seen one completely happy man."

My friends and I heard and saw as much as we could crowd into seven days and nights. Some of it was fascinating, and all of it was to be learned from. There were, however, three unique old ladies then on the recital platform.

All of them were dubbed "Madame," all were singers of sorts, and all of them drew capacity audiences consisting of the musical cognoscenti, chiefly the celebrated singers of opera and concert. Two of the ladies also attracted composers and critics. The third did not. None of them was the possessor of much of a voice. All of them sang the most difficult repertoire, and all, though in one way or another fondly remembered by those fortunate enough to have been anywhere from twenty-five to forty-five at the time, are now long dead.

The two who attracted the most "musical" public (including critics) were Madame Povla Frijsch from Finland, a longtime resident of New York, and Madame Eva Gautier.

Madame Frijsch was moderately tall, and when she walked onto the stage of Town Hall, she lifted her knees (under her dress, to be sure) so high and tossed her head back in such a spirited manner that she reminded me of a circus thoroughbred entering the center ring. On the other hand, Madame Gautier was short and stout and always seemed to be wrapped in an ample scarf against all possibility of draft. She had charm but belonged to no such thoroughbred ancestry as did Madame Frijsch. The latter's clothes were usually elegantly black, studded sporadically with black beads, while Madame Gautier appeared to have been costumed from odds and ends that on other occasions lay carelessly across her piano.

Each was always greeted with enthusiastic applause, the kind that tells you that the idol is the personal property of every member of the audience.

As each lady braved her first song, it was frequently difficult to suppress a wanton giggle or to make a silent self-inquiry: "Why am I here? And surely she can't sing!"

However, the first song provided, and simultaneously resolved, the shock: the discovery that indeed the empress was wearing no clothes! Afterward, there was no escaping the spell that each wove. Both ladies were impeccable artists, and it is my guess that they were both bright enough to know that with their limited vocal resources they must present seldom-sung art songs if their careers were to continue. This both of them did, and it was very seldom (after the first song) that their limitations called attention to themselves.

Their programs were rendered with consummate taste. They sang in French, German, English, and Italian; Madame Frijsch had Finnish to herself. They did world premieres and New York premieres, but most of these were to the greater credit of the nonsingers than the noncomposers. However, these new items did add special distinction to their evenings and often turned them into semioccasions.

The third of this triumvirate leaves an unresolved riddle to posterity. Like the aforementioned ladies, Madame Florence Foster Jenkins had no voice. Unlike the other two, she sang only familiar songs and arias, the combination of which would have been suicidal for the greatest of divas, in that they ran the gamut of vocal demands.

I was taken for the first time to hear Madame Jenkins by Madame Gaudenzi, Walter Lawrence's teacher, who took it for granted that *everyone* knew about Madame Jenkins. In my case, she erred. We arrived in the auditorium (the Grand Ballroom at the Plaza, I seem to recall), and it was so crowded that we were ushered into the very first row. Inasmuch as the seats were not reserved, it occurred to me only later that everyone else had come early in order to sit as far away from the stage as possible. And everybody else included the most famous opera singers in the world.

Before the event began, Madame Jenkins (or one-quarter of her— a considerable amount) could be plainly seen peeping out at the audience from the wings. The audience played its part by pretending not to see anything. Finally, the lights were lowered, the stage lights were brightened, and out shuffled a lady who *had* to have been in her seventies. She was quite tall and extremely weighty. Behind her walked her accompanist, Cosmé McMoon, who wore, in addition to white tie and tails, a large artificial handlebar moustache.

Madame Jenkins looked at the audience through fish eyes, settled herself in the arm of the grand piano, and, after a few Handelian chords, opened her mouth and screamed what was once thought to have been an aria. Never at any time that evening—or any other— was she on pitch, a matter that threw the audience into a laughing panic, suppressed but audible. The room shook. I was taken by such surprise that I had to ram my handkerchief in my mouth and cover my face with the program.

Although this was the gist of this and subsequent evenings, a few details will bear telling. When she sang the "Vissi d'arte" from *Tosca*, she managed to get down on her knees, but at the end, two stalwart stagehands, hardly dressed for the occasion, and the moustachioed McMoon were required to raise her again to her feet. The applause was deafening and managed to cover the entire episode.

When she came out to sing Lakmé's "Bell Song," she was followed by a string quartet and a man carrying a tambourine, which he managed to play sporadically and at the wrong times. A flautist tried hard to keep up with her cadenza, but one of them was simply not doing it correctly.

There was great clamoring for an encore and Madame Jenkins took forever to reappear, but when she did, she was wearing a gypsy costume with a wicker tray of artificial flowers secured around her neck by a red ribbon. She sang the Spanish "Clavelitos," during which she ungracefully hurled the flowers toward the audience, which, in turn, threw them back at her.

During the intermission at one of these recitals, Madame Jenkins's husband was pointed out to me. As I passed, I heard him say, "You know, Madame's voice is not what it once was, but her artistry is flawless."

Over a period of perhaps ten years I attended several similar evenings, the last of which was sold out at Carnegie Hall. It occurred to me then as now that perhaps—just perhaps—Madame Jenkins was "having" the audience and earning a considerable sum of money. If she was aware that she was being laughed at, she never disclosed it. Because the audience thought she was deadly serious, the fun became much greater; the laughter—great as it always was —nevertheless had to be suppressed. It seems to me that if we had been free to behave as we might have watching, say, Beatrice Lillie, once would have been enough. Under the impression that we were *stealing* our fun, we continued to be Madame Jenkins's body slaves to the very end.

Strange, but these three old ladies—two on one side and one on the other—drew almost identical audiences. We went to hear them sing, the one thing that none of them could really do at all.

Work with Goldmark at the Juilliard continued for four years, until the old man felt he had no more to teach me. During those four years, I was required to do quantities of writing—good in that it helped to create a valuable habit of work. I composed all day, every day. My writing, however, had to be done in conventional idioms because Goldmark could not understand or criticize any others, but he was content for me to write as I pleased after I had completed what he assigned. I began leading a schizophrenic creative existence that became increasingly complicated until several years later when Roger Sessions, the composer, took it upon himself to help me coordinate what I had learned with my creativity.

I went everywhere, met everyone, and worked hard every day. I learned to love New York and especially the Village; lower Fifth Avenue enchanted, turned into a park as it passed through the Memorial Arch in Washington Square, the charm of old houses lining the Square, the peacefulness of residential blocks that empty into the Avenue, the absence of ostentation of the rich and of shyness of the poor, the springtime wagons ablaze with potted geraniums, the children who still rolled hoops noisily around the fountain in the Square, the bulging crowds that jammed the sidewalk cafe under the Brevoort's awning to be insulted by the snooty French waiters, Luchow's and the Lafayette, the careless little gardens in everybody's back yard, the back yards that became restaurants in the summertime, the unremitting garishness and clamor of Fourteenth Street, the haughtiness of Gramercy Park, the rotting and deserted docks beyond the Washington Market still ample for lovers strolling, the night sounds on the river and the lights—gliding, weaving in and out, blinking, fading softly away.

Most of all, it was New York that mattered. There was so much to be seen and experienced, so many people and such a variety of places. These, combined with the opportunity to create, could only have happened in New York, in our land, in our time.

The discussions I could be a part of mattered most, I think. They involved the theater, music, painting, poetry, and the dance, and they had tremendous value for me, not because everything that was said was profound or even infallible but because the discussions caused me to think about things that had not before even occurred to me.

On the one hand, theater, concert, and opera excursions absorbed our serious attention; on the other, a crowd of us often went to Harlem late in the evening and did not return home again until dawn. The places we visited were "private" apartments, not cabarets with public licenses. They were crowded with bawdy people, overflowing with cheap gin: the Pleasure Dome of Kubla Khan. In our lives, even at that time, these night trips were exhausting intermissions between working days. Some of us eventually tired of them and exchanged them for less depleting ones. For many other young people whom we customarily saw in the Harlem joints, work was only necessary as the provider of this important pleasure. We lost them there—nowhere.

When summer came around again, there were no lessons, no concerts, no opera, and fewer shows. But summer in New York could be happy. The daytime working was often hot and wilting. But the nights and the long, slow weekends could be filled with fabulous pleasures that were available to everyone. In my time, what was more extraordinary than a ride atop the elephantine double-decked buses that waddled from Washington Square up the length of Fifth Avenue and along the Hudson on Riverside Drive? Was there ten cents worth of anything else in the whole world that was so gay? And for five cents, you could lean across the rail of a ferry to Staten Island, watching the black waters churn in the boat's wake and the receding of New York's blinking canyons, or you could hail the Statue of Liberty at the boat's side, or trace the boat's course at its bow as it weaved in and out of the paths of other boats. And for nothing you could stroll in Central Park and lose yourself by the lagoon or among the hills and rocks or loll on a grassy bank under a swaying tree. New York hovered around nearby, but—especially at night—it rested unseen beyond the jungles of the park. These were peaceful pleasures for a summer night. So also were the beaches of Brooklyn and the Battery Park at South Ferry, where you could hear the water lapping at the wall and watch the boat lights slide noiselessly by, or you could stand on Brooklyn Heights and see these same lights and the outlines of bridges in one vast smoothly working design.

You could walk before the lighted shop windows of Fifth Avenue —dressing, exchanging, furnishing, remodeling, traveling, or assembling libraries, linens, toiletries, luggage, silver, or lithographs. When you were tired, you could rest beside a silent dusty lion on guard against nothing before the Library. Through it all you remained invisible, for were not the lovers invisible who sat locked in each other's arms on top of the bus, their hair tangled together in the riding breeze? And were those other couples not invisible who lay together on the grass in the park, who walked hand-in-hand along the Avenue, who stood kissing in the darkness of the boat deck? Only in New York, where men and women move together in crowds, can they thus remain peacefully invisible in the summer night.

On a Sunday morning in summer you could walk tieless into the silence of a garden cafe. You looked through the pages of your heavy newspaper while your coffee cooled. Your silence was respected. The music ended with your drinking on Saturday night. Nobody turned a dial on a radio. "Good morning!" was a complete conversation. After breakfast, you could walk for hours in and out of many different worlds separated from each other only by the turn of a corner. Along the rotting wharves there was warm languorous sunshine in keeping with the listless motion of the water. Through the streets of the slums, pushcart peddlers darted about like bees on a honeycomb. The day was busy and confused by the variety of meanings attached to Sunday by the hodgepodge of ghetto groups. Farther downtown, Wall Street had one understanding of the day. The narrow streets and lanes between the dizzy-high buildings were deserted and neat, like the cities in a Tom Swift adventure. Now and then a sharp shaft of sunlight pierced the cool shade. Two pigeons sauntered across a street with dignity, then flew up without warning to be lost in the high recesses of the buildings.

All of this was New York in summer. And New York was much more, for it had to be lived with if it were to be understood. Walt

Whitman knew it. In the many decades since his white beard disappeared from Central Park, more than the makeup on its face has changed. It is a face that I once loved.

And New York can be the city of life, of beginning, accomplishment, growth, development, attainment, fulfillment. It is the place where a talent may be nourished and fostered, engendered—if in itself it is insufficient—through contact with other talents, and the broad achievements of many other talents, so that at last it may become solely itself—matured, unique, perhaps even monumental. Or this talent may be much less than monumental and still may sparkle for one great moment, catching the rays of public fancy, and in New York, even in that moment, every face may turn to behold and wonder. This, too, is a fulfillment—the easier kind—the long shot, requiring not the long preparation, nor the long view, nor the deep gift, nor the great development, but only the lucky, proper facade at the proper lucky time. Like the quick flash of sunlight caught for an instant in a mirror, it may dazzle and then forever disappear.

All of this is the public aspect of life and New York, the result of the struggle of big talent and little talent and often of no talent. They could not grow into life anywhere else in this land, in our time. It is the city that, like a mother (sometimes, even cruelly like a mother), discovers and presents it. She performs the symphony with her orchestra, produces the opera and the drama on her stage, sets the feet of the dancer to moving in the likeness of her own rhythms, hangs the pictures on the walls of her museum, puts up the signboards and the lights to announce the achievements to the many others who need it for their own very lives.

And sometimes New York can be the city of oblivion, the only city in this land, in our time, in which people can be lost: the boys and girls from Pine Bluff, Sioux Falls, Cedar Rapids, and White River can come here—come away from the families and neighbors who know them and their every dream and their every dress and suit and the cut of their hair and shape of their nose and the days on which they were born and baptized and graduated. They can leave the familiar and come here to the strange. They can become integrated with the millions like and unlike themselves and, of necessity and not necessarily to their misfortune, alter the dream that will not work, so that life itself here at last can take on the only true meaning it could ever have had.

But oblivion in New York can mean the beginning of life, too. It can mean the relinquishing of sometimes unattainably foolish dreams foisted on the young by the fond ones at home. In New York, our City-Mother opens the eyes to the real world. The young, transplanted here, find in the living oblivion, the blessed falling-away of heavy responsibility. No longer will John be a failure because while walking in the shafts of sunlight filtered between the mountain-buildings, he perceives that he will never be president. Here in New York, it is not incumbent upon him to be what he was not meant to be—not meant to be by his own impulses and potentialities. No longer will Mary be a failure, because while walking out through the drafty alley of a stage door, she knows by her own self-honesty, newborn, that she never was and never could have been the great ballerina Mrs. McNair predicted she would become after her recital last year at home. New York has helped these girls and boys to settle it for themselves, once and for all, so that now at last they are free to live and grow, as and for themselves, in the ways that will most nearly make them happy. The momentary sting of disappointment suffered in this oblivion will pass quickly and perhaps leave no scar at all.

In personal ways of life, this oblivion of New York can be no less loving. Not everyone who grows up in Pine Bluff and Sioux Falls and Cedar Rapids and White River needs New York for the opportunities of learning and doing. Many boys and girls come here, nevertheless, just to get away from families and neighbors who seemed to know their every dream (or did they?) and their every dress and suit and the cut of their hair and shape of their nose and the days on which. . . . Here in this truly loving anonymity, they are able to avoid the patterns of life that to most seem most desirable: the dates (or the failure to have them), card parties, showers, clubs and the expectations of marriage and homes and families (or the oblique questions when the pattern is not conformed to). Here the City-Mother does not ask, demands no answer. She is deaf and without the power of speech. But more importantly she vibrates with life, and all who live in her great house vibrate with her. In our land, in our time, here is fulfillment.

4: Under Way

JOHN MARTIN, CRITIC of the *New York Times*, made me acutely aware of the modern American dance movement, and Harry Losee, whom I met through the Clarence Adlers, was the first of many dancers I was to know.

Harry and his friends seemed to me both fascinating and evil, and I was dazzled by their cheap glamor. They were the embodiment of the storybook New York, but their behavior—far from being harmful—helped me to grow up, to observe, to learn, to reject what was not compatible with me.

Harry, a tall, well-developed man in his mid-thirties, lived in a cheap hotel, a hangout for infrequently employed vaudevillians. He was always surrounded by other dancers, booking agents, hangers-on (but to God alone knows what). Because of prohibition, he himself produced quantities of gin. We stayed up very late every night because as a friend of Harry's it was futile to try to leave whenever he wished you to stay. I wrote music for him, which he used in a free recital at Wanamaker Auditorium—his gesture toward "art." He wanted, as many performers want (in an abstract sort of way), to be a "great" artist, but he was unwilling to sacrifice anything from the frippery of his foolish, wasteful life for sustained work. He needed people to such an extent that even his pathetic attempts at creation became private performances for just anyone who would sit about with cocktails watching him improvise. On several occasions, because he could not pay his bills, the hotel locked him out of his room; then a week's engagement at the Roxy would take care of him temporarily and provide the excuse for celebrating in a new money-draining series of parties.

One engagement brought Harry to Radio City Music Hall early in its existence. Harry worked on a dance number for himself, a female partner, and the resident corps de ballet. A day before the opening performance, it was discovered that the music he had worked with (Ravel, I believe) was not available.

Harry called me to the Music Hall at about midnight prior to a scheduled 10:00 A.M. orchestra dress rehearsal, asking me to compose new music. Two exhausted dancers lay on the floor of a small office where I worked at a piano. When I would complete a phrase or two, the dancers would come alive, stand up, try out the steps to the music, then lie down again. A music-copyist would appear at regular intervals to take a section at a time to an assembly-line of orchestrators and copyists. (This went on all night.) At 10:00 A.M. the orchestra played the music, and the dancers changed none of their choreography. I was paid seventy-five dollars.

The dances that Harry and I had done together contained every idea he ever had. Under new titles, with different costumes and music, the same dances were reproduced time and again. Years later, when he choreographed skating sequences for Sonja Henie's films, I saw the same things once again.

If Harry Losee initiated me into the profane order of the dance (and there were many others like him along the way), it was Martha Graham, who, unknowingly, beckoned as a high priestess.

When I first saw Martha Graham dance (about 1930), I had such an overwhelming experience that it became imperative that I compose music for her. Although we had never met, I was a good friend of John Martin's, and I could therefore claim some common tie with her. I sent her a letter requesting an appointment. She did not reply. I telephoned her studio and wrote to her again. After several months of fruitless pursuit I was at last given an appointment to meet her and her accompanist, Louis Horst, at the latter's apartment. At the designated time, I rang the doorbell, received no reply, waited an hour, then went away. This did not prevent my writing again.

After several more weeks of trying to see her, she made and kept

Martha Graham about 1932.
Photo by Soichi Sunami

an appointment at Louis Horst's apartment. They listened intently
to my music. Both were sympathetic and promised that we would
collaborate.

It was in the fall of 1931 (only a few months later) that we
actually began work. We did many compositions* together during
the next three years, and they involved me totally. Martha created
most of the choreography in advance of my seeing anything. She
would perform alone or with the girls in her group to "counts." I
would comprehend an overall mood, write down the counts, notat-
ing phrases or accents or climaxes or places where we agreed there
should be silence. Martha would talk to me, usually in terms of
qualities or general essences like "the stillness of sunrise" or "the
sound of a forest at night" and I would go away, wrapped in a kind

* *Ceremonials* (1932), *Ekstasis* (1933), *Transitions* (1934; this included "Sara-
bande"), *Marching Song* (1935), *Imperial Gesture* (1935).

of magical mood of her making. Then I would compose to this framework of mood and counts and return with what I had written. She would listen, comment (usually enthusiastically) about the style and quality, and then dance to it, counting and listening at the same time. Here she felt there were too many notes. (I would thin them out.) Here the music should sustain while she moved, or the music should move rapidly while she sustained. Always there had to be complementary interaction. Much of the most concrete work was done in the final week and even on the day of performance—in an atmosphere of terror.

But the experience of working with Martha Graham was among the sublime moments of my young life. The ideas that she ulti- mately used germinated slowly. Whatever she did came as the result of an irresistible inner compulsion. Often I think she sensed that a work-in-progress might not turn out well but that she had to com- plete it and perform it before she could discard it and proceed clearly to the next work, whatever it might finally be.

The night before the premiere of *Ceremonials*, a long work draw- ing on Indian lore, she decided that the girls' costumes were not "right." She herself sat on the floor and cut, fitted, and pinned to- gether new ones for the waiting seamstress. The next morning, she had a bad cold, and several of her girls were ill from exhaustion. At the lighting rehearsal in the theater, Louis spoke so sharply to her that I feared she might collapse. I spoke up, begging him to be less harsh. He smiled, confiding that at these times Martha might "fall apart" if he let her alone. He had found that by quarreling with her, making her fight back, she kept her spirit and energy up and would not then stop.

The performance was jittery. The girls were still visibly counting their steps: one and two, turn, walk, two, three, four, stop. But there were exciting and moving moments. It failed with the critics, al- though my music was received favorably. Martha presented it once again in a much-altered state, but she was still not satisfied, and so she dropped it altogether from her repertoire.

Martha of course never had any money. She usually paid me an "outright" fifteen dollars for a score (orchestration included).

One time, perhaps ten days before a recital, her announcement circulars arrived from the printer but Martha did not even have the money for the postage. I think she borrowed eleven dollars then.

In one of our long "collaborations" Martha asked if I would object to begin writing the music of a sizable middle section. She explained that in one part she wanted the music to be like wallpaper—real background without melodic contour or rhythmic interest. After watching her rehearse this section to counts a number of times, I agreed to commence with it. She said there were eighty-seven counts of "seven."

A couple of days later I returned to her studio, where she characteristically sat on the floor (her hands covering her eyes) to hear what I had written. She was very well satisfied with the "feeling" and then decided to "try it on." I played, and Martha danced. After two bars we were not together. We tried again with identical results. Finally I asked her to dance to counts aloud. What I heard to my horror was "1–2–3–4–5–6–7–pause." Her "sevens" were "eights"!

Martha not only taught me much about dance and music with dance but also exercised on me a profound influence in an incalculable variety of other ways. I was able to employ her ideas of music-movement complementarity when I began writing incidental music for plays. I merely substituted word motion for body motion, the musical principles being nearly identical. I always recalled her saying that a bodily movement *must* be carried through to completion if it is to have any meaning. This was my most valuable single conducting lesson. It taught me the necessity of full, positive, energetic gestures and the sense of strength especially needed in guiding an orchestra through quiet, seemingly relaxed passages. It was from her that I learned that relaxation in a performance can only *seem*, not *be*.

Because Martha was great, my music was serviceable, and the newspapers had some good words for me, more dancers wanted me to write music for them. Within three or four years I had written for practically all the concert dancers in America. I had become a vogue. (Almost everyone at some time does become a vogue.)

Martha Graham is a great artist and innovator. Her choreography lives on even without her physical presence as a performer. Now in her eighties and still in possession of enormous technique, she has had the good judgment to teach younger dancers the roles she originally created for herself. She will not—cannot—die.

The people I was meeting belonged more to the theater than to music. Through Max Leavitt (then an actor, later founder of the Lemonade Opera), I met Julie (John) Garfield, Sanford Meisner, Robert Lewis (all soon to become members of the as-yet-unformed Group Theatre), Gerry Butler, Lucian Scott, and Hiram Sherman. Also Paul Goodman.

Although I was still a student at Juilliard, I had begun a career. Through friends, I organized an amateur chorus (I learned by doing). I composed a chorus called *Rain*. Marguerite Dessoff performed it with her choir in Town Hall, where it was well received. I acknowledged the applause from a box, smiling down at Mr. Goldmark, who sat below with Miss Leo in the first row, his hand cupped questioningly around one ear. Again, the papers wrote well of my music.

Also through Cincinnati friends I had met Aaron Sapiro, the Ford-slander lawyer,* who was on the board of the Music School of the Henry Street Settlement. I had become familiar with Kurt Weill's children's opera, *Der Jasager*, and Sapiro put up most of the money for its production at the school simply because he liked me.** Sandy Meisner staged the opera. That went well, too. I had learned by doing.

I wrote criticism without pay for the *Musical Leader* and helped Louis Horst found a little magazine, *The Dance Observer*. I persuaded the editors of the *Leader* and *Musical America* to allow me to write interviews with Arnold Schoenberg, the great German composer, soon to arrive in America. I was an extravagant admirer of his music, and this was to be my sole opportunity for coming into personal contact with him.

Somehow in November of 1933, I found myself at the docks, saw Schoenberg disembark with his wife, his daughter of less than two

* Mr. Sapiro, a New York City attorney, sued Henry Ford for a remark against the Jews. Ford settled the case out of court and issued a public apology.

** On opening night the professional lighting man refused to work without first being paid and Mrs. Elinore Stettenheim (now Mrs. Marvel), a board member, came hurrying downtown with her own money.

years, and his dog. I trembled, but this did not prevent my approaching, introducing myself as an interviewer *and* composer, and I was told at once that I could spend the time with him during the next few days, when he would be going to prearranged interviews with other writers and at NBC.

Schoenberg was small, dark, and bald, with sensitive eyes. He spoke English, which he had not studied since he was a schoolboy forty-five years before, with difficulty. He appeared to be nervous, but this may well have been caused by the strangeness of his surroundings and to the strenuousness of receptions and interviews. He was neither vigorous nor aggressive; his voice was peculiarly unresonant. When he occasionally expressed himself in German, his personality expanded, but this was not to say that when he spoke in English he was not also compelling. He was modest when alluding to himself and his work and was kind and indulgent toward everyone. Although he was fifty-nine years old, he showed no sign of advancing age.

In my several brushes with Schoenberg I carried a small notebook on each page of which I had written a question. I reproduce the exact replies to some of them as I wrote them. The awkwardness of some of his answers was caused largely by his limited English, but I think the reader should know *exactly* what was said. The words in brackets are my own additions made in an attempt to clarify what Schoenberg had to say.

What is the connection between classic harmony and counterpoint?

It is the same thing—another manner. Same thing. New thoughts. Another method of the same thing. There is no rule for following harmony. Melody only.

Do you think race-traits are felt in music? Don't you feel that your music presents definite Hebraic characteristics?

I hope, but I don't know. As a Jew, I show a measure of thinking certainly Jewish.

In America there is no musical past. What do you think of the musical future? Indians? Transplanted Negroes?

Yes, if they will comprehend not as different but as if it is tradition.

Do you have any new aims regarding your music?

Always one aim, to be concise. Never to write something which is only there to accomplish only formal necessity. Each teacher is a good teacher if the pupil is good or is bad if the pupil is bad. It is not necessary for pupils to know classics, but I prefer it.

Tell me something of the pictures you painted during composition of the Gurrelieder.

For many years I had seen these pictures in my mind, and one day I have had the courage to write them. People pretend it [music] is "abstract" but it is not. It is "music." Art is only the new. Art means *new* art. Bach created a new art. Even today it is not approximated. He extended music from seven tones to all twelve. The polyphonic style of Bach is founded on all twelve tones. Handel is like a slice of bread. Simple. Square. Bach used all kinds of music, discord, etc. Offers a marvelous quality of melody. He first employed the principle of variation, which is the basis of Haydn, etc.

Difficult to be up to date today. . . .

Pathos is a sign of romanticism. . . .

Art is nonexistent without participation. It does not dispute [the] right of [the] majority. . . .

First flights are not done by majority. Matter for single persons. . . .

Artist must not paint what he cannot see in a twinkling of an eye. Otherwise [it will] never be a unit. . . .

Like life—one situation grows out of another. . . .

My public? I had none. My friends had applauded for me—not [my] works. . . .

After revolution of 1918 [there were] no attachments.

Leaders of music grew more stupid, more superficial. . . . Leaders of music do not follow my direction. [They] consider it a duty not to understand my music. . . .

[I] thought in my youth, *profession* of conductor to understand compositions. Not even understand the classics, why *mine?* . . .

Leaders only misguide. . . .

Audience [is] present to judge [rather] than enjoy. . . .

In 1924 [I] conducted *Pierrot Lunaire* in Italy. Puccini was very kindly. . . .

A fact is a fact and not a problem. . . .

[A question about the pictures.]

Not pictures. It is music tones. But musical themes, tones, and melodies I call "quasi-pictures." A musical story in musical pictures. Not a real story and not real pictures.

Fancy is the dominant force which drives the artist. . . .

It is not of great difference to me whether the idea is a practical idea, a program or a pure musical idea. For a musician can always say only music and the cause is of no importance. I am not against program music. If a composer can write good music describing spring, country, sun rising, skyscrapers, why not? The cause is of no importance. . . .

I am always writing that [which] my fancy gives me and always I can only write if I have seen a musical idea. . . .

When you have seen a musical idea, how do you seek to express it?

I receive an impression of musical form and extension of the whole and of the parts. By and by I am seeing this form more exactly and begin to hear themes and sonorities, and I begin the writing with the pen—sometimes with sketches and sometimes I write the music directly.

Do you think that in time the public will come to understand your music?

I only hope that it will not be so long, but I am not sure. The difficulty for the public to understand is the conciseness. I never repeat. I say an idea only once.

At first, did this [lack of public understanding] discourage you?

I was always offended by it, for I think that the public could know that I have worked with the greatest earnestness and sincerity and I think I have the right to demand the respect of the public for my work.

What do you think is the greatest need in music today?

What we need in music today is not so much music but men with the courage to express what they feel.

Henry Cowell,* the most energetic and enterprising of the many composers I was coming to know well, asked me to organize and

---

* Cowell published my unfinished *Job* in his *New Music* as "Three Excerpts from *Job*," along with a piano piece by Ruth Crawford, the mother of Pete Seeger.

preside over a weekly radio series of lecture-broadcasts on American composers. There was to be no remuneration, but I would be able to do an interesting job, would help to create an audience for the music and for myself, and would meet many performing artists who would appear—also gratis. (For this series I took speech lessons to eradicate my southern accent.)

One of these was Harry Cumpson, a concert pianist and teacher. He was close to the American composers, especially Roy Harris, Carlos Chavez, and Aaron Copland, and played many of their pieces at his concerts. A year after our meeting, Harry arranged a series of lecture-recitals with me, and until he passed away in 1970, he was to be counted as a devoted friend.

Although I was busy with my Juilliard studies, doing the radio series, rehearsing *Der Jasager* for the Henry Street Settlement School, and a dozen other things, I undertook composition of a ballet, *Phobias*, based on a libretto (and with decor) by John Vassos for the Dance Center, headed by Gluck Sandor and Felicia Sorel.* Because of my whirling schedule, I could not attend regular rehearsals. But having discovered the propensities of dancers as a class to distort music (by making repeats and cuts and by altering tempi at will), I insisted upon seeing a run-through of *Phobias* the night before its opening. Since the music at that rehearsal was played as written from beginning to end, I was satisfied that there was to be none of the nonsense I had feared, but it did seem that the dancers were incredibly confused.

The following night at the premiere, *Phobias* (forty-five minutes of music) lasted nearly two hours! There were innumerable repetitions. Naturally there had been confusion the preceding night because the run-through had been presented only for my approval and the dancers had actually been forced to improvise for me for forty-five minutes!

In spite of spiraling activities, I was occasionally able to compose something solely to indulge myself, to "express" myself. On one of these rare occasions I set to music a poem by e.e. cummings, whose work I knew intimately and admired extravagantly. My song was small and insignificant, but I required the poet's permission for use

---

* At this time I became acquainted with another young composer, William Shawn, who for many years now has been distinguished as editor of the *New Yorker*.

of the lyric. Fortunately, I had come to know a very shy, sincere, and wealthy young painter named Howard Rothschild; I had seen some of his pictures and liked them, and he in turn believed in the music that I was writing. When he learned that I wanted to meet cummings, he treated it as the easiest thing in the world to arrange. (I contend that, without exception, no matter how uncelebrated we are, we somehow meet someone who knows someone we would like to know.)

Late one afternoon, he took me to 4 Patchin Place, where cummings lived with his wife, a former model and then an actress. Patchin Place is an alley and is unique in New York. It is embedded in the Village between Sixth Avenue and Greenwich Avenue. It runs only one short block and is separated from all that lies before it by a wrought-iron gate, which is not used so much to shut in or to shut out as it is to define. The little alley divides two wall-to-wall sets of four-story houses at once simple, unostentatious, and in no way distinctive.

When Howard and I arrived, we were greeted by cummings. He was vigorous, cheerful, plain, and always—then and later—flourished a wonderful sense of humor. He closed the white door that no longer fit snugly in its frame, and we were in a tiny sitting room with a fireplace, undistinguished furniture, and a beautiful woman, Marion, his wife. I think I have never known more cheerfulness and have never had such a warm welcome.

We had tea and cookies. We laughed a great deal and almost continuously. I told cummings how much I admired his poetry and that I wanted to set some of it. He seemed "delighted" (his word), and he put no obstacle in my way.

Somehow cummings, Marion, and I (without Howard then) became friends. As happens in New York, the years passed and we spent an evening together about once a year. Often it was in my apartment where we had dinner. Just as often I took them to a restaurant.

cummings (by the way, everybody called him that except on rare occasions when Marion addressed him as "estlin," his second name), liked to play little jokes. Once he took a volume of his poems from my shelf and below my signature he wrote, "Glad to see he reads."

When there was a new set published or a new edition, he invariably gave me a copy.

Once we agreed to see a movie after dinner. I never quite understood whether cummings had never seen one or had simply not seen one in a long time, because he literally jumped in his seat every time the picture cut from one scene to another. He became so unsettled that we left, and we all laughed.

Often when the two of them were in my apartment, cummings would ask me to read some of his poems aloud. One request was enough, and we were off. Every so often I would stop to ask him if I had understood what he meant, and he invariably agreed.

He had as much success, I imagine, as any American poet could have had in his own time. He was published and written about, and once in a while he would give a lecture—usually under august auspices. However, he never had any money.

He died while I was out of town with a show. I wired Marion, and when I returned, I telephoned and asked her to dine or do anything with me that would please her. She would never accept an invitation and seemed to be steadily and deeply sad. It was not long before she too died.

My personal friends, as distinguished from those I knew personally on an artistic level, continued to form the spine of my life. I never exchanged one for another or one in one category for one in another. Both groups of them only began to grow in number and along seldom converging lines.

I had begun to accumulate credits. I had begun a career. Max Leavitt brought me to the attention of Herbert Gellendré, head of a "theater studio," the Repertory Playhouse Associates (RPA), where I was engaged to form a singing chorus out of a group of actors. We performed madrigals because I had just discovered them myself and loved them, not because I really knew anything about them. But again I was learning by doing, and this was to become an important experience in learning and loving for me.

In the summer after I had been notified of my graduation from Juilliard (a mere letter-formality), I went to Vermont with the RPA to conduct the chorus and to compose incidental music to a play, *It Is a Strange House*, by Dana Burnet. It was the first time I was ever paid enough money to live on (my parents had supported me until then and my schooling had been free).

Walter Lawrence was still studying singing but had not yet sung a song—nor did he he ever sing one. Through Walter, I met a young writer, Joe Ginsberg, later called Joel Graham. We had a great deal in common in spite of the fact that I did not like his writing, which, as it turns out, was not what he seemed to have been cut out for.

Joe Graham came to Vermont to spend a week with me and told me of his friend Mildred Fellner, whom he had known for a long time. They were to be married soon, and he wanted us to meet. I could hardly have known it then, since friendship is a result rather than a plan, but together Joe and Mildred were to become my most constant friends—if not my family. There were others in time who were also close, but the Grahams demanded nothing, understood me, often waited patiently while I explored and then tired of some new passion in my life, and were always there lovingly, especially whenever I needed them.

It was during that summer with the RPA in Vermont that a "fluke" occurred. On a Sunday in August 1934, I read an announcement in the *New York Times* that Sean O'Casey's play *Within the Gates* was to be presented in New York in the fall. An actor in the Vermont company owned a printed copy of the play that contained the songs and choruses written for the original London production (I did not think highly of them). Realizing that a conductor would be needed, I wrote a letter to the producers requesting an interview, but with no real conviction that I might get the job. To my amazement I received a prompt reply, inviting me to drop into their office on my return to New York in September. I had had so little experience to recommend me for the job that I was not hopeful, but I did call at the producer's office. Hundreds of actors were storming the place, but since I was not an actor and not in competition with them, I dared to push my way through to announce myself.

Inside, the familiar movie-profile of Melvyn Douglas confronted me. As he was to direct, he was casting the play. Although we spoke together, I don't think he ever looked at me. I stressed the fact that I had conducted choruses and that *Within the Gates* contained much choral singing. This information seemed not to affect him, but he nevertheless invited me to accompany him that very afternoon to the home of Milton Lusk, a friend of the producer's, to hear Lusk's new score. Trembling with delight, I accompanied him and Lillian Gish, who was to be the star of the production.

I was happy that the English music had been scrapped, but imagine my disappointment when, upon hearing the new music, I found it amateurish and unimaginative. Lusk was a successful businessman and a quarter of a century earlier had been a school friend of the producer; he had written music for school shows and club affairs. Music was his hobby.

After we left the apartment, Douglas was silent, and his eyes still behaved toward me as if I were the little man who wasn't there. He invited me to have a cocktail. In the bar, I decided to take my future with Melvyn Douglas into my own hands. I said that I did not like the music.

For the first time, his head inclined down from Olympus, and his eyes focused on me. He was happy. He had found an ally, for he had also hated the music.

"But where can we get new music?" he asked. "Time is short. Rehearsals begin in a week."

"I can write it," I said. "I can have it finished by tomorrow morning."

He might have had me carted off to Bellevue, for what I had said must have sounded absurd. Actually, to me it seemed easy. There were five choruses, four songs, and some incidental music to be written, but I was accustomed to writing quickly. In any case, Melvyn (as I have called him for a long time) agreed to come to my apartment the following morning to hear what I had done. The music was completed, and he was enthusiastic about it.

In the course of rehearsals Melvyn and I developed a friendship that goes on today, nearly forty years later. Back then, at the end of a day we would drive in his car through Central Park, dine somewhere magical to me and often go to theater. It was Melvyn who first introduced me to Gilbert and Sullivan and D'Oyly Carte.

When his beautiful wife, Helen Gahagan, came east from Hollywood with her firstborn, Melvyn had to go west to make a film, and Helen and I became close friends.

And so my first show on Broadway (1934) was under way and

nonsensical under the circumstances that I—on my own say-so—should conduct it, accidental that I should compose the music.

Sean O'Casey, the great man himself, came to America to witness the final rehearsals of *Within the Gates*. He squinted through his thick-lensed spectacles, never wore anything but a turtleneck sweater under a tweed jacket, fought noisily against what he did not like, but was lyrical and warm when he was happy.

When he saw James Reynolds's realistic set, he swore murderously. He liked the cast and my music and me, and he often made false excuses to the producers in order to go with me to lunch. He seemed to shuttle between two worlds: the one of poetry and dreams, the other of "God-damn-it" worldliness.

In 1936, two years after *Within the Gates* O'Casey addressed the following letter, quoted in part, to Melvyn Douglas:

> I want to ask you, if you still happen to be in touch with Lehman Angell [*sic*], to see if he could let me have a copy of the music he composed for *Within the Gates*. The Old Vic Theatre here—that specialises in Shakespeare productions—(and often does them badly) thinks of putting it on next season, and I much prefer the American score to the Irish score (most of it my own, and terrible!). I have often thought of Lehman, I think he has a fine talent, I hope he may get something after that will be worth his while to help—like *Within the Gates*, for my dear Mel, with all its faults, and God knows (and you know) the play had many: but it, I think and still believe, it was worth his trouble, and all the energy and thought you put into it. . . .

One day during rehearsals of *Within the Gates*, I timidly invited Lillian Gish to lunch at Schrafft's near the theater. This was Lillian's thirty-fifth birthday. Ladies passing our table spoke in loud voices to one another as though we belonged at Madame Tussaud's: "She certainly is well-preserved for her age." "She certainly doesn't dress very well." "My goodness, I'll bet she's a million if she's a day."

Lillian was not disturbed. This was during the time of five-year-old Shirley Temple's great success. Lillian had been sixteen when she became a D. W. Griffith star. She smiled to me: "Twenty-five years from now Shirley Temple will have passed into history. She will be thirty but people will assume she is a well-perserved ninety."

Lillian was a model of star behavior. She was usually the first at every rehearsal (half an hour early to change into working clothes) and always the last to leave, remaining afterward to go over troublesome spots with Melvyn. She not only did what she was told to do, but she actually begged for direction.

Within the Gates was not a success, though my music was praised, and after it closed, years went by before I again saw Lillian Gish. Once it was on a crosstown bus on Fifty-seventh Street, where she lived. She had gone to a pre-sale at Mainbocher to buy dresses at a reduction. Years later, the Brooks Atkinsons, Lillian, and I had dinner on a number of occasions. I was struck by the fact that now, at seventy-three, she has the legs of a young girl, she needs no glasses for reading, no aid for hearing, and she works constantly.

Our meetings at dinner and at other people's parties have continued for some time. I saw her quite recently at a cocktail party in honor of Dolores Del Rio, who looks just as she did in movies more than a quarter of a century ago. It was in the apartment of my lawyer, Arnold Weissberger, and Milton Goldman, the agent.

When Lillian entered, she limped a bit and sat down almost at once. After greeting her, I inquired of her health, to which she replied, "Mama always said that someday I'd pay for those three weeks on the ice floes in *Way Down East*."

Also in *Within the Gates* was Mary Morris, who played the Old Woman. Mary and I became lifelong friends. I knew her through many reverses—professional, physical, and financial—but she never outgrew her basic optimism. She had begun as O'Neill's Abbie in *Desire Under the Elms*, passed through an acting career often praiseworthy but too sporadic, was fortunate in being added to the faculty at Carnegie Institute of Technology, and then, after retiring, suffered a long illness that only death would free her from. She was unusually honest and cheerful, and her life became an ironic comment on her sense of unreality.

Before I could conduct *Within the Gates* I had to receive permission from the musicians' union Local 802. I had been a member of the union in the Jackson local since I was sixteen, but I had failed to file a transfer in New York. It was necessary to have deposited a transfer with the New York local for six months before one could accept "steady" employment. Under these circumstances, I was ineligible to conduct my own show!

As I stood before the executive board I conceived a plan: I pleaded that I had composed the music, that this was my only chance to earn a living through it; I told them that I had persuaded the producers (this was true) to employ seven musicians instead of four and that I would use only four (this was untrue) if I were not allowed to conduct. It was blackmail, but under the circumstances I thought it was legitimate. The board asked if it could appoint a "contractor" (the man who engages the orchestra personnel for the job). I readily agreed, and the union in return granted me permission to conduct. The then-president of the local turned up as the contractor, replete with a union-election-time revolver strapped around his waist. Backstage during performances, he often, playfully, used to chase me, pointing it at me.

Among the seven musicians, however, there was a cellist, Morris Stonzek, who befriended and advised me, was helpful in this difficult situation, and took a great interest in my future. After *Within the Gates* he continued to be a close friend, and as I went along, he engaged my orchestra personnel (whenever I was allowed to use him, which was nearly always) for the rest of my life in theater, radio, recordings, and television. He and his wife Lee and I have been friends for nearly forty years.

As conductor of *Within the Gates* I was paid $75 weekly. The contract for composing and arranging was not signed until opening night, and I was paid an outright $125. (This was one way in which I paid for my opportunity.) More costly to me, however, was the printed program which read: "Music by Milton Lusk [large letters] and Lehman Engel [small letters on the line below]," as though I had perhaps added a note or two. In time most critics came to know that I had composed it.

After only a few months *Within the Gates* closed, leaving me with a feeling of responsibility. I had had my Broadway debut. Now would I have another opportunity?

A consideration of even greater importance (though I doubt that I appreciated its vital significance at the time) was the fact that I had actually and for the very first time earned my own living. This constituted an essential proof of success in the eyes of my family. That and what the newspapers had said about my music were tangible, almost monumental, marks of arrival. I could look to them and their world for the approval I needed. After all, this was still my world—and for a long time to come it would remain my most important world.

I had arrived. But now I had to go on. There would need to be a nearly unbroken earning of dollars and a steady flow of complimentary printed words to assure those back home that I was in public favor. Then they could also afford to approve, being unable to make any evaluation themselves.

With the closing of *Within the Gates*, I was faced with still another problem. I had spent four weeks rehearsing, which meant literally living with some fifty people I had never known before. I was not only friendly by nature but, being twenty-four, and the youngest and most inexperienced person involved in the project, it was inevitable that everyone would be friendly to me. After the rehearsal weeks we performed together for several months. Then the play closed and the theater was no longer home, and the theater family dispersed in many different directions. This left me in a strange state of confusion. I had come to feel that the theater personnel were my friends, and I had an irresistible urge to "keep track" of them, to continue to see them, and to prolong our relationships.

Of course, I recognized the hopeless folly of this, but the urge was present and with considerable sadness and frustration, I resisted it. I kept the real friends: Mary Morris, Morris Stonzek, Melvyn Douglas, and Lillian Gish. For the others there were hellos in passing on the street, but little more. After a few months some of the cast even failed to recognize me. In any case, it was a kind of hurt. I was fooled by the closeness of our association, and I made certain assumptions about the theater family that, fortunately, were false. Had they not been, I would by now have a theater family of some twenty thousand! But I had to learn.

In the summer after *Within the Gates* I went to Bar Harbor with a theater school to write and direct music for an alfresco production of Aristophanes' *The Birds*. The actors included an unknown, Van Heflin; a child, Katherine Bard; and Philip Tonge.

At the opening performance we had an audience of distinguished summer residents, including Walter Damrosch, several former diplomats, and founders of America's great soup and soap industries.

In Bar Harbor, Maine, 1935, following a performance of Aristophanes' *The Birds*, for which I had composed the music. Walter Damrosch rushed to congratulate me. *Photo by Tom Kelley*

Throughout the performance one could hear Walter Damrosch. He shouted, roared with outrageous laughter, and applauded out of all proportion. At the conclusion a photographer from *Town and County* asked me to stand for a picture. As he was about to snap it a great commotion of good cheer brought Mr. Damrosch scurrying to congratulate me. We were photographed together. The congratulations and Mr. Damrosch departed with the photographer.

Although I had made a beginning in New York, my total earnings for five years fraught with ceaseless activity and blessed with consistently favorable attention was much less than two thousand dollars. Without Mama and Papa—nothing. But with them and their view of things—the only view that I could have—I was on my way to a fairly quick and remunerative success that would compel and (to a point) serve me but would in the end never provide me with anything like the promise and the vision in the garden.

5: WPA Days

In 1935 the WPA (Works Progress Administration; later, the Works Projects Administration), was set into operation by President Roosevelt to provide employment for those armies of men and women who could not be absorbed into private enterprise and, in the case of the arts projects, to return to the taxpayers some education, entertainment, and culture.

I became involved in much WPA work, and like everything else in my life, it was to provide me with inestimably valuable experience.

I had at one time played Mendelssohn's "Scherzo," and that *did* presuppose that I was an "artist." The theater—my Broadway kind of theater—was not included in my born-and-bred idea of what was "artistic." After all, it was not "serious," and besides, I personally did not walk across the stage in funereal clothes and take a bow. It is possible that I had not put two and two together at that time, but my creation of the Madrigal Singers was my answer to the Dying Poet.

Officials of the newly formed Federal Music Project—a subsidiary of the WPA—asked me if there was something I would like to do in the project. I was a promising lad in my mid-twenties, and it would never have occurred to anyone that I too might have used the weekly $23.86 that everyone was paid. Me? (The aura I exuded often got me things simply because I appeared not to *need* them.)

My newfound loves in music were madrigals and other music of the Renaissance. Through auditions I brought together a group of

The Madrigal Singers about 1936. Was I conducting or about to dance a fandango? *Photo by Ben Pinchot*

eighteen singers and an accompanist. During four years of work, only seven singers were ever changed.

They were a heterogeneous bunch, at first called the Madrigal Group and later the Madrigal Singers. They had come from everywhere and included two Catholics, five Jews, one Spiritualist, and a variety of Protestants. One soprano was black. Their ages ranged from the twenties to the sixties.

I was in absolute charge—which was more responsibility than privilege. We rehearsed two and a half hours each day, five days a week, which accounts for everything we accomplished. Approximately two months after we began, our first concert took place in a Harlem YMCA. The singing and the ensemble improved steadily, although the vocal quality and intonation always left something devoutly to be wished.

The difficulties, benefits, and pleasures were endless. The first category included the behavior of some members toward each other, but in time they grew to be like a family. There was the usual day-to-day pettiness. One singer would tell another that she sang flat. All of them had poor opinions of each other's vocal abilities, which they rarely refrained from expressing (a common disease among singers). The presence of the black girl caused a "progressive" coalition to interpret everything said to her critically as anti-Negro-inspired. (After all, wasn't I born in Mississippi?) There were also anti-Semitic rumblings, which seldom fell on unsympathetic ears. My assignment of a solo passage to one singer was enough to promote a protest meeting against favoritism. (They refused to accept the principle that all people are not created equal.) Schedules of rehearsals were arranged like the pieces of a jigsaw puzzle, to allow members to earn extra money at church services, funerals, weddings, appearances on Major Bowes's Amateur Hour, or teaching.

Audiences were as varied as the music we performed. Once at a settlement school, I came out on the stage for a serious lecture-concert only to discover that I was addressing five hundred little girls, identically dressed, between six and eleven years of age. After I recovered from the initial shock I began by asking questions.

"Who knows anything about Sir Walter Raleigh?"

Many hands flew up. I pointed to one child.

"He put his coat across a mud puddle so Queen Elizabeth wouldn't get her shoes dirty."

"Does anyone know that Sir Walter Raleigh wrote poetry?"

Much confusion. No hands.

"Well, he did and I want to read you one."

I then read "What Is Our Life?"

"Also, a man named Orlando Gibbons wrote music to that poem."

Quiet attention.

"How many of you have fathers and mothers who, after dinner, sometimes play cards?"

Many hands went up.

"How many of your parents invite two friends to play with them?"

Just as many hands.

"Do they sit around a table to play?"

Vocal assents.

Then I explained about madrigals and how four people sat around a table and spent an evening singing new madrigals.

Audience participation little by little became so free that we were able to present our entire program (including a Palestrina mass) and the little girls listened enthusiastically to the end.

We were never free of rumors about discontinuance of the WPA, which had become a hot political football, and I think all of us knew that sooner or later this would be more than mere rumor.

After nearly four years of uninterrupted association, during which we had enjoyed continuous success with public and press, our parent, the WPA, at last began to collapse. I ran around frantically to concert managers in a death-throe effort to establish the Madrigal Singers on a commercial footing, but it was all to no avail. At the end we gave a benefit concert for Sigma Alpha Mu, my college fraternity, in Town Hall, and it was good. It was a credit to our nearly four-year daily association and an honorable conclusion to something unique in America—the end of an artistic accomplishment born out of governmental recognition of poverty.

Through the Madrigal Singers I had proved that there was a public that found our kind of repertoire alive, sometimes amusing, sometimes moving. Our concerts—nearly a thousand—also provided the stimulus for other singing groups with similar, though necessarily smaller, repertoires. And for me, personally, aside from its career and educational value, the Madrigal Singers provided me with my finest musical experience.

All that remains of my Madrigal Singers is a good memory. The singers had provided me, at twenty-seven, with an artistic past though I had also experienced too soon the end of one phase of my life. I had bad financial times to thank for its existence and bad politics to blame for its demise.

While the Madrigal Singers occupied my attention in the Federal Music Project, I was also busy with the Federal Theatre Project, at first composing music for T. S. Eliot's *Murder in the Cathedral*. I remember scarcely anything about it until opening night, roughly three months following my first meeting with Halsted Welles, the director, a young man who had previously staged the play at Yale. I recall preliminary conferences and then his frequent disappearances

Standing in a corridor at Carnegie Hall (about 1936) before a concert with the Madrigal Singers.

on motorcycle trips. His rehearsals were never scheduled together with mine until just before the opening of the play.

Edward Goodman,* the Federal Theatre producer, gave me everything any composer ever dreamed of working with. I had a speaking chorus of about fifteen, a backstage singing chorus of nearly a hundred, an orchestra of about forty-five—all personnel taken from relief rolls.

The play itself (prior to opening) also made very little impression upon me. I liked the poetry as such, but I distrusted the religious implications against which, admittedly, I was prejudiced.

Many of the people I had to work with were old and disgruntled. At first they violently opposed everything I directed them to do, and they were openly hostile to my music. I insisted quietly and in time they acquiesced.

I do remember vividly that at the final rehearsal I said to Goodman, "I am sorry for what I have done. The critics and the public will be shocked. It is too bold." I will always appreciate Goodman's reassuring smile and his pat on the back.

* Director of the Washington Square Players (circa 1917), which eventually provided the nucleus of the Theatre Guild.

At about twenty-five in New York. Marcus Blechman, whom I had first met as a Charles Weidman dancer, was the photographer.

I conducted the opening performance, and as it unfolded before me, I saw the play for the first time. I liked it so much that I conducted every time I was free enough of other work to do so, and I believe it was the best theater job I ever turned out. I had no reason to fear the critics, for evidently the music was so much within the frame of the play that no one took exception to its violence. The success of the entire thing was unequivocal.

After *Murder in the Cathedral* Goodman acquired rights to a terrible musical comedy script, *A Hero Is Born*, by Theresa ("Terry") Helburn, one of the executive directors of the Theatre Guild. I was asked to provide the music. I cannot claim that Eddie Goodman's motives in producing *A Hero Is Born* were anything but sincere. My own connection with it was definitely insincere. It was to be my third show on Broadway. I felt I could not afford to be choosy; perhaps my judgment was not sound, but I was not uninspired by the thought that my collaborator was an executive director of the Theatre Guild. My music, written without conviction, was a horrible confusion of innocuous operettalike ditties and inexperienced jazz. The cast included Margaret Wycherley, the eminent Irish actress. Miss Wycherley, I think, undertook her role out of friendship for Eddie and Terry, but she also wanted to utilize this opportunity to sing for the first time. (This new desire was destined to become a disease among musically unqualified actors.) During rehearsals, her one song had gone so badly that I wanted to eliminate it if only for her sake, but Miss Wycherley became offended at the idea.

On opening night the accompaniment of her song began. Miss Wycherley stood in the center of the stage wringing her hands (suddenly it was the sleepwalking scene), unable to remember how to begin. When the last section of the song came round (it was like the first), she began singing from the beginning. The orchestra (I was not conducting) concluded according to the written page, and she continued singing without accompaniment until the very miserable end.

The WPA Children's Theatre twice engaged me to write incidental music: for Charlotte Chorpenning's *The Emperor's New Clothes* and for *Horse Play* by Dorothy Hailparn. I undertook the first as a favor to the director and signed a contract paying a royalty of three dollars per performance. I wrote what was needed in one afternoon. So many productions and performances were given in so many cities that I earned more than three thousand dollars in a year. I then tackled *Horse Play* with enthusiasm and nothing at all came of it.

During my multiple involvement with the Federal Arts Projects I received a telegram from President Roosevelt requesting me to attend a meeting at the White House. I felt honored, accepted readily, and presented myself at the appointed time.

I was greeted by a black butler, who ushered me into a small room very near the entrance. I had expected to be a member of some large group and was stunned to find that I alone had been summoned. Seconds after my arrival, the president was wheeled in in a chair, and I was shocked at seeing him unable to walk. He greeted me warmly, thanked me for coming, and then explained that he had been advised of my varied activities in the WPA and that I might provide him with useful answers to questions that concerned him.

The president consulted a yellow legal pad where he had made some notes. All of his questions were cogent, important, and realistic. Did I think the projects provided adequate employment for the unemployed? Did I feel that the various artistic presentations were helpful to the public at large? Under these difficult circumstances, were the projects being administered effectively? Did I feel that the participants might eventually bridge the great gap between government subsidy and private employment? Did I think that some permanent inroads on popular taste and art-consciousness might conceivably be made by the offerings being presented throughout the country? He made it quite clear that he wanted my personal opinions in every case. It was a relaxed and easy meeting, and the president was at all times pleasant and considerate.

We spoke for about an hour, during which time he made some jottings. Finally, the attendant who had brought him in entered and informed the president that he was to go. The president thanked me profusely and said that "a friend of yours [obviously Mrs. Roosevelt, whom I had met on many occasions] wants you to have tea with her."

I was deeply flattered but insisted that Mrs. Roosevelt could, I was certain, use her time better. I was pleased but thought this was a quite unnecessary bonus.

We parted. It was not to be our last meeting.

During these WPA days I became acquainted with a talented young man named Orson Welles—then about twenty—who became director in a WPA theater of which John Houseman was producer. Together they did some of the most original and exciting productions ever seen in any New York theater. Despite his youth, Orson was in full charge of whatever he undertook. When he was inclined to lag, Jack sped him on his way. He was inventive, witty, alternately lazy and energetic, and knowledgeable. His thinking was bold and his work usually produced sensational results. He lived only a block away from me, in a basement apartment on West Fourteenth Street, and we saw a great deal of each other.

Orson already carried much white flabbiness on a large frame. His head always belonged to a foetus. His agreeable bass speaking voice was pitched even lower in performance than nature had intended it. He was given to quick, noisy, nasal laughter. Although he had patience with actors, he had none with himself. In directing he never tired of going over the smallest detail hundreds of times in order to have it precisely as he wished it. His own performances happened suddenly for good or ill. They were or they were not at the very outset.

I knew him well for perhaps five years, and even during those early years he was driven to being overbusy. When he was not busy, he was lonely and miserable. He would often call to ask if he might go with me to a rehearsal. He seldom abided by his own rehearsal schedules, seldom violated a performance one. He was, always has been, and still is, a boy: a Peter Pan too heavy for flying.

I first worked with Orson on the steel-strike opera, *The Cradle Will Rock*, by Marc Blitzstein, who had asked me to conduct it.

This was the first of many associations with Marc that would span more than two decades, until he was mortally injured in Martinique. Marc was an original. His mind and talent were theater-bent and leftist-politically saturated. He was nervous, full of laughs (often derisive), somehow "tight," impatient, and—it was always my feeling—bent on self-destruction or failure. His lyrics were brilliant and were served well by his music. Often his music was almost brilliant, but when it became too promising, Marc seemed to need to prevent its successful conclusion: he would do just anything to frustrate a desirable resolution. Or so I always thought. Withal, he was most likable and thoroughly brilliant.

During the early days of *The Cradle Will Rock* Orson rehearsed little. A sunny day would send him out of the theater for a long lunch. An interesting group of friends were sufficient excuse for canceling his evening schedule. These were the first weeks. Later he would start at ten in the morning and often not leave the theater. He might dismiss his cast at four the next morning, but when we would return at noon, we would find Orson sleeping in a theater seat. On these occasions Anna Weissberger, Arnold's mother and the mother of "Gusty," Orson's secretary, would rush down the aisle carrying a pot of homemade chicken soup.

Orson not only staged the show but, according to his custom, also designed the mechanically complex sets. During this period I was on the faculty of the Music School of the Henry Street Settlement for the second time; the new director, Grace Spofford, wanted me to do something "theatrical" with the chorus. (I had conducted Weill's *Der Jasager* at the school before Miss Spofford's tenure.) The talks she and I had with Aaron Copland resulted in his composing an opera for children, *The Second Hurricane*, which we asked Orson to direct.

ABOVE: *The Second Hurricane* company on the stage of the old Grand Street Playhouse (1937). L. E. stands in the center of platform. RIGHT: *The Second Hurricane* was broadcast over the CBS Network shortly after its premiere. Pianist Everett Roudebush (*left*), Aaron Copland (*center*), and I examine the score prior to going on the air.

Orson had the concept, and it was good, but between continuing rehearsals of *Cradle* and a thousand other budding things, one of his actors and an old friend of mine, Hiram Sherman, attended to most of them. Joseph Cotton played the only adult role for ten dollars a performance. I think that this *simpler* work—simpler because it was composed for children—became a most important development in Aaron Copland's creative life.

But back to Orson and *The Cradle*. After months of rehearsing we were ready to open in May, but government officials in Washington, for one stated reason or another, were continually pushing back the date. Finally, one was actually set, and an invited audience at a preview the night before, received it with enormous enthusiasm. The day of opening was filled with pleasurable anticipation. The house was sold out, and public interest was high. Official order for opening had not actually arrived, though it had been promised, and Archibald MacLeish, the poet and friend of many of us, fearing some mix-up, went that morning to Washington to see Harry Hopkins, then head of WPA. Returning in the afternoon, MacLeish assured us that approval for opening was definite and official, that a confirming telegram would arrive at any moment.

Orson, Jack Houseman, Marc, Gusty Weissberger, MacLeish, and I were gathered together in Orson's basement office in the Maxine Elliott Theatre. By five, when no word had been received, MacLeish phoned Hopkins only to be told that no one knew his whereabouts. In Hopkins's absence, WPA matters were handled by his assistant, Mrs. Ellen Woodward, former congresswoman from Mississippi. I phoned Mrs. Woodward, who seemed pleased to hear from me until I told her of my connection with *The Cradle*. I assured her naively that a grave error was being made in withholding the order.

"The house is sold out," I said. "Think of the scandal if the audience arrives and is not admitted. The WPA approved the show months ago. It has rehearsed for months. Much money has been spent."

Mrs. Woodward was adamant. MacLeish seized the phone, and the two of them had a noisy exchange. Nothing came of the talk except a clear, final realization that no opening order would be forthcoming from Washington then or ever.

It is probably necessary to explain that *The Cradle Will Rock* is

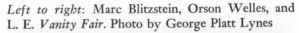

Left to right: Marc Blitzstein, Orson Welles, and L. E. *Vanity Fair*. Photo by George Platt Lynes

satirical of the rich and powerful and strongly advocated labor unionism. It was considered radical, even Communist-tainted, and it became a cause célèbre.

Orson and Jack resolved that there would be an opening as planned that evening. Jack was able to lease the Venice Theatre, a barn of a place on Seventh Avenue at Fifty-ninth Street, for two hundred dollars in cash. All of us pooled our cash, and the deal was set. We could not use the orchestra, because the union scale for that many men (there must have been thirty-five) was too high, and so, someone ran into the street and stopped a homeward-bound drayman for the hauling of Marc's own piano to the stage of the Venice.

One of the members of the cast, acting as deputy for Actors' Equity (the actors' union), telephoned Frank Gillmore, its head, for permission for the appearance of the actors at the Venice. Gillmore cautioned that actors appearing on any other stage while on WPA payroll might be considered "employed" and subject to dismissal from relief rolls. Such an appearance could be costly.

Jack Houseman, who listened as this message was relayed to the bewildered cast, offered a plan: "I am the producer of the show at the Venice," he said. "No one can prevent your sitting in the audience, and only I could stop you from standing up at your seats to sing an occasional song."

It was a technicality, but to most of the actors it was logical, and all but three or four elderly people entered into the spirit of the occasion.

Meanwhile the audience was gathering on the sidewalk at the Maxine Elliott. Will Geer, the Mr. Mister of the cast, entertained them with guitar-accompanied songs while plans were completed. At length, Jack announced that the show would be given at the Venice, sans costumes, lights, orchestra, and scenery and that he would collect the WPA tickets at the door without destroying them so that he could turn them in to the government, en masse, for refund the next day.

The chorus sat in the front row with me. The actors were scattered in every part of the theater and no one quite remembered which ones would or would not participate. Marc sat at the piano on the stage. Orson made a too-long speech to explain the situation, the scenes, the deficiencies of this kind of presentation. But there was something that Orson did not know, and perhaps there were few of us then who realized it: with Orson's scenery—realistic, heavy, and cumbersome—no longer a participant, and with the audience relying only on its own imagination, the show was better, and Orson— serendipity at work—was never to be debited with this cluttered nightmare production.

The orchestra came as spectators, but the accordion player, who had brought his instrument, remembered much of his music and from his place in the audience played along with Marc from time to time. Scene after scene unfolded. Duets were sung by actors seated on opposite sides of the theater. The funny scenes were funnier, the poignant ones more poignant. Marc supplied the missing roles. Everything actually gained in this kind of presentation. I have seldom seen such enthusiasm.

The papers printed the story on front pages. The *New York Times* said:

STEEL STRIKE OPERA PUT OFF BY WPA
Many among 600 gathered for preview charge censorship . . . because of radical plot. . . . Officials deny any curb. . . . Say delay until July 1st is to reorganize. . . .

Less than a year later John Houseman and Orson left the WPA and established their own Mercury Theatre, which became highly successful. Marc did the music for their effective *Julius Caesar* in modern clothes and clearly about Fascism. I did the next music for Dekker's *Shoemaker's Holiday,** which was not only a great comic romp (with Hiram "Chubby" Sherman as Firk), but another lesson in Orson.

His rehearsals ran counter to those of most directors. He seldom told an actor "why" but told him the "what" in copious detail. The style of his *Shoemaker's Holiday* production depended upon the precise machinelike interplay of movement, music, curtain, and lights. It was the director's expression. The actors were his puppets.

Orson rehearsed each minute section of *Shoemaker's Holiday* over and over a thousand times. Usually he demonstrated movements of

* The cast included George Coulouris, Frederic Tozere, Joseph Cotton, Vincent Price, Whitford Kane, Norman Lloyd, Hiram Sherman, Elliott Reid, Stefan Schnabel, Arthur Anderson, Edith Barrett, Marian Warring-Manley, and Ruth Ford.

hands and feet in detail, speaking the lines in precise time relationship to them. Then he would have the actors imitate him.

In ordering the music from me, he practically dictated it just as he dictated the acting performances. He beat out rhythms to go with planned action and "walked off" space to indicate duration. He never miscalculated.

During an evening rehearsal the night before the announced first preview, Orson sent messengers to the stage doors of all Broadway theaters, inviting actors to an impromptu midnight preview of *Shoemaker*. The theater was filled to capacity with the kind of audience that actors—when they think they are good—love to play for. Hiram Sherman was a riot, and *Shoemaker's Holiday* was altogether a great success.

The Mercury's life was not long *because* it was a great success. Orson had conquered something else and had to go on to newer fields. This time it was Hollywood and first off—presto!—*Citizen Kane*.

Before his departure, he was the star on one of the Texaco Star Theatre radio programs of which I was the music director (incidental-music composer, orchestrator, and conductor). The broadcast, emceed by the well-known critic Burns Mantle, was presented in a theater before a live audience. It was customary to introduce the star to the audience just as we went on the air so that the broadcast began with the sound of applause. Orson bowed and as he walked slowly toward the microphone at center stage, he dropped his script, which fluttered away in dozens of pieces. *Everyone* was nervously on his hands and knees picking it up and trying feverishly to collate the pages. (The scripts were read, not memorized.) Orson continued toward the microphone and with the entire production staff in a state of hysteria he produced *another* copy from the inside pocket of his jacket!

While I was a sailor at Great Lakes during World War II, Orson, then newly married to Rita Hayworth, invited me to Sunday lunch. He showed me his beautiful wife while she slept. Orson was suffering from a hangover, which could only be endured with more drinking. We never got around to lunch, but after a number of drinks Orson asked me to escort him to a private dining room where he was scheduled to make a speech. Realizing that he was unsteady, he affected the use of a walking stick on which he leaned heavily, making his unsteadiness appear to be the result of some ankle accident.

About fifteen years later, I ran into Orson in a book shop on Fifth Avenue, and inasmuch as many people gathered to watch, he hugged and kissed me, then departed. Exeunt.

6: Accelerando

Dᴜʀɪɴɢ ᴛʜᴇ ғᴏᴜʀ ʜᴇᴄᴛɪᴄ and rewarding WPA years in which I conducted the Madrigal Singers, wrote music for *Murder in the Cathedral* and *A Hero Is Born*, edited four *Renaissance to Baroque* volumes, conducted *The Cradle Will Rock*, and contributed incidental music to two children's plays, I also composed music for nine Broadway plays; conducted one musical show and one opera; was commentator on a radio series; conducted choruses in six schools; wrote a small symphony, a piano sonata, a ballet, and a number of choral pieces; and helped to found the Arrow Music Press, Inc.

Having become increasingly aware of serious American composers' needs for publication, Aaron Copland, Marc Blitzstein, Virgil Thomson (the composer-critic), and I met for discussions as to what we might do to be of help. Since the press was my idea, I was made president, although I was the least known and the youngest. The meetings were hilarious because of our personality differences. Aaron, who was the secretary, was a "giggler"—a pushover for every kind of joke—but perfectly informed about every financial detail: our bank balance, sales, amounts due, distributors, composers, printers, and so on. Marc was a listener and frequently an arbiter—as indeed was I. Virgil was vocally active, serious, and contralto. He often exhumed legal technicalities that were unknown to the rest of us. He had the knack of reversing "to whom we owe" to "who owes us." He was intensely businesslike and so outrageously proper in tone that he often seemed like the Mad Hatter. Virgil and Aaron were the active ones.

Often at our gatherings we would find ourselves in a bind because Aaron, Marc, and I would agree on a point, while Virgil felt oppositely. When this happened he usually teased us with, "Well, I guess the American Jewish Composers' Press . . ." and so on.

After months of meetings with my attorney and friend Arthur Strasser, we became incorporated as a nonprofit group. We could agree on no pertinent name for our company but on a Sunday morning when the four of us sat over breakfast in the Automat on West Twenty-third Street, we saw the sign on a lunch wagon across the street: Arrow Cafe. And so, we became the Arrow Music Press, Inc. We collected gifts of money from wealthy friends. Aaron secured a lease on the Cos Cob Press, Inc.—important but then nonoperating —from its owner, Mrs. Alma Morgenthau, which enabled us to start off with a basic catalog.

Our Arrow Music Press offered composers an opportunity to print and distribute their music inexpensively, and with virtually no bank account we published in the first five years, through composers themselves and friends, fifty-four works, most of them of major proportions and importance.

In time the need for continuing our press lessened. More native composers were so frequently performed that commercial publishers sought contracts with them. After about two decades we allowed composers who wanted their music together under a single publisher to remove their stock, and we dissolved the press as such, giving the residue to Boosey and Hawkes, Ltd., for continuing representation.

With my engagement at the Neighborhood Playhouse Studio, a theater school, I began my varied career of part-time teaching. Martha Graham, Louis Horst, and Sandy Meisner were members of the faculty, and while I was there, we had many talented pupils, including Edmond O'Brien, Nicholas (Richard) Conte, Gregory Peck, Anne Jackson, Eli Wallach, Efrem Zimbalist, Jr., Betty Garrett, and Patricia Morison.

At Walden School and at the Ethical Culture Society I also conducted choruses, but I lasted at the former only a few months because the students—being educated "progressively" and encouraged to "express themselves"—were never silent long enough to hear a single word I ever spoke. In the middle of a class, I "expressed" *myself* and left.

At Katherine Gibbs (secretarial) School, all of us had a jolly time, and I continued my work at Henry Street.

My real failure, however, was at Sarah Lawrence College, where I also conducted a chorus. The composer William Schuman, a friend of mine, was also a member of the faculty, and it was because of his enthusiasm for my work with the Madrigal Singers that I was engaged by the college.

I was so busy that I failed to give this college the special attention it merited. After all, I knew that my success in similar positions had largely been a result of my employment of a repertoire of light music. But I failed to take into account the fact that Sarah Lawrence students were more seriously interested in the arts than those of most other schools. I lasted one season only and accomplished nothing for the school or myself. Schuman took up my job and performed the very kind of music that had first attracted him to me at my Madrigal Singers.

The nine plays for which I wrote incidental music began with *Shoemaker's Holiday*, already spoken of. The next was to be Margaret Webster's production of Hamlet.

I first met Margaret ("Peggy") Webster at a party given by Orson, and I liked her at once. She was bright and witty, precise and kind, warm and outgoing. We got to know each other well, and when Maurice Evans planned his uncut *Hamlet* (1938) with Peggy as director, she asked me to compose the music. I did most of it during a vacation in a garden in Cuernavaca.

It was a wonderful experience to work with Peggy on *Hamlet*. She knew the play from memory and therefore had an extraordinary freedom and certainty about everything she did. Always, she worked from the inside of the play out. Physically, she was a "thing" to behold. Generally, she wore slacks. Her short hair fell in strips across her face. A cigarette always hung precariously out of the corner of her mouth, the smoke menacing her eyes and provoking violent fits of coughing. She was everywhere in the theater at once and never accepted any nonsense from anyone. She was the first to laugh raucously at a joke, but her work was concentrated, and it proceeded without interruption from the first day of rehearsal to the last.

Peggy's scheduling of rehearsals, contrary to Orson's—and for that matter, almost all other directors'—was a model of planning. She knew exactly which actors were to be needed. Each day for at least the first two weeks she began with two or three only. Then they were joined at a set time by one or two others, until everyone was present for the big ensemble scenes. At these times, placement of people was quick and precise (not improvised), since it had all been meticulously worked out in advance.

Peggy also understood discipline. She could persuade an actor when that tack seemed in order. She could outscream anyone when provoked. Sometime later, when we worked together on *The Strong Are Lonely*,* an abysmal flop, I saw her triumph over temper in quite an unusual way.

As we sat together during a run-through (no one else was in the theater), Dennis King, the star (with Victor Francen), surrounded by a large cast, stepped downstage in the middle of a scene and delivered a noisy diatribe against the other actors (standing nearby), against the play, and against Peggy. His screams seemed to go on for hours. Peggy did not move. The cast was frozen. As Dennis had no antagonist, he had to continue. Finally, little by little and even a bit pathetically, he "ran down" like a mechanical toy. Then silence. He stopped talking and froze like everyone else. After an interminable pause Peggy spoke up strongly and pleasantly: "Dennis, if that's all, we'll take the scene again from the top!"

Dennis had lost his battle. At the end of the scene, Peggy called a five-minute break, and Dennis hopped off the stage to embrace her and apologize.

"Oh, that's alright, Dennis," she said. "But I do think you owe the cast an apology."

I knew Peggy through eleven subsequent productions. She was a dear, loving friend, one who never complained about anything that bothered her personally. She died recently after several years of

---

* The cast included Nils Asther, Philip Bournef, Frederick Rolf, Wesley Addy, John Straub, and Stuart Vaughan—now a successful director.

intense suffering, a blessing for her but a great loss to all of us who had the good fortune to be near her.

Maurice Evans was a special sort of actor-manager, never taking advantage of his position to command anything. Criticism was accepted with interest, and he behaved at every rehearsal as if he had been employed by Peggy rather than vice versa.

The opening of the uncut *Hamlet* was important. The audience arrived in daylight before 6:00 P.M., in evening clothes. There was a happy air of expectation. Although I am seldom nervous about my own performances, I feel helplessly edgy about the performances of friends, especially when my music is involved and I am not guiding it myself.

Before curtain time I wandered backstage and spoke to the musicians. Wishing them luck, I started toward the auditorium. As I passed Maurice's dressing room, I had an urge to wish him success. I paused, thinking of all the reasons for not disturbing him. Against these, I knocked at his door.

"Come in," came Maurice's high-pitched voice.

"Oh, Lehman," he said. "I'm so glad to see you. I wanted to ask if you minded if we raised the trumpet fanfares a half-tone at the beginning of Part Three. It would make them more brilliant."

"Of course I don't mind," I stammered. "I'll go and tell the musicians."

"Oh, that's all right. I have an entrance right by them and I'll tell them myself."

He remembered and he told them.

Because Maurice wore a white collar on his black coat in *Hamlet*, Dame May Whitty, Peggy's mother, used to refer to him as "Little Lord Fauntleroy."

About the time of *Hamlet*, I went to Philadelphia, where Eddie Dowling was having difficulty with *Mme. Capet*, a play starring Eva Le Gallienne. I was summoned to invigorate a French revolutionary mob with songs and orchestrated shouts, but nothing could have prevented the play's poor reception in New York. Hal Welles, who had directed *Murder in the Cathedral*, had me do some music for Stanley Young's *Robin Landing*, which suffered a similar fate. Hal also did an "experimental" tryout of Stephen Spender's *Trial of a*

Judge for WPA. I wrote some organ "cues," and we got an impression of a vastly interesting poetic drama, which, in our time, could only have been unveiled apologetically as "experimental."

Next was *Johnny Johnson*,* with a book by Paul Green and the first musical show written in America by Kurt Weill, the only one produced by the fledgling Group Theatre, the first of the enormous number of musical shows I was to conduct and the only one that had no pre-Broadway tour.

The Weills (Kurt and Lotte Lenya) had arrived in New York a season before, and as they had an introduction to me (how times had changed!), they came to the Village to my one-room apartment to tea one afternoon. As I was acutely self-conscious, I struggled to make conversation. I was twenty-five, the Weills about ten years older. I did not know that Mrs. Weill was Lotte Lenya, but I was to discover it embarrassingly that afternoon.

In my desperate need to make conversation I spoke of *The Threepenny Opera* with sincere enthusiasm but added that the female singer on a recording I had was terrible! The Weills smiled indulgently and said that I must have the French recording. No, I persisted, I had the German one. It was then that I found out that the singer was Lotte Lenya, my guest! In my young life I held pear-shaped vocal tones sacred, and it was to be many years before I could comprehend any other kind of singing. When I did, I was to worship at the shrine of Lotte Lenya.

This incident was not held against me. Aaron Copland was close to the newly-formed Group Theatre directorate (Lee Strasberg, Harold Clurman, and Cheryl Crawford), and he had recommended me. Sandy Meisner and Bobby Lewis, by now "old" friends of mine, were Group Theatre actors. Besides, several years earlier I had conducted Weill's children's opera, *Der Jasager*, probably the first performance of any of his music in America.

Kurt Weill was a short, likable man in his late thirties. He wore thick glasses, was nearly bald, inclined toward stoutness, spoke with

---

* The cast included Robert Lewis, Tony Kraber, Phoebe Brand, Roman Bohnen, Will Lee, Curt Conway, Russell Collins, Sanford Meisner, Lee J. Cobb, Art Smith, Albert Van Dekker, William Challee, Elia Kazan, Joseph Pevney, Luther Adler, Jules (later, John) Garfield, Paula Miller, Paul Mann, Ruth Nelson, Morris Carnovsky, and Orrin Jannings.

a thick German accent, and smiled squintingly. In work, I found him Germanically pessimistic.

The Group Theatre members who made up the cast were, as a whole, more intelligent and interesting than most of the people in an average cast. They were especially considerate of each other's neuroses and idiosyncracies, which were legion.

As I had never before put a musical show together, I was uncertain about everything, and my insecurity—the incessant fear of doing the wrong thing—must have stuck out all over me like sores.

At the last rehearsal, Lee Strasberg, the director, came to me while I was conducting: "Stop thinking of what somebody has told you about the music. It is yours now. Give a performance!" That remark meant the whole world to me than and for all time.

Johnny Johnson was not a success, although many things about it were admired. The collaboration between Green and Weill was a violent stylistic dichotomy, since Green is American in style and Weill was essentially German and Jewish.

The preparation of *Johnny* was unique among musical shows. Since it was done with actors saturated in the Stanislavsky Method according to the gospel of Lee Strasberg, the show was studied, improvised, and dissected for a period of about three months prior to the beginning of actual rehearsals. There were no singers in the cast, and the songs were worked on chiefly from an acting point of view.

I recall a dress rehearsal when the actors had to encounter Donald Oenslager's scenery for the first time. The chief problem suddenly became one of self-preservation in climbing out of World War I trenches and of making costume changes with no allowable time. The acting problem then became secondary despite the protests of the director.

Once during the brief run, Sandy Meisner (by then one of my oldest friends) whistled rather than sang a song. In the intermission, I protested and he slapped my face. Afterwards there was a meeting of the Group's tribunal, which sent me an apology.

At a matinee performance, at the rise of the curtain, a stout actress came out on a porch. I was conducting an introduction to a song (umpa umpa) and at the proper time "cued" her to begin singing. She merely stared at me open-mouthed, pulling heavily on a post, nearly collapsing the scenery. She was drunk. Her fellow performers were filled with sympathy until she repeated her performance that evening. Then the tribunal replaced her.

Kurt and I remained friends. A few seasons later he asked me to audition singers for his new show, *Lady in the Dark*. Moss Hart, author of the book, and Hassard ("Bobby") Short, the overall director, charged me with choosing sixteen boys and girls who *looked* no more than twenty-one, had very good figures and attractive faces.

At the Equity call, nearly three thousand singers jammed the empty stage of the St. James Theatre. Among them there were as usual a countless number who were not young or were too fat, too thin, and anything but attractive.

Up to this time in my life, I had always listened briefly to everyone at auditions, but with the physical types so clearly specified by Moss and Bobby, it would have been an obvious waste of everyone's time to do this.

I made a speech.

"In this show I can only use trained voices. Only people who *look* no older than twenty-one, with good figures and pleasant faces need wait to be heard. I cannot accept anyone looking older than twenty-one. Please do not wait if you do not belong in this category." (Naivete at thirty-one!)

Long pause. Total freeze. The old ones began to look older, the fat ones fatter, the ugly ones hideous. But all were immobilized. And so for the first time in my life I had to eliminate by type.

The two stage managers lined up the females, then males, ten at a time. The people in each line stood breathless as I tried to assess possibilities. It was embarrassing for all of us: like selecting animals. (My grandmother used to choose chickens by pinching them.) This selecting-and-rejecting process took an entire morning, then the singing began.

It is usually true that the best-looking can do the least, and so I heard a couple of hundred—all I had kept for type reasons—before I found about thirty-five (needing sixteen) who were vocally acceptable. Kurt was pleased with the results. He felt somewhat embarrassed because his old friend Maurice Abravenel (lately arrived from Europe) had been engaged to conduct *Lady in the Dark*, and he made speeches to me about my conducting his next show. He thanked me for my helpfulness and said that he had a present for me that he knew I would like. He would send it to me.

Needing money, I was taken aback by the idea of a "present" for my hard work. (Always one learns.) I had completed a job that had lasted nearly a week and was worth at that time hundreds of dollars. The "present" turned out to be an autographed vocal score (retail price $2.50) of *Johnny Johnson* to which I, as its original conductor, should, in any case, have been entitled.

During the next four years, while I was in the navy, I saw Kurt and Lenya here and there. Nearly three years after I returned to civilian life I ran into Kurt in the New York Public Library, where he was copying out American folk songs. He greeted me warmly and said he would call.

A few days later—I was to leave soon for my first season in Dallas —Kurt did call and invited me to lunch. He told me of his new show *Lost in the Stars*, which he wanted me to conduct in the fall.

On my return in September he called to say that the production was to be small, the orchestra small, and the budget was so small on so chancy a show (blacks in South Africa) that he wondered if I minded *this* time if he engaged a new young conductor who would work for less money than I! I said I did not mind.

Lost in the Stars was not a hit. Sometime after it opened, I ran into Kurt as I came out of Sardi's one day after lunch. He was obviously happy to see me, spoke of our getting together, and said he would walk with me then wherever I was going. We chatted in a warm way, and when I reached my destination, he promised to call.

A few days later I read in the newspaper that he was in the hospital, having suffered a heart attack. A few days afterward I telephoned Lenya to ask if I might send flowers.

"No," she said. "Kurt is recovering nicely and he'd rather see you. Call tomorrow and if things are alright, come pay us a visit."

The next morning's paper contained his obituary.

7: New Shows

Since all the musicals I have *conducted*—more than a hundred—have had much in common with one another in their preparation and through the Broadway opening, I will try to describe them in general from my own point of view as musical director. The inevitable differences concern personalities, accidents, and special events that will be told separately.

I calculate that I have spent perhaps twenty-five years of total time in preproduction discussions, auditions, rehearsals, pre-Broadway performances, and openings on Broadway. This time does not include the widely varied run of the shows or the thirty-eight plays I have composed incidental music for. I tell it because I think few people know what goes on.

To begin, let us say I have been engaged to conduct *Ring Around*. The rehearsal dates are set to begin September 1. By mid-July the producer has set up meetings, and the composer will want to play his score for me. I spend a day reading the script and half a day hearing the score, which at first seems unlearnable for a variety of reasons from the simplistic to the ultrasophisticated.

The meetings with the producer include most of the staff: scene designer, costume designer, stage manager, composer, lyricist, stage director, author, producer, orchestrator, and musical director. These meetings are essential, time-consuming, and too often thoughtlessly planned. Nothing relating to costumes and scenery concerns those in the music department and vice versa, and so, too often, many hours are wasted.

What is important to me involves producer, composer, stage manager, orchestrator, and sometimes the orchestra contractor, because it is then that we freeze the show's instrumentation, discuss the number of orchestral players and singers allowed in the budget. We begin with essentials or "unavoidables." The producer has limited the size of the orchestra to twenty-five—the minimum required by the musicians union. The choreographer requires two drummers. A piano is usually desirable, as is bass. The arranger wants four trumpets, three trombones, five reeds—each man doubling on saxophone and one or two legitimate reeds. The composer will want a harp and perhaps a guitar. The arranger, because of the musical "color" of some of the songs, will want a French horn. This makes a total of nineteen out of the available twenty-five. The remaining choice is small. How do you balance six strings against four trumpets, three trombones, and five saxophones? And how will you divide six strings? Perhaps one cello, one viola, and four violins. Or two cellos, two violas, and two violins. Does it make much difference?

Finally, there are the auditions for singers. Whether sixteen or eight are to be made available, you will want to hear everyone who is physically acceptable for the particular job. The Equity call (for members of Chorus [or Actors'] Equity only) will occupy one whole day: boys in the morning, girls in the afternoon. Then another day is spent at the "open call"—a free-for-all. While most of these people are untrained and unprepared, they must be heard, since they will also include the most recent New York arrivals. (At one of these auditions a quite sultry, beautiful, and shapely girl sauntered out. She was well dressed, and although she appeared shy, there was something about her that suggested she was a "striptease artist." I asked her if she sang: she shook her head negatively. I asked her if she danced. No. Was she an actress? This time, she replied, "Well, ahee can read lyons.")

The best singers who are also the likeliest physical types are called back for "finals" on a third day. All the brass will be present in order to have a vote in the final selection. There is argument and discussion and eventually, after they have been heard, the choreographer has seen them in some kinds of movement, and everyone has expressed preferences, they are selected one by one. Everyone on stage and off breathes a sigh of relief.

A week or two later, rehearsals commence. Equity restricts each person's working to seven out of ten hours and requires that each have one day each week off. Good. But this seldom affects the staff. A production schedule will have certain people come in at 10:00 A.M. Lunch will be from 1:00 to 2:30 P.M. At 2:30, the other performers are scheduled, and so we have an entire company until 6:30, when we break for dinner until 8:00. At that time only those who began at 2:30 will return and work until 11:00. This schedule is altered daily.

As for the day off, it is possible that ensemble singers and dancers will be given one day off, while the principals will have another. In this way the staff has personnel to work with seven days a week and from 10:00 A.M. until 11:00 P.M. If meetings are needed, they will be called at 11:00 or perhaps at 9:30 A.M. the following day.

During the rehearsal period each department head argues for more rehearsal time. This is reluctantly surrendered here and there. One day the choreographer needs everyone for four hours; another day the conductor needs everyone for an equal amount of time. Meanwhile, the stage director—the big boss—is unhappy, and he usually ends up with a lion's share of daily time.

For many years now rehearsals have taken place in a series of studios, all under a single roof. This practice began when theaters were less readily available than today. In many ways it is a good thing, for it allows many simultaneous rehearsals and no loss of time if one director needs one or two performers out of another director's rehearsal for a few minutes. There is usually a large studio for the stage director, a similar one for the choreographer, perhaps a smaller one for chorus practice, and one or two closetlike cubicles for solo song coaching.

Most rehearsal studios contain very old and badly out-of-tune upright pianos. Often there are to be found half-empty cardboard coffee containers with a thin coat of cold coagulated cream floating on top, opened waxed-paper lengths containing bread crusts of once self-respecting sandwiches, ash trays spilling over with half-smoked cigars and cigarettes, and a variety of other unpleasantnesses.

The new company almost invariably arrives on schedule, but many individuals, looking like they have just awakened, carry in a paper bag containing coffee and a piece of Danish pastry, which they attempt to consume surreptitiously during the preliminary announcements.

The first day is easily recognizable to the initiated. Since anyone can be fired or replaced by the end of the third day, there is a general walking-on-eggs attitude. Affability is overdone to the point of foolishness.

Each of the directors is finding out how well people work individually. In my case, when the singing ensemble is given to me, I discover and rediscover that when personnel is selected for voice and appearance, there is too frequently no room left for brains and musicianship: most of the singers cannot read music! They learn slowly and what a bass (for example) may learn with difficulty is too easily corrupted when he sits next to someone—anyone—singing a different part.

I see the same people with the dance director. They are too often incapable of sustaining a fixed rhythm or have four left feet or have never learned to distinguish right from left.

The stage director "reads" all of them in order to select small-part actors. He needs a man to run on as a Western Union messenger. He must say, "Telegram for you, sir. Sign here," receive a tip, say "Thank you," and exit quickly. Nearly all singers become instantly frozen when trying out for this difficult cameo. They run like hippopotami and declaim as in a Handel oratorio. The dancers end up with most of these jobs.

Whenever the stage director works with an ensemble and does not require the presence of most (or any) of the principals, they go to an available pianist to practice a song or pace the corridors, script in hand, trying to memorize their parts.

Everything must be readied for run-thoughs and musical numbers, which after the second week of rehearsal will have to be meted out, one by one, to the orchestrator, who will be growing ulcers from waiting and knowing that in another two and a half weeks he must have *everything* scored and orchestra parts copied for the first orchestra reading.

Solo songs cannot be given the arranger until they are learned thoroughly and staged. Dance numbers must be completed, certified by director, producer, composer, or others, and usually cut down in length.

Sometimes on the last Saturday afternoon at the end of four weeks of rehearsal, there is a "gypsy" run-through, so-called because other theater people—"gypsies"—are invited to see it. The performance is given on a bare stage lit most often by a single dull "work" light, without scenery or costumes. A single piano represents the orchestra-to-be. The purpose of this run-through is to subject the cast to an audience and to observe its reaction.

That Saturday night, the conductor, the pit pianist, the two drummers, perhaps the concertmaster, first trumpet, and maybe the first reed player go to Philadelphia (or Boston or just anywhere outside of New York) because the first orchestra reading will begin on Sunday morning at ten.

The conductor, after settling himself at his hotel, usually visits another where the arranger (by now with three or four assistant arrangers and an assembly line of copyists, perhaps six to ten) is working vigorously in a series of connecting rooms against time and mounting fatigue. There will be coffee percolators everywhere and plates of Danish pastry and sandwiches. When one of them cannot possibly continue, he throws himself on a bed, sleeps for twenty or thirty minutes, is awakened, drinks a cup of coffee, and returns to work.

The orchestra usually begins to assemble in a hotel ballroom by 9:30 A.M. A ballroom is used instead of the theater because electricians and stagehands are utilizing the theater to hang scenery, to hang and focus lights, and to move in furniture, costumes, and set decorations.

A ballroom is the worst imaginable place for an orchestra reading because the sound is too "live," but there is ample space not only for the orchestra but for the cast, which will usually join the orchestra by the following Wednesday. Nevertheless, there are five or six New York players and nineteen or twenty local musicians arranged for in advance through telephone conversations between the New York and the local contractors, A sleepy copyist arrives with armloads of scores and parts and distributes them on the various music stands.

This first "reading" requires lots of time: notes must be corrected, phrasing and dynamics indicated, some heavy instrumentation thinned out, and so on. After the lunch break, more scores and parts appear. After dinner, still more.

It continues Monday morning, and throughout the day. By the end of Tuesday, perhaps, all of the music will have been received and read. Then the conductor has to "routine" the show—that is, have the players put all of the music in proper sequence. He will have them write the word "segue" at the bottom of many pieces indicating that the orchestra goes immediately into the next piece. Sometimes a "stop" is joyfully substituted.

By Wednesday the cast arrives from New York, and they report to the ballroom. I begin conducting, from the beginning, the music which, until this moment, they have not heard an orchestra play.

Usually I omit the dance numbers from the routine order because I want to rehearse them with the dancers when the rest of the cast has been dismissed. Stars and other solo singers come one by one to stand beside me as their songs are played. They are very nervous. The sound, because of the ballroom acoustics, is much too loud. (I explain this many times.) The principals sing but often have difficulty finding their starting note. When this happens, I begin the number again; otherwise, it is once through.

The chorus stands behind the orchestra and sings. When all of them have gone through their numbers (this takes perhaps two hours), the cast, except the dancers, is dismissed. Then I go through the dances, watching them for visual cues (*my* first time through) and often I repeat each number.

The company then has a call at the theater from 7:00 P.M. until midnight. (The rule now before opening is ten hours out of twelve, with twelve hours between calls.) At the theater the purpose is a so-called "technical" rehearsal. Translated, this means a rehearsal with actors to "try on" the scenery, costumes, and lights, to accustom everyone to entrances and exits, to make certain that there is enough time for costume changes, to see if the lighting produces its desired results.

This rehearsal is accompanied by piano. Performance, ensemble, and such are not thought about. If everything works out properly, if planning has been correct, it will require twenty hours to go from the start of the show to the finale: Wednesday night, five hours;

Thursday, noon to five and seven to midnight; Friday, noon to five and Friday night a full, nonstop dress rehearsal with orchestra. Perhaps there will be a second one on Saturday afternoon to which soldiers, nurses, or institutionalized people will be invited. Saturday night—the end of five weeks' work—will be the start of the show for the public.

After each performance, the "brass" has a meeting lasting many hours. All aspects of the show are discussed—often violently. A song does not work and needs replacing. Another needs only to be deleted. Another ought to be reprised in Act Two. A scene is too long or too dull and must be cut down and/or rewritten. A performer needs to be replaced. A dance is much too long. A line thought to be humorous gets no laugh. A scene is too dimly lit. And on and on.

The stage manager and I are the two workers among the group: the rest have sat taking notes during the performance. We need a sandwich, and everybody needs a drink. Not nearly every problem can be tackled at one time and so a decision is reached as to what is to be done specifically at tomorrow's rehearsal.

This will start at noon and go until 5:00 P.M. Several problem places will be indicated and cuts will be made. The scene, song sequence, or dance that has interior deletions will have to be rehearsed.

I must keep a clearly spelled-out list of all the changes that involve music. Sometimes a scene underscored with music is shortened, and so the music has to be correspondingly cut down. A chorus is taken out or added to a song. An ending is shortened. A song in Act Two takes the place of one in Act One and vice versa. The list is always long.

I can speak to the orchestra only fifteen minutes before curtain time at night. I have each player bring his music to the basement, where I will have to dictate the changes carefully, clearly, and swiftly. While this is going on, the stage manager is shouting directions over his public-address system. As the basement also houses the wardrobe department, there will be bustling and shouting there also: a dancer cannot find the belt to her first dress, a singer's collar button has broken off, a zipper fails to function, and so on.

The musicians listen and mark. The almost inevitable response from some player will begin, "In other words . . . ," and I have to rephrase what I have already said because someone has not understood. These "talk-downs" are extremely difficult, important, and dangerous. If anyone fails to mark his music properly, he may, for example, start in the wrong place and continue playing when everyone else has stopped.

The stage manager descends to the basement: How much longer will this take? The show must get started. I assure him that I will dispatch the orchestra members to their seats in the pit as soon as I have finished and will then go to the stage manager and await his orders to begin.

These nightly meetings and preperformance changes go on endlessly. The only departure from this routine occurs when a new song or new orchestration has been written. This must be "read" by the orchestra and gone through at least once with the singer it involves. The union allows a one-hour call for musicians prior to an evening performance, and so the new music is generally rehearsed at that time and put into the evening performance.

I believe that nowadays Equity requires one weekly day off out of town. Throughout my career, no such rule existed. As a result, on Sunday, when there was no performance, the director, authors, and others took advantage of the available extra time to change whole scenes either in writing or staging. Rehearsals began at noon, stopped at five for dinner, resumed at seven, and ended at midnight. Sometimes as a result of this allowable time, a practically *new* show was tried out on Monday night. This necessitated long, exhausting, rigorous talk-downs on Monday night.

The critical and audience response in whatever town the show first opened will have its effects. Good press notices often breed smugness, while the more objective ones among us will fear that the proper out-of-town work will not be done. Poor reviews breed discouragement and hysterical resolutions to replace just about everybody from choreographer to stage doorman. Audience reaction in Boston and Philadelphia *prior* to New York reaction is seldom valid or in some cases overly enthusiastic. When you have done as many shows as I have, every laugh at what in your opinion is an unfunny line is the equivalent of a nail in the show's coffin.

After four weeks in this town and usually after the Saturday night performance, my four or five or six musicians and I take a sleeper to the next town. The company will travel next day (Sunday), while we are preparing a new orchestra.

I notice that a second trumpet here is better than the one there or that a second reed is going to be a disaster, but there is nothing to be done about it: the choice is too limited, and "making waves" is pointless when it will fail to have any effect.

The most appalling thing is discovered at this first reading, which now lasts only about six hours: some one or two players in the last town *memorized* their cuts and changes but failed to make a single mark on the music! This means that those unmarked parts have to be carefully edited and explained to the new players. I do not remember a single time when this phenomenon failed to occur (pencil shortage, no doubt).

Otherwise the daily and weekly routines are identical: performances, reviews, meetings, changes, rehearsals, and all for perhaps another four weeks.

Again, after the last performance the musicians and I go at once to the next town—this time, New York. We will carry with us a certain optimism concerning the show's fate, a definite feeling of discouragement, or a guarded wait-and-see attitude.

The orchestra this last time around will be the permanent one, provided, or course, the show itself is permanent. More time will be spent in polishing the performance. I have often had occasion to remark that out-of-town theater musicians as a whole may play less well than their New York counterparts but read at sight more quickly.

There will be a dress rehearsal and a couple or a few weeks of previews. New York taste is reflected by the audiences' reactions. Sometimes this is better than ever, sometimes dishearteningly poor.

Opening night draws a conglomerate audience. Critics occupy a large number of seats, and they do not react audibly, at least during the performance. Backers will have tickets, as will friends of cast members. If the show enjoys an advance reputation of distinction, no seats are available to the unconnected public. Too often the backers and their guests and the relatives and friends of cast members go overboard in the noisiness of their response; they cheer, try to promote standing ovations once reserved for distinguished artists, applaud as well as laugh at jokes, and so on. This not only fools no one but has a decided tendency to irritate the more sober-minded, including the critics.

Backstage, before and after, there is pandemonium. The narrow passageways are crowded with flowers and gifts. Messenger boys run in and out of the stage door all evening delivering hundreds of telegrams. Afterward there is a general crush of friends and relatives. Then the company dresses, goes to a party given by the producer or a backer, and stays up most of the night indulging in free food and liquor.

Most dangerous is the custom of turning on the television while reviews are being given and of having press agents hurry in and out of the party with copies of newspaper reviews yet to be printed. These are read aloud to an anxiety-ridden cast with crossed fingers and legs. When the reviews are favorable, there is cheering. Too often, they are not favorable and a deep depression sets in.

If the show appears to promise a run with or against these notices, on the following Sunday there will be a recording session. The musicians will start at 10:00 A.M. Cast and chorus are carefully scheduled, since no one can record more than seven hours out of ten and everything must be completed on that one day. The sessions will be divided into three (10:00 to 1:00; 2:30 to 5:30; 7:00 until completed). Any time in excess of three-hour periods means overtime pay for the players, who are generally and understandably so tired by 10:00 P.M. that the thought of some extra pay becomes a secondary matter.

Then there is whatever run of the show there is. Failure means a waste of time and energy ending in joblessness and, if lucky, another arduous ride on a similar merry-go-round. Success means eventual boredom: an eight-times-a-week repetition plus some inevitable rehearsals for brushups and corrections.

This is the general pattern.

8: Mostly about Monty Clift and Charles Ives

WITH *Johnny Johnson* I began for the first time to earn a weekly salary that I could live on and I would never again be able to exist without it. I still clung hopefully to the creative dream I had always had, and I continued to work at composing music every day of my life. The "show," I thought, would form only a brief intermission in my own work. That intermission would last a mere four weeks while I rehearsed. After opening, all of my time—all day, every day— would be my own again. But the "free" time was from the beginning and ever afterward a delusion, for I had not figured on the extra tolls in the time budget, and the extra energy tolls because of the time. Wednesdays and Saturdays still gave me free mornings for work before the matinees until I came to need to rest in order to have energy for the expensive activity that lay ahead. Then on Thursday and Sunday—days following double performances, I needed to recoup the expended energy. On other days, at intervals, there were (and always are) rehearsals, auditions, understudy re-hearsals, chorus brushups, friendly requests for tickets, and so on, all of which are always time-consuming. And after the evening perfor-mances, unwinding takes several hours, so that sleeping time comes later and waking time proportionately, though unwillingly, comes later. In no time, there is no time. The paper-schedule of eight weekly performances requiring a total of twenty-four hours with all the remaining time available for my own work (my "real" work, as I thought of it) dissolved into a certain nothingness. It was to continue this way, but it was to be nearly twenty years before I was able to recognize it for what it was. I earned, and I paid—all in one single transaction. The one canceled out the other.

I wrote music for *Everywhere I Roam* and *Family Portrait*, both of which, like *Johnny Johnson, Mme. Capet,* and *Robin Landing,* failed, and music for *The Time of Your Life* which failed to survive the pre-Broadway tour.

Everywhere I Roam, a play about the growth of America, was written by Arnold Sundgaard, a talented young playwright, and directed and rewritten during production by Marc Connelly. Connelly, the successful older man, versus Sundgaard, the young man with fresh talent and part of a play, could not possibly have "collaborated."

During dress rehearsals of *Everywhere I Roam,* the choreographer Felicia Sorel brought a young actor to the theater who wanted to take photographs. He was nineteen, and his name was Montgomery Clift. After extensive picture-taking, Felicia invited Monty to join us for tea. I had never met so lively and vital a boy. He was interested in music, painting, studied photography, had studied acting with a variety of teachers, spoke several languages fluently, and was an avid reader and theatergoer. He had already acted in stock and at fifteen on Broadway in the Cole Porter-Moss Hart *Jubilee.*

A few weeks after our first meeting, Monty turned up in the first row at a lecture I gave in Stamford, Connecticut (I was then twenty-nine), and we returned to New York together on the train. This was the start of a long friendship.

For several years Monty and I went to the theater, museums, and took trips together. He made everything seem exciting. Once he called me early in the morning.

"Mon vieux!" (his frequent term of address to me), "there's a Blake exhibit in Philadelphia. Why don't we go?"

We met at Penn Station and spent nearly two days looking at pictures.

He was always full of pleasant surprises, one of which he had arranged—and at nineteen!—on that jaunt. As Orson Welles was playing in *Five Kings* in Philadelphia, Monty had booked tickets.

We saw it in the evening and went to supper with Orson afterward.

Monty and I made periodic excursions on the sight-seeing boat around Manhattan, to Boston on the night boat, and once, when I was most tired, we flew to Boston for the weekend to sleep, walk, and see whatever was to be seen. On this occasion, we stayed at the Ritz-Carlton and on a wintry Sunday morning set out for a walk in the Public Gardens just opposite the hotel. There we ran into Moss and Kitty Hart, who had run into others whom we all knew, and the Harts invited us all for cocktails in the late afternoon. Boston became—pleasant as it was—a transplanted New York.

In the summer I decided to go to Cuernavaca in Mexico for the second time to combine writing with resting. As I had little money, I booked passage in a crummy cabin accommodating four—on the *Orizaba*, the old ship from which Hart Crane, the poet, had disappeared a few years earlier.

As soon as my plans were made, Monty's mother asked if Monty might go along with me. I was delighted and at her request gave her my ticket so that she might "book something nearby" for Monty. When the two of us arrived for the sailing, Mrs. Clift had taken the only suite on board for us and had filled it with flowers, candy, cookies, liquor, books, and everything that could turn a journey into a dream.

Monty and I had a little cottage in the back garden of the Hotel Marik, with a swimming pool and a nearby "forest" of orchids. Julie (John) Garfield and Robbie, his wife, were in Mexico City only two hours away, to help exploit Julie's latest film, *Juarez*. The altitude bothered them, and so I asked them to our lower, more comfortable town. Only a moment after they arrived, they decided to stay.

In a few days, Rose and Miguel Covarrubias (the artist-caricaturist) and the Misrachis (a cultivated Jewish antique dealer) descended upon us, and Monty and I had a houseful. The later arrivals came to dinner but stayed on several days. Each morning Rose Covarrubias was up early to go to the flower market, where she bought exquisite fragrant white flowers for her raven hair, and every day—like the flowers—her coiffure was new.

Finally, the Garfields had to return to Hollywood. As we had heard of lovely beaches on Mexico's west coast at Acapulco, the Garfields planned to go there and pick up a ship for California.

Left to right: John (Julie) Garfield, his wife Robbie, L. E., and Monty Clift in the summer of 1940, before the cathedral in Taxco, Mexico. *Photo by Recueido*

Monty and I decided to go along, and so the four of us and a driver set out first for Taxco, where we spent the night.

Next day we were in for a dreadful ride to Acapulco. The highway was hardly begun, and we were principally occupied with stirring up swirling clouds of dust as we bumped along the dry hot road. As we were very thirsty, and drinking water anywhere was a thought not to be cherished, we stopped to buy cold beer here and there. We were hot and tired and ill, and our stomachs were painfully upset in every way.

At that time, Acapulco consisted of a tiny, cheap, but new, hotel on the beautiful beach and an older one high above on a cliff. There was nothing else except open fields.

Julie and Robbie embarked a day later, and Monty and I discovered an airline that would take us up to Mexico City the following day. (It was inconceivable that we return by car.) We were in-structed to await the plane in a grassy field where a single cow grazed. The plane at last set down. It undoubtedly belonged in a museum: the door was held together with hairpins, and the various meters were denoted by empty round holes where they had once resided and functioned.

After takeoff we had to gain considerable altitude immediately as Mexico is almost entirely mountainous. It was soon obvious that the pilot had lost his way and the trip lasted five hours instead of forty-five minutes. Both Monty and I had been frightened, but Monty was really ill. He returned to New York within a couple of days, and doctors discovered that he had amoebic dysentery, against which he spent several years in treatment.

Our careers drove wedges between us, and our meetings—always warm and friendly—became less and less frequent. World War II came, and I was soon in it. Monty was touring with the Lunts in *There Shall Be No Night*, and we corresponded. He looked to me for advice, and years later, after World War II, although I seldom saw him, he continued to depend on me when he needed to make a decision. His movie career, which he had postponed several times on my advice, at length began, and he became a big star. He brought quality to his films.

My blooming career and his lengthy stride to the West Coast and sometimes abroad made our meetings less and less frequent. He began to have a new family of friends and I had mine. His personal-ity had gradually altered in the meanwhile. He was no longer the free little boy of nineteen—happy and energetic, eager to learn—but was now a man in his early forties who seemed driven by some mysterious self-destructive urge.

Some years after the war, when I was again busy with my own work and seeing Monty only rarely, I returned to my apartment one afternoon and as I opened the door the telephone was ringing. My old friend Norris Houghton, with his cohort T. Edward Hambleton on an extension, was calling for help. They were at their Phoenix Theatre, where a dress rehearsal of *The Seagull* was scheduled to begin in an hour, but Monty, they said, had insulted all of the ladies in the cast, which included his teacher, Mira Rostova, Judith Eve-lyn, and Maureen Stapleton, and had created such difficulties that a scheduled dress rehearsal—or for that matter anything further—seemed impossible. Norris and T. said that Monty (and the ladies) had agreed that they would abide by whatever decision I made if I would arbitrate. It seemed to me that I had no choice, that Monty was in trouble and I must go at once.

A very few minutes later I arrived on the Phoenix stage, where Monty, Norris, and T. were awaiting me in one group near the door of the bare stage and the various ladies—alone or in little groups—clung to the bare brick back wall.

I no longer remember the causes of the crisis but two things—both, I considered, Monty's fault—had to be settled. I took Monty by the arm and asked him to walk around the block with me. In essence what I said (after he had expressed his unhappiness with the actresses) was that he must have been aware of his feelings from the beginning, which was the only time he might have expressed himself so strongly; that it was now too late; that the scheduled dress rehearsal *had* to be under way since the first preview was to take place a day later; and that under the circumstances I felt it was Monty's responsibility to apologize and placate the actresses.

Monty agreed.

A few days later he called me, and we sat together briefly after a performance. He was intensely unhappy but incapable of knowing why. He had a distinguished talent, a worshipful public, and success nearly always. Whatever it was that bothered him, that drove him in a self-destructive way, I never knew.

We later spoke on the phone once in a while, but I never saw him again alive.

His young laughter and enthusiasm and taste are unforgettable. *An American Tragedy* was more than the basis for one of his many films.

Robert Edmond Jones,* like Monty, I came to know in *Everywhere I Roam*, for which he designed the scenery. He was one of

* I had known Bobby Jones earlier when he had spent much time listening patiently to my "serious" music. Through him and his assistant Rose Bogdonoff, I also came to know the distinguished designer Jo Mielziner, whose talent was equaled only by his charm.

the greatest men the American theater has ever produced: a great scene designer, a great man of the theater, a distinguished mind, and a sublime human being.

He was profoundly interested in new talented people and was bitterly disappointed if his good opinion of a talent had to be altered. He always found time to listen to a new musical composition, read a manuscript, see a dance, or view a stage design. He said only and precisely what he thought, and if he admired the talent but disliked the specific work, he could make even devastating criticism sound encouraging.

On one occasion he told me that "real" materials on stage look phony. As illustration he said that if he wished to effect cloth-of-gold he would probably use gold-sprayed burlap even if real cloth-of-gold were available.

One day after lunch he returned to rehearsal upset.

"What's the matter, Mr. Jones?" I asked.

"People talk about American art in the silliest way," he sputtered. "American art has no roots, they say. Why does it have to have roots? Who says it's a plant? Maybe it's a bird, and wouldn't a bird look funny with roots?"

Once he gave me several of his designs merely because I admired them. I am particularly proud to have a watercolor for a scene in the opera *Wozzeck*. He promised me the entire series. Somehow he kept forgetting to locate the others. Years passed, during which he developed a tragic mental condition and destroyed many of his designs. After his death, it was discovered that my *Wozzeck* design was the only one extant from the series.

Family Portrait, also a kind of folk-play and done that same season, was about Jesus' family. Judith Anderson played Mary the Mother, and Peggy Webster directed and played Mary Magdalene. At the opening, Peggy sat with me in the theater. She dressed for her own last-act scene during the second intermission but returned to sit with me after the house lights had gone out for the final act. As her scene came round, she sprinted around onto the stage, played the scene beautifully, and returned to her seat in time to shed a few tears with me at the play's end.

In the spring of 1939 the Westminster Choir at its school in Princeton presented a Festival of Contemporary American Music arranged through Roy Harris, the composer, who taught at the school. My new choral piece, *Rest*, was on the program. I was not invited to any rehearsal, and consequently, I had no opportunity to offer any criticisms. At the performance the choir sang as always with rhythmic precision and accuracy of intonation. My very delicate piece was given a cold, hard, and loud rendition, devoid of sensitivity. It was also placed disadvantageously on the program between two showy and more conventional compositions. *Rest* was lost. There was polite and feeble handclapping, which barely got me out of my seat for a bow, but as I rose a boy-soprano-like voice said, "Bravo!" The small single commotion embarrassed me until at the end of the program Roy Harris told me that it was Professor Albert Einstein who had shouted. Roy had hardly finished telling me this when Professor Einstein sought me out. He spoke warmly. His eyes gleamed. He said he thought I was very talented. He hoped he would have the pleasure of hearing more of my music. He said goodnight and left the hall quickly.

Last of the productions during the season was the Aaron Copland-Edwin Denby school opera, *The Second Hurricane*, of which I have already spoken.

In the summertime Peggy directed four of Shakespeare's plays in one-hour versions for the Globe Theatre—part of "Merrie England" in the New York World's Fair. I wrote music for *A Midsummer Night's Dream* and *The Comedy of Errors* for recorder and virginal. Peggy and I would meet before 8:00 A.M. out in the Globe Theatre in Flushing Meadows after she had played Mary Magdalene (*Family Portrait* still clung briefly to life) until nearly midnight. I remember her affectionately on those mornings, her eyes scarcely open, the familiar cigarette drooping out of one corner of her mouth. The theater itself was still in the process of being completed as we held final rehearsals in it. Time was short and labor somehow scarce, and so Peggy climbed ladders to nail up curtains, helped to alter costumes, and completed all kinds of odd jobs that normally did not come within her province.

On the opening day five people (including Peggy and me) saw the first matinee. The Globe also closed in a very short time.

Now in my collection at
Millsaps-Wilson Library,
Jackson, Mississippi.

While I was conducting the Madrigal Singers, I saw a photostatic copy of *The 67th Psalm*, by Charles Ives, and I wanted to perform it. I wrote Mr. Ives and received an immediate reply asking me to visit him. Although he was then in his middle sixties, he had the physical bearing of a man twenty years older. He had a ruddy face with a chin that seemed particularly sharp because of a closely cropped grey beard that came to a point slightly below the limits of his face. His cataract-infested eyes seemed sharply penetrating, and this effect was heightened by a squint, which doubtless allowed him to see a bit better. His lean frame was slightly bent, and he displayed surprising agility when he moved, often darting about.

I went to his house in East Seventy-fourth Street, where he lived with his wife, Harmony, and their daughter. It was a quiet, modest, polished house with a dark plainness: no decorative features, no fanciness, no opulence, but one could be certain that its occupants were not poor.

He always rose from his couch and leaned down over the bannister to greet me avidly as I came up the stairs to the second-floor living room. Often, when we entered into a discussion, he would become violent and prance around the room, pounding his fist on a table or shaking it in my face to enforce a statement, punctuating it with an asthmatic laugh. Exhausted, he would fling himself on the couch (interrupting himself in the middle of a sentence) and pant loudly before being able to continue speaking. When I first saw this I was frightened, but Harmony, a strong, but placid, white-haired lady, would pick up the conversation in an airy way as if I were not to notice her husband, all the while continuing with her rocking and her knitting.

On one of my visits Ives wanted to illustrate some point at the piano, which was in a kind of attic two flights higher up. He led the way, literally crawling on his hands and knees, and when he had recovered his breath he banged away at the keyboard in a manner that undoubtedly proved the point to him but meant little to me.

The subject of my first visit was of course his *67th Psalm*, which I intended to—and did—perform. We also subsequently recorded it for Columbia, and this was the first recording of any of his music by a major company. In speaking of the piece written in two concurrent keys, he said that he had always thought that the Danbury (Connecticut) Choir sounded as if it were singing in two keys. But everything he composed had for him a realistic origin.

Ives's response to our first performance is contained in a now-famous letter he wrote me, dated May 18, 1937:

Dear Mr. Engel:

Many thanks for your letter telling us of the Madrigal concert last week. The news that the *67th Psalm* was so warmly received by the audience and critics was much appreciated—but it was something of a surprise to me as it brought back the memory of the trouble it made, and the scowls it brought from some of the pews (but not from the pulpit)—about forty years ago because of its two-key tonality basis. But evidently in music, custom, habit and easy ear-learning, static rules based on even vibratory sounds are having less to say—at least not the whole say—today.

Your remark "the lazy ear has been an enemy to musical progress" is well taken. Yes, and it has been a help in keeping it not always, but too often, from stronger ways and bigger fields and higher mountains. You ask if there are any objections to having the record of the *67th Psalm* made. No, there are none, we are very glad to have it made.

I am afraid some of the manuscripts of some of the other early chorales are not legible and rather difficult to read. The *Harvest Home* pieces—for chorus, organ and some brass, etc. used to go well sometimes after some rehearsal trouble—they are a kind of outdoor music and have something in common with the trees, rocks, and men of the mountains in days before machinery.

Probably the old ladies (male and female) would not—but there are some men who would like to hear some of the choruses with orchestra today, especially those about the world problems of the people, etc. sounding up over the stone walls, and "west mountain."

The one called *An Election* (in the original score) was called *Down with the Politicians, Up with the People*. I think you have a copy of this score, if not, would be glad to send one on and with it the Unison Universal Chorale *Majority—Thanksgiving and Forefathers Day*. The last movement of the Symphony *Holidays*— "Our exiled fathers crossed the sea; for freedom of body and soul."

These are about things that are not discussed enough by the people in this world today. I feel strongly that the great fundamentals should be more discussed in all public meetings, and also in meetings of schools and colleges, not only the students but also the faculty should get down to more thinking and action about the great problems which concern all countries and all people in the world today, and not let the politicians do it all and have the whole say.

I have often been told that it is not the function of music (or a concert) to concern itself with matters like these. But I do not by any means agree. I think that it is *one* of the things that music can do, if it happens to want to, if it comes naturally, and it is not the result of superimposition—I have had some fights about this.

Now I will stop and let you finish your symphony. Again many thanks for the fine work you and your singers are doing.

With best wishes, in which Mrs. Ives joins, I am,

Sincerely yours,
CHARLES E. IVES

P.S. At the end of the *Election*, published as an arrangement (for voice and piano) is a footnote, referring to a suggested Twentieth Amendment that the people may have more of a direct say in the important public matters which concern us all. Will send a copy to you.

During a period of several years, I visited Mr. and Mrs. Ives a number of times and usually with similar experiences: the excitement, anger, humor, breathlessness, and so on.

Few composers knew him, for his illness prevented his meeting people generally, but he always followed accounts of their work in the press. For reasons that were never clear to me there were some he would never consent to meet. He lived a full creative life in loneliness with the discouragement of too few performances and no acclaim of any kind.

Ives always spoke of America and of his father. He told stories of Danbury, where he had grown up, and of the Danbury Choir and band, and what "Pa said to Lincoln" or vice versa.

It was just prior to my first meeting with Ives that Aaron Copland, Virgil Thomson, Marc Blitzstein, and I had founded the Arrow Music Press. Once I asked Ives, who had made a financial success in the bond firm of Myrich and Ives, if we might publish some of his music, and I explained the terms. He was quite willing for us to do any of his works, left the choice to us, and agreed not only to pay the costs but to give the income to the publishing of young composers' works.

During one of my subsequent visits Ives spoke about the compositions of one of his old friends and he wanted me, as president of the Press, to have our board publish this composer's symphony at Ives's expense. Knowing Ives's temper, I hesitated to criticize his friend's music but then decided that too much was at stake to remain silent. While I considered what I should say, Ives launched into a discourse on his friend's life: he had worked hard and sincerely, he had gone without material necessities, he had always provided for his family's needs, he had had no recognition, he had gone on composing (like Ives himself) in spite of every discouragement. I replied sympathetically that I was aware of these things but that I deeply regretted feeling that his friend's music—in spite of its sincerity—was worthless. There was a silence, then Ives burst into tears acknowledging the truth of what I had said and cursed life, which could fail to couple industry, self-sacrifice, and sincerity with talent. We agreed that publication would not serve any purpose.

Early in 1942 I went into the navy. Ives and I exchanged letters, but I never again saw him.

9: I Love You Truly

ALL ALONG IT HAD BEEN theater that I wanted, but it had been *musical* theater. Now it was theater with music—a great difference—and the quality now was generally far lower than anything I had ever nodded to in a nightmare. The sounds, the thoughts, the gestures were puny. As I dreamed them, they had been grand.

I was now settling for a compromise. I would work honestly to do what I could, and do it as well as I could. But it was not what I had wanted, and I knew it. I even suffered guilt, like the child who plays with his marbles when he knows he ought to be doing his finger exercises at the piano. Marbles were sometimes fun too, in an unimportant way, like this substitute theater.

But each of us does what he is driven to do, neither more nor less. We dream, translate the dream to plans, but then sometimes we are lured where we never planned to go, to do what we had never dreamed of doing. We do (we say it is temporary), "we could have done differently" (we say), until we find with a shock that we cannot, that truly we never could have done any differently, done anything else.

It was my dream that brought me into the theater, but by the time I could take stock of my surroundings and my own relationship to them, I was already running ahead, dashing successfully nowhere. For the dream, even as I saw it in my mind's eye, had already been shaped for me by the still stronger ideas instilled in me by my whole upbringing.

Within a space of about ten years, I moved to several different and always better apartments, always in the Village. The last of these before the war had a terrace not large but bright, and it allowed a hairlike view of the Hudson. The day I was to move, alas! was one on which I had to meet an important, unchangeable, airtight schedule which took me away from my to-be-abandoned home early and would return me to my new place about midnight. I had no idea what I could do about seeing my possessions safely and wholly out of one place and into the other.

Paul Dupont, the costume designer who was connected with the Group Theatre and my many friends there, volunteered to oversee the switch, and I was of course relieved at the thought of shedding my responsibility. There was no reason at all—not especially close friendship or anything conceivable—why Paul would inflict such a thankless task upon himself, but he did offer and I could scarcely refuse his generosity.

When I entered my new apartment just before midnight, I was stunned by what I saw. Paul was seated in a chair in my new living room, reading. All the furniture had been carefully arranged as though by an army of stage-set dressers, and draperies had been made and hung! The experience was staggering until, upon retiring, I opened a closet door and was set upon by an avalanche of clothing and luggage. It was great, somehow, to realize that not *everything* was perfect! Even God had not created the world in a single day.

Settled in my new apartment, I began what was to be a long association with my Anna. She was large, black, and generous. She made out of me the "gentleman" she wanted me to be. It was an easy role, for it was also the one in which my mother had cast me.

With Anna, I made a permanent home away from home. She was my usually invisible hostess who planned the meals, cooked, and served them (dinner twice a week). Always next day she would deliver penetrating autopsies on the guests. Although basically she was a snob (and Southern), her appraisals were seldom incorrect. Everything she served was good. Anything less—as in Jackson— would have been disgraceful.

I met a radio-theater director, Tony Stanford, who because of my experience in theater composing-conducting, engaged me for a series of Texaco Star Theatre dramatic broadcasts. I worked quickly, so that I usually spent only one morning each week composing the necessary music. Of course, unknowingly, I was being had. I think I received $175 weekly for composing, orchestrating, and conducting with its necessary rehearsals. But we always pay for our opportunities, and it did not matter to me only because I did not know any better. Nearly every popular theater star appeared at some time on this program: Helen Hayes, Ethel Barrymore, the Marches, John Garfield, Dennis King, Mady Christians, Ruth Gordon, Henry Hull, Louis Calhern, Luise Rainer, Victor Moore, Lee Tracy, and countless others. Out of the entire series Joan Bennett was the only one who ever came late for a rehearsal, and Charles Laughton was the only difficult one.

The only program horror happened when an actress had a miscarriage on stage during a dress rehearsal. After a rest-intermission, however, she put on an evening dress and gave the scheduled performance.

While working on the program, I became involved in several theatrical productions.

First, there was William Saroyan. What seems now to have been only a fad began with an "experimental" and quite beautiful production of Saroyan's *My Heart's in the Highlands*, directed by Bobby Lewis. It was special, appealed to a special audience, and was poetic; it seemed then that a fresh new voice was being heard in the land.

The Theatre Guild then decided to produce Saroyan's *The Time of Your Life*, with Bobby again directing. The stars were Eddie Dowling and Julie Haydon. I was engaged to compose the incidental music. Martin Ritt was cast as the hoofer—and now (thank you) he is a very successful film director.

Throughout rehearsals, Saroyan was still on the West Coast having, I believe, a mad affair with his typewriter, so he did not appear until we were in Boston preparing to open.

The script of *The Time of Your Life* had the longest stage directions I have ever encountered. He called for what could best be described as "sensitive" effects, and all of them were accompanied by lavish descriptions of music. (That was where I came in.)

Bobby directed the play with scrupulous honesty. What Saroyan had set down was carried out explicitly. I wrote all the music as nearly as possible as it had been described. Boris Aronson's set was magnificent, and it too adhered faithfully to the author's meticulously detailed intentions.

I was first aware of Saroyan's presence the morning after the first dress rehearsal in Boston when he stood in the back of the theater with Lawrence Langner and Terry Helburn, the heads of the Theatre Guild. Their conference or powwow or whatever it might have been called was scarcely argumentative, since no one seemed to disagree with anyone else.

Finally, the three of them slithered slowly down the aisle to the first row, where Bobby Lewis was seated, and they began a powwow with him. Voices began to overlap and grow louder. There was war. Bobby was fighting for the preservation of what Saroyan had written and Saroyan, now represented by the Theatre Guild management, was in full agreement with the others that—"well, you know . . . well, I didn't really . . . ," and lots of other things that only seemed to reinforce my earlier belief that Saroyan was indeed having an affair with his typewriter! What he created with it was to be only their very private own. *Entre nous*, you know. Naturally, *anybody* would know that it was not to be taken literally and undressed just like that before the public.

Well, Bobby asserted all two hundred pounds of himself. If the production were to be watered down he would leave, but he refused to denature it. He strode up the aisle and out. Finis.

It became instantly clear that this course of action had commenced somewhat earlier, because Eddie Dowling, the male star, immediately took over the direction. To my horror I observed Langner and Dowling go up on stage and physically tear down artificial flowers, uproot grass mats and other parts of Boris Aronson's scenery, which had been stipulated expressly by Saroyan. It was the day of the butcher.

I walked over to Terry, with whom I had had a disastrous WPA collaboration, and suggested that under these circumstances my music would no longer be appropriate. She protested, but I said I would return to New York and come back to Boston when and if needed. I was never called.

The Time of Your Life opened in New York with a young actor named Gene Kelly as a replacement for Marty Ritt. (It seems curious to me that Ritt had been engaged as an *actor* who could not dance well—the very idea of the character—and was replaced by a superb dancer who was *supposed* not to dance well. Logical?) There was no incidental music beyond Ross Bagdesarian doodling on the harmonica and Reginald Beane playing the piano for the dancer. Nothing original.

There were many beautiful things in the version of the play I worked on that were never seen. *The Time of Your Life* was a moderate success. Then there were a couple of other "interesting" Saroyan plays. And now? That was more than thirty years ago. No Saroyan in quite a long time. Somebody should ask his typewriter.

During those years New York was still a safe place for walking at night. As usual I was conducting some Broadway show, and for this one I wore tails. Each night in the late spring when the weather had become balmy I walked to my apartment on Fourteenth Street and Seventh Avenue. In the first floor corner of the building there was a garishly lit Stewart's Cafeteria. By the time I reached there, customers were few and many of the remaining ones were so drunk that they were scarcely present.

Meanwhile I had staggered along the way and had had—here and there—three or four scotch-and-sodas, so that when I arrived I wanted only a glass of milk before going to bed.

The cafeteria stayed open twenty-four hours, and there was a young night manager who was most pleasant. Of course, he treated me deferentially because I was dressed in evening clothes. After I had come in a number of times, he took to bringing himself a cup of coffee and sitting with me. I learned that he was in his final year at New York University, that he had a girl in a Far West town whom he would marry after graduation, and that he had a job awaiting him at a college in the same place. He worked all night at Stewart's, was a waiter during the lunch period at school, had some hours there in the bookstore, and was happy to be able to do his work while supporting himself. He would graduate at the beginning of summer, and all of this would be in the past. Neither of us ever knew the other's name.

Our nightly visits went on for some weeks until one night I found him looking depressed: He would not be able to finish school until sometime the following season because he had had to give too much time to supporting himself.

"However . . . ," he sighed.

I sympathized with him but asked if he quit his jobs, how much money he would need to finish at the time he had planned.

"Two hundred dollars," he replied.

I said goodnight and left. I was bothered. I had only three hundred dollars in the bank, but what was two hundred dollars to me? I knew what it would be to him.

Next morning, I drew out two hundred dollars and put them in an unaddressed envelope because I did not know the young man's name. The following evening I stood in the shadows of the building opposite Stewart's and saw the night manager disappear into the kitchen. Then I ran to the cashier seated immediately inside the front door, handed him the sealed envelope, and said, "Give this to the night manager. It's very important."

I returned to the shadows across the street to watch. The night manager returned to the front of the cafeteria. The cashier handed him the envelope with a shrug of his shoulders. The manager opened the envelope and found the money. He looked stunned and did not move for some time—this unnoticed by the cashier who was busy ringing up checks for departing customers.

The next night, I returned to the cafeteria, drank my milk, and observed with the greatest happiness I have ever known that the night manager was no longer present.

Bobby Lewis called on me to compose music for Albert Bein's hobo folk-legend, *Heavenly Express*, starring Julie Garfield, Aline MacMahon, and Harry Carey. This was Kermit Bloomgarden's first production. Like many other art works in an unfinished world, *Heavenly Express* was an unfinished work of art that refused to respond to all the surgery it underwent.

One of the pleasantest parts of this association was being with Julie Garfield again, for he was always genial and happy, and we had been good, if sporadic, friends for some years.

During rehearsals we dined one evening in Sardi's. As we

emerged hurriedly after dinner, Julie was overwhelmed by a mob of autograph seekers who snatched at his handkerchief, tore buttons off his coat, removed anything detachable to be kept as a memento, all the while squealing "Johnny! Johnny!" sexually. Julie hurriedly signed probably fifty autograph books, then as we pushed ahead toward a waiting cab, he said politely that he was late for a rehearsal and had to refuse to sign any more. We entered the taxi, but the people pushed their pencils and pads through the half-open windows. The driver could not move for fear of injuring them. Julie declined to sign any more books and begged the crowd to stand clear of the car. As the cab began slowly to push away, the crowd grumbled, then clearly took voice and as we rounded the corner they shouted, "Garfinkle!" It was still the voices of the Kane brothers calling "Sheeny!"

Meanwhile, I had become friendly with Harold Rome, the composer-lyricist, who was enjoying great success with *Pins and Needles*, a small, brilliant satirical revue, produced by the International Ladies Garment Workers' Union. Harold's music was freshly melodic, his lyrics engaging, and his personal warmth shone through everything he did.

Harold asked me to conduct his new musical comedy, *The Little Dog Laughed*, to be produced (nominally) and directed by Eddie Dowling, to be financed by Louisa Carpenter (a Dupont heiress), and to star Milli Monti, a nightclub singer of infinitesimal talent, and Paul Draper. (The principal female dancer was Marjorie Bell— now Marge Champion.) This was the beginning of a lifetime association with Harold, who subsequently asked me to conduct every show he ever wrote.

Much of what this show lacked might have been remedied had it not been for the fact that Milli Monti, the raison d'etre, was not "right" for the show, and most changes were vain attempts to show her off to better advantage, or at least to conceal as many of her inadequacies as possible.

The Little Dog Laughed spent its final rehearsing days in Atlantic City, and the tune was always the same. Miss Monti needed a new dress. Miss Monti needed a new coiffure. Miss Monti needed a new orchestration. Miss Monti needed a different colored light. Miss Monti needed less orchestral volume. The show needed a new star,

and I needed benzedrine to stay awake during the opening performance.

The premiere lasted half the night. Milli made her first entrance
and stood stock still as if the orchestra had played a fanfare. No one
applauded. Everyone asked who *she* was. Paul Draper walked
through the same door in his simplest manner and brought down the
house.

A magician symbolizing "propaganda" (which can turn white
into black and black into white) reached in his cape for a concealed
fishbowl, and before he could disengage it, splashed the water over the
stage. He "materialized" a white dove, which misbehaved in his hand
and then fled for safety to the center chandelier in the theater. Next
the magician accidentally burned a large hole in a handkerchief borrowed from a gentleman in the front row. Dozens of other errors
ended in the fouled-up disappearance of the magician himself. One
week in Boston followed the Atlantic City engagement, and nothing
else followed at all.

It was by then midsummer—a bad time—which contained no
prospects of any work for me. In New York, I had promises of
many jobs, but the projects themselves failed to materialize. After so
much work it seemed incredible that I could now be jobless.

In the midst of an incomprehensible vacuum, Tony Stanford
(former director of the Texaco broadcasts) did a few broadcasts
with Gene Autry and engaged me to compose incidental dramatic
music for palpitations of the purple sage and "conduct" Autry's
creamy coyote calling. It was in the cause of Wrigley Chewing
Gum.

Autry himself told his musicians—most of whom were with him
permanently—exactly what he wanted in the accompaniments.
(The Lord knows that I didn't know.) I "lifted" the original music
from my memory of the orchestra in the Majestic Theatre in Jackson, where I saw the only Wild West pictures I had ever seen.
Autry, an amiable man, always addressed the studio audience before going on the air. He would indicate me at the end of his usual
presentation: "An' folks, I want you to give a hand to that director o'
them Texas Wil' Cat Fiddlers, Lehman!"

From Palestrina to the purple sage is really not as far as one would think. (And Elia Kazan watched amused from a front-row seat.)

The season was clearly under way without me. And I was nowhere. Everything that I had done before was an experience, not alone, isolated, but a key to the next better experience, an education, a new step. No single work was an end in itself. Each was valuable only as it led to the next. And the income also was constantly essential, and because of the intermissions there was never anything left over.

Of course, I was still active during this hiatus but not creative because I felt too insecure: all time must go into making contacts, mingling with people, doing anything that might keep me moving. I had to move.

When this interim time comes (and you pray that it is only an interim), you think of all the advice you have so often given others to look elsewhere, to work in other areas where one thing can lead to another, where a job well done usually leads to another and perhaps better one. But in my position, and with already so much past activity, this thought was an impossibility. I could not turn back and I could not let go. I was the "who" I had become, and just the upkeep of that "who" was a continuing and insatiable problem for which I had no solution.

My old friend Mary Morris, then teaching at Carnegie Tech, and Henry Boettcher, head of the drama department, aware of my dilemma and of my ambition to someday stage a show, invited me to stage *The Beggar's Opera* by John Gay at Carnegie Tech. I was happy at the eight-week earning prospect and excited with the anticipation of a new work experience. Because of the continuing activities of two of my school choruses, I was obliged to commute between Pittsburgh and New York.

At Carnegie Tech I was able to accomplish all the things that made me want to go there, for although Henry Boettcher did not agree with my ideas for the production of *The Beggar's Opera*, he did everything to help me accomplish it.

The day before the first performance the leading man became ill and another student with a reputation for great facility was brought in. We canceled only one performance and in those two days the new Macheath learned all of the songs, dances, most of the lines, and performed with gusto. His name was William Eythe.

As I was finishing in Pittsburgh, Peggy Webster asked me to do the music for an Experimental Theatre production (two matinees and no fees) of *The Trojan Women*, with her mother, Dame May Whitty, Peggy herself, Water Slezak, Tamara Geva, Joanna Roos, and Frederic Tozere in the cast. Dame May, then in her late seventies, never complained of fatigue, stood for hours delivering Hecuba's long speeches shedding real tears, carrying in her arms the hulk of a nine-year-old child who appeared to be more dead weight than dead.

The winter season had proved to be a zero to me, and I could expect nothing from the summer. The irony was that everyone called me for advice or help, that I was able to find jobs for dozens of friends but none for myself. I got Burl Ives his first radio network engagement; sent a soprano on a European concert tour; introduced Arnold Sundgaard through Morris Stonzek to Kurt Weill, a meeting which culminated in *Down in the Valley*; helped a lady explorer get a fellowship that resulted in an Arctic expedition; sent a young actor off to a brilliant movie career; installed a floundering singer in a permanent teaching position; helped to put another into an important recording job; and clarified the thinking of dozens of others so that they were able to become not what they longed for in utter frustration, but what they were truly equipped to be.

Everyone thought I was so busy (and I was) that it never occurred to anyone that I could need anything. Nobody would have offered me a small job. I was listed in all of the encyclopedias: proof of success. Big jobs were not then to be had, but all of the possibilities for the future were big. They usually are. I pursued them delicately, but the projects themselves dissolved into thin air. The bright future was surely only removing her gloves before knocking at my door. Any moment.

Finally Janet Cohn, a literary agent and friend, persuaded the Bucks County Playhouse to let me put on my version of *The Beggar's Opera*. I used Jane Pickens, Walter Cassell, Richard Hale, Edith King, and T. C. Jones in the cast, and Howard Bay designed ingenious scenery.

In spite of my own disappointment with an inadequately rehearsed production and poor newspaper reviews, the indestructible *Beggar's Opera* was sold out for the week, and an extra matinee, added at the last moment, was likewise sold out at once. Two spectators each offered—unsolicited—to invest ten thousand dollars toward a Broadway production. My next goal then was to raise the balance of the money and find an interested producer.

From among the many discussed projects, *Macbeth*, starring Maurice Evans and Judith Anderson and directed by Peggy Webster, did emerge. I was engaged to compose music. Although the fee was small and without royalty it had psychological importance for me. Also I was "at home" with Maurice and Peggy and Judith and many other friends, including Mel Ferrer and John Ireland, who had small parts.

Rehearsals went along smoothly. Judith made her sleepwalking scene memorable in spite of the fact that she referred to Lady Macbeth as a "walk-on." She studied for the scene by observing an exhibition of hypnotism.

When I was called to Boston to make a few minor musical alterations, Maurice invited me to lunch and poured out his heart (a delayed message for Peggy) on the subject of love scenes in Shakespeare. The Bard, he contended, had written female parts for boy-actors and therefore never intended them to be played passionately. Judith was apparently overdoing the sex angle. I then had cocktails with Judith: she was having to chase Maurice around the stage whenever she wanted to hold his hands. Compromises were made, and the New York opening was successful.

Many busying things followed in rapid succession. None of them was important from any point of view. None of them resolved any of my difficulties. Cheryl Crawford produced a revival of Barrie's *A Kiss for Cinderella*, starring Luise Rainer and Ralph Forbes. On the day of the opening I was called in to straighten out the hodgepodge of incidental music. Nothing was salvageable.

Louise Crane, a wealthy and socially prominent friend of mine, commissioned me to stage and conduct an opera for her protégée, Ellabelle Davis, a Negro soprano whose musical education I had already supervised for several years. I found an eighteenth-century "entertainment" by William Boyce and put it on for a single performance at the Museum of Modern Art with Ellabelle, Carol

Bruce, then a magnificent unknown contralto, and two male singers. I conducted some combined school choruses in Brahm's *Requiem* over NBC and took a quintet of vocalists (The Lehman Engel Singers) on tour in half a dozen concerts.

I was still plugging along to raise money for a New York production of *Beggar's Opera*. I lunched with agents, dined with managers, called on producers, drank with professional money-raisers. Many times I thought that something was going to happen. Nothing did. As a last resort, I called on Terry Helburn and Lawrence Langner at the Theatre Guild. After weeks of conversation, Langner arranged for a meeting at his home the following Sunday for making definite production arrangements.

For the first time in two years, the outlook was exciting. At last the show would go on, and it was to mean everything to me both as an artistic enterprise and as a source of perhaps large and long-overdue revenue.

As if the hope of the production itself were not enough, I was dining in Sardi's alone one night when I saw a tall English sailor enter the restaurant. I was certain that he was Michael Redgrave, the distinguished actor whose recording of *The Beggar's Opera* I much admired. I would want to meet him, of course, and discuss the possibilities of his appearing in my forthcoming production. As he joined the table of an actress who was currently in Maurice's *Macbeth*, I sent a note asking them to have coffee with me. They accepted, and the sailor *was* Michael Redgrave. He was an able-bodied seaman, and his chores (as he put it) included carrying large sacks of potatoes. He added, however, that his private assignment was reading aloud to his commanding officer, Lord Mountbatten. As England was at war with Hitler, Redgrave could make no commitments, but that meeting was the beginning of a long friendship.

The following Sunday, a cold sunny day early in December, I left my apartment in high spirits, bound for the Langner house a few blocks away. I climbed his front steps and rang the bell. The maid who admitted me seemed hysterical. The radio was blaring away, and Mr. Langner was at the telephone speaking in an excited voice. The air was electric, but it could not possibly concern me as my own business had not as yet begun. I removed my coat, sat down, and became gradually aware of the message that was just then coming over the radio: Japan had attacked the United States at Pearl Harbor. I had not heard the name Pearl Harbor before, but hearing it now effectively blocked any discussion of *The Beggar's Opera.* One personal thing at least was settled: I would definitely enter upon a new life in a short time. No longer any uncertainty at all.

Christmas was soon. CBS engaged Sir Thomas Beecham to conduct a Christmas Eve midnight program, but Sir Thomas was ill and uncertain of doing the performance. I was asked to prepare it and be available to conduct the broadcast at the last minute in the event that Sir Thomas was unable to appear. Rehearsals had gone well. The old man did appear about nine o'clock on Christmas Eve. He asked me to run through the carols, which were unfamiliar to him. He seemed pleased, went through them once himself, and gave no criticism. He took the orchestra through its paces and conducted the program at midnight.

One day, soon afterward, I ran into a scriptwriter at CBS who suggested that I ought to enlist in the Navy at Great Lakes where her friend, Lt. Comdr. Eddie Peabody (the banjo player) was in charge of entertainment. Until that time, I had thought only of letting the draft take its course. My friend called Great Lakes, and then, after some correspondence, I went to meet the "little" commander who eventually offered me a billet (without commissioned rank) to conduct concerts. I enlisted.

My parents came to New York. I gave one long last party at my apartment before it was dismantled. Billie Holiday sang beautifully and endlessly. Everyone came to say goodbye—all except Brooks and Oriana Atkinson, who by that time had become very good friends of mine.

Next day, bit by bit, furniture disappeared to various buyers. Books and music vanished inside large packing boxes. The stage was set for the final act of *Cherry Orchard.* The doorbell rang. It was Brooks Atkinson. I thought he had mistaken the day. No, he said. *This* was the day, the really difficult one. He came in, regarded my empty living room, remarked about the good times we had had in it, patted me on the back, and left quickly. My Anna—large as a house —and I shook hands after the last packing box was carried out.

"When the lights go on again. . . ," she said.

10: Parenthesis

THE DRAB RED-BRICK gates to the Great Lakes Naval Training Station were everybody's nightmare of death. Other-world zombies dressed as guards admitted me, and my name was listed in the Great Book. The Great Father was expecting me. An escort marched me block after block past building after building through all Eternity. Arriving at the office of the commandant and with hardly a pause, I was ushered into the august presence of God. He was a small, rotund man with more than a twinkle in his eye, and he addressed me, his arm around my shoulder, as "My boy."

He was apologetic that he could not offer me a commission and still hold on to me at Great Lakes, where he did wish to keep me. He did not think I ought to take "boot training," and when I asked what that was he laughed, Santa Claus fashion, but did not explain, thinking my question was a joke.

The first day, the captain made me an official member of his family, designating me yeoman, third class. I was given an identification card at once so that I would not be restricted to the station, and I was put in the care of one of my "shipmates," a young man who was to expedite the red tape. Not the least part of all this kindness was our being able to use banjo-Commander Eddie's car to transport me around the vastness of the station, where I had to collect my heavy gear.

The barracks housed members of the Band and Entertainment Division exclusively and everything was superclean. There was even a kind of housekeeper—Master-at-Arms Mullins (called "Moon"), a warm, dried-up little man whose only life had been the navy.

As I had never before lived with anybody, I had qualms about living in the barracks. Now I was to share one vast dormitory with 250 men. I learned quickly to my surprise that all of them sincerely wished to be helpful.

The first morning when I went to shave I experienced a shock. Having always, as a hobby, collected special colognes, after-shave lotions, and such, I had reluctantly given them all away when I departed civilian life. I had brought with me the most chaste and common of shaving lotions—the only one I would not have previously owned: Aqua Velva. My first morning at Great Lakes I had a rude awakening when I found myself flanked by men using Aphrodisia and Woodhue.

Commander Peabody put me in charge of organizing a symphonic concert band, although I had never conducted one. Once again, the United States (as in the WPA) was giving me a free education. With the commanding officer's authority, I wired draft boards requesting assignment to us of special draftees, and eventually we received some of the finest instrumentalists in the world. Out of the entire division—overlapping—there were several dance bands (Ray Anthony was the head of one), a large symphonic band, a radio orchestra, and smaller concert-band units.

The largest group I conducted was employed at weekly concerts in a fine modern auditorium. Soloists included Tibbett, Thomas, Sayão, Milstein, Piatigorsky, Kreisler, Menuhin, Robeson, Pons, Grainger, Ganz, Horowitz, and many others. Horowitz's appearance at Great Lakes was of course a great event. Afterward Valodya (as he is called by his intimates) and Wanda, his wife, who is Toscanini's daughter, stayed in Chicago for some time. I was invited several times to hear Valodya play pieces new in his repertoire. Everything he did became a superhuman feat, but I found myself saying over and over again, "It's too fast for the music."

One night he was soloist with the Chicago Symphony Orchestra, playing Rachmaninoff's fiendishly difficult Third Concerto. Wanda invited me to sit in her box. The contrast between Wanda and me was absurd. I was wearing my sailor suit and was very, very fat. Wanda looked like an Arabian princess. Her hair is straight and jet-

L. E. conducting part of the concert band near Great Lakes in 1942. The paunch was developing rapidly.

black; her complexion, swarthy. She wore no makeup nor did she need any. Around her neck was a triple strand of sizable diamonds, set simply—one by one—in a platinum chain. At the back of her neck was an enormous diamond clasp. Everything else had to have been simple, and it was.

When I commented about the diamonds, she explained that Valodya knew how to evaluate precious stones and that she had a great deal of beautiful jewelry because Valodya liked to accumulate valuables that could be taken out of a country at a moment's notice. No banks for him after Russia.

The concert, under Fritz Reiner, was magnificent, and the concerto which closed it was breathtaking. Of course, Valodya got an enormous ovation.

Wanda and I sauntered slowly backstage. Valodya, who was perspiring heavily, wrapped himself in a muffler and topcoat, and then we three began the long journey through the stage door and alley where hundreds of his admirers stood applauding, begging for autographs, kissing his coat. A waiting limousine drove us to the Drake Hotel, where the couple was staying.

No sooner had we arrived than there was a knock at the door. Two detectives received the diamond necklace and handed Wanda a receipt. (This was the first time I had seen such a transaction.) Valodya sat rather tensely and silently on a stool, his hands together prayerlike between his knees. Wanda, knowing of my passion for gin rummy, asked if I would like to play. The two of us sat playing, while Valodya sat noncommitally watching us.

I felt great pangs of guilt that the little man who had just had such a triumph should be sitting there without any attention.

"Valodya, wouldn't you like something to drink?" I said.

"Yes," and he smiled like a little boy.

"What?"

"I don't know. What do you think?"

Then I answered as though to a child, spacing my words slowly and deliberately, "Well, how . . . about . . . scotch . . . and . . . soda?"

He beamed.

"And wouldn't you like something to eat?"

He beamed again.

"How about . . . scrambled eggs . . . and toast . . . and milk?"

He was ecstatic.

Wanda picked up the phone and gave the order. We returned to our game. Valodya watched, his eyes sparkling.

A smaller unit out of the large navy group (about forty out of a hundred) was used for concerts in front of the admiral's house and at the station's several hospitals.

It was not easy to maintain authority over men in the navy where authority is chiefly measured by sleeve decorations. Many of the men outranked me, and as most of these were "regular" navy men lately returned from the fleet, they were not easily convinced that they ought to be put in such a position: the archangels under a novice. Many of the players were experienced bandsmen. They were, however, patient and helpful. At the end of each day's rehearsal period, I had the task of assigning two "sweepers" to clean up the quarters. The names were assigned alphabetically. The commander had mentioned that "of course" I should not participate. I took the view (and as it turned out, correctly) that I would *never* have any authority if, under the circumstances, I treated myself differently from the others. And so when the day for my name to be called arrived I was aware of the intense listening. I called my own name. There was general relaxing and even mild rejoicing. It was the smallest possible price to pay for an ounce of esteem.

For the weekly Admiral's Concerts, I deposited mimeographed programs in the letter boxes of the high-ranking officers' homes. These concerts took place in a Victorian bandstand literally in the front yard of the admiral's house. As far as we knew, nobody ever listened, but the concerts took place weekly in all kinds of weather. Often the admiral was not even "aboard"; nevertheless, the concerts were played.

It was my duty to line up the men before concerts and march them to the bandstand. The first time this was to happen (I had had no military training) I asked the advice of a regular navy man. He told me to order, "Fall in, in twos." When the twenty pairs, laden with instruments, were in line, I called out with a beckoning gesture, "Come on, fellows!" They fell out—but on the ground, laughing. After that I became known as "Come on, fellows," or sometimes

"Kettle," which had to do with my figure, especially in a sailor suit.

Once, on the day of an Admiral's Concert, the weather was so cold and damp that I asked permission to cancel the concert. The thermometer stuck rigidly at forty degrees, and the rule was that we play unless the temperature was *below* forty. Morale was so low that the men played wrong notes deliberately. Also, because of the damp cold, the instruments were badly out of tune. Suddenly, during the *Tristan* Prelude, I spied the commandant's wife, swathed in fur, sitting on a bench! I decided that I must offer her some explanation of the awful sounds. As I approached her and before I could speak, she said, "Oh, Mr. Engel, I don't see how you do it, it's so wonderful!"

John Charles Thomas was soloist at the first regular concert in the new auditorium, at which I employed a much larger group. The audience (then and always) was enthusiastic, and the highest "brass" on the station attended in mezzanine seats. At the conclusion of the program the admiral's aide came backstage to inform Mr. Thomas that a supper party was being given in his honor by the admiral. I then said goodnight to Mr. Thomas, explaining that as an enlisted man I was ineligible to attend the party. To my horror Thomas sent word to the admiral declining the invitation: It had been largely my concert, he felt, and he in turn invited me to be his guest at supper in Chicago. In record time the aide conveyed Thomas's message to the admiral and returned, *ordering* me to the party. After that, I was ordered to all of them. In fact, before long, I *arranged* the parties and issued the invitations.

Many men within our division did not play band instruments. Danny Hoctor was a dancer; Billy de Wolfe and Larry Storch did monologues then, as they do now; Carroll Huxley made attractive orchestrations as he had previously done for Kostelanetz; Bob Elson, sports commentator, was a lieutenant and assistant to the "little" commander. Bob Linden (now a Broadway and Los Angeles production assistant) worked out the staging and lighting of everything anybody did in the entertainment division; and Lou Mindling, a former agent, arranged the bookings of guest celebrities.

I was included in much Chicago society. Ruth Page, the dancer, and her husband, Tom Fisher, made their simple home mine. Near them in Hubbard Woods were the Max Epsteins, whose palatial home was always open to me. (The Fishers referred to it as their "annex.") There at Sunday dinner each week I met as heterogeneous a group of distinguished guests as has ever been assembled anywhere: theater visitors to Chicago, ambassadors, cabinet ministers, and business tycoons. We wined and dined under Botticellis and Rembrandts and Van Dycks and Watteaus. We swam in the pool and enjoyed the most lavish hospitality, but always identical menus: chicken.

Frequently, I spent a night or a weekend at the Epsteins, where I was assigned a room which became my own, like a place at a family table. On the first such occasion the old butler, Carl, who was both genial and proper, came to help me retire, and I was nearly hysterical watching him try to hang up my sailor suit. It was he who brought breakfast to my room at six the following morning, but not before Mr. Epstein, fearing that I might not be awakened on schedule, padded down the hall in his long white nightgown to make doubly certain. Then the chauffeur drove me to the naval station.

My real oasis during my nearly two years at Great Lakes was the Parkway Hotel, where I stayed most of the time because my cousins Gene and Sara Schweig lived there permanently. Sara did everything to make me feel at home and, I enjoyed lunch with them nearly every Saturday. My uncle Bob Engel and Renie, my aunt, also lived in Chicago, as well as my Aunt Mildred and Uncle Harold Schweig, and we were all together often. Joe and Mildred Graham came from New York to see me, and in many ways, life in the navy was much like living in the suburbs of New York.

Sometimes Carroll Huxley, Hoctor, and I would dine in the Ambassador Hotel's famous Pump Room, where we came to know the hospitality of patriotism. No sooner would we be seated than some waiter (all of them knew us well) would "sell" a patron the idea of sending us cocktails. This sort of thing became contagious, and before long, somebody else had sent cocktails; then someone would insist on picking up our dinner check (poor sailors!), and finally, the waiter would fill our empy coffee cups with cognac (never younger than seventy-five years), which was never added to the check. Dinner at the Pump Room was seldom more expensive than the waiter's tip. Often the waiter refused even that.

My pianist friend Harry Cumpson (*left*) and I at Pennnsylvania Station, New York, in 1942, on leave prior to my return to Great Lakes. *Photo by Sam Hood*

During my nearly two-year stay at Great Lakes, I became acquainted with Claudia Cassidy, the incredibly powerful critic of the *Chicago Tribune*, and her husband Bill Crawford. Sometimes she invited me to accompany her to concerts or the theater, but more often I met with Bill at a small neighborhood-type bar and together we waited while Claudia wrote her review and subsequently joined us.

I fail to understand the hostile attitudes of many people toward Claudia. True, she was often stern in print. She refused to tolerate second-rate theatrical companies sent to Chicago, where their producers often meant to cash in on the strength of a better company's Broadway success. She supported top-flight conductors of the Symphony and lambasted their inferiors. She was a genuine crusader, and it was Chicago's entire cultural life that she was trying to shield against mediocrity.

Also she was then—more than thirty years ago—beautiful, with fiery hair and enchanting dimples; and today—that much later—this loveliness continues to hang about her like the trappings of an Irish queen.

That nearly ancient friendship has become intensified with time, and the silence of distance and infrequent meetings has done nothing to alter it.

When Secretary of the Navy Knox discovered at the Epstein's that I was one of his boys, I was ordered to "put in" my papers for a commission, and I was directed to take my physical examination. I encountered a lieutenant-commander doctor who was unfriendly and resentful (it was an old navy tale) because I was a musician. As luck would have it, I was suffering from a hangover. He made a urinalysis and was happy to report that it showed too much sugar for me to get my commission. He advised my coming in at eight the next morning for a redoing of the same test as well as completing the examination.

Next morning the urinalysis, disappointingly enough, was satisfactory. I was standing nude before the doctor as he proceeded with the examination, when we became aware of a tremendous hubbub in the corridor outside. The noise grew louder and at length the door of the examining room burst open. In walked my friend the commanding officer—a wonderful, rough old man who had seen a lifetime of naval service, Commodore Robert Emmet—and with him his entire staff wearing all the gold braid and battle ribbons that could have been assembled. Standing at naked attention, I was most embarrassed to be the subject of this hubbub. The commander had heard about my encounter of the previous afternoon and he was irate.

"Why do you think they want him in Washington? Do you think he's going to command a battleship? He's needed in Washington, and you're going to pass him at once, and with no nonsense," he shouted at the doctor.

Then he asked me what I wanted for lunch, what kind of cocktails I wanted, and ordered me to report to him after I had completed the examination and procured my new uniforms. He wanted to "swear me in" himself.

When the commodore and his party had gone, the doctor hastily concluded the examination, hardly daring to speak to me; he nervously erased "Overweight, requiring waiver," and substituted "Very muscular."

I was met at the Washington train station by my old friend Walter Lawrence, who, as a sailor in the OSS had returned to Washington from duty abroad. He had answered a newspaper ad—"Room and bath to let"—that proved to be an ideal setup, with the John Schuster family in the vicinity of my station.

Next day when I checked in at the Photographic Science Laboratory, I was escorted inside by marine guards. As a new officer, I was especially apprehensive that my newness would show. My worst fears were realized when I saw a stout sailor who turned out to be Hiram Sherman, the actor. He greeted me loudly with, "Now, isn't that the cutest little lieutenant you ever saw?"

After my two years in the service as an enlisted man, the sudden transformation to officer without transition or training was a shocking experience. I had the constant feeling that I had forgotten to zip up my trousers. I was self-conscious around all classes of navy folk, feeling that enlisted men resented my newly conferred authority, while officers felt that I did not "belong." Still the high school misfit.

I was assigned as assistant division officer to Lt. Emil Velazco, formerly an organist at the Roxy Theatre, who understood authority only through rank. Under us there was a small staff: Louis Palange, a fine arranger; Chief Petty Officer Shipp ("Chief Shipp, will you bring me a chit?"), who attended to routine matters; four WAVES used as music copyists; an enlisted man who was a would-be arranger; and an expert film-music cutter from Hollywood and his two assistants. Velazco did a certain amount of composing, but within a short time I wrote practically everything with Palange, who also composed (poor fellow), having to orchestrate as rapidly as I could compose.

In addition to completing musical assignments that came fast and with early deadlines, as an officer I had to perform military duties. Most of these consisted of routine inspections, about which I knew nothing, and once in every ten days I had to be officer of the day, a twenty-four-hour duty in which I assumed responsibility for the security of the entire laboratory.

To be fitted for this duty I had to attend a weekly gunnery class to learn about handling a .45. The prospect of this was frightening, as I had never even seen a pistol, and I was afraid of how I might

behave because of the "kickback" and the noise. I became part of a
class of about twenty new officers. The first lesson was all talk.
Finally, we were marched out on a firing range. The single pistol
was passed around among the officers in alphabetical order. Most of
the men ahead of me missed the target-board altogether, so that by
the time my turn came, realizing that nothing was expected of me, I
was more relaxed. Still, when the instructor handed me the gun
I apologized that I might behave nervously. I aimed at the target
and hit it dead center with the first shot! All of the other shots in my
three rounds came within the first circle around the target! The
chief, not believing my sad tale, discharged me from the class and
asked me never to return.

Not too long after I was settled in Washington, Lieutenant
Velaszco resigned because of age and I became head of our music
division. One day I was ordered to attend a meeting headed by
President Roosevelt, at which he explained that he wished to have
one man edit and put together two films of animated battle plans
(the invasions of Iwo Jima and Okinawa) and "cut-ins" from other
films, to be scored musically by me so that the men in the fleet
seeing the whole on the eve of an invasion would comprehend the
plan and be excited to action.

I remember realizing when I emerged from the meeting that I
was in possession of a really important secret (no dates were known
to us) and that I must not afterward venture far afield. I never again
saw the president.

Some months later he died. The whole world seemed to stop
breathless. In Washington people could not speak. The radio for
many days played only solemn music. Movie houses and theaters
remained closed. On the morning of the funeral I took my little
division to watch the cortege. The streets were lined with soldiers,
sailors, and marines. We in the crowds stood behind them. It was an
unseasonably hot day with rapidly shifting clouds. No one spoke,
and there was no sound of any kind. Presently, the procession came
by, and even the most stouthearted of the marine guards wept without shame. Mrs. Roosevelt alone in the short, simple procession did
not weep.

At four o'clock the funeral services began in the White House. I
stood in the crowded park across the street. The silence was ca-

thedral-like. A heavy rain fell. No one moved. The rain stopped as suddenly as it had begun.

Assignments came to the Music Division so fast that we often worked forty-eight hours without stopping. As soon as we completed the composing, arranging, and copying of a film score, the Navy Symphony Orchestra, which contained some of the finest musicians in America, recorded it.

In those days (and prior to Roosevelt's death) I conceived a plan that I thought would greatly benefit the government. Hundreds of accomplished musicians in the military services (composers, arrangers, instrumentalists), were not used to the best of their special abilities, while the government spent millions of dollars annually with civilian agencies for the composing and recording of music for educational, documentary, and propaganda films. If all of the choice musicians could be brought together in one department, the needs of all government agencies could be effectively taken care of without the expenditure of any extra money.

Since I had once conferred with President Roosevelt during the WPA days, I wanted to get this plan to him. I wrote Mrs. Hallie Flanagan, formerly head of the Federal Theatre, because as a navy man I could not write to the president without going through the chain of command. Mrs. Flanagan (then director of the Drama Department at Vassar) thought so well of my idea that she wrote Mrs. Roosevelt, who in turn spoke to Harry Hopkins, the president's trouble-shooter. His secretary set up an appointment with me at the White House.

The day I went to see Mr. Hopkins was extremely hot. I experienced some embarrassment in extricating myself from my station because I had told my commanding officer of my appointment. When he asked tremblingly why I had been called, I told him that I had been instructed to tell him nothing. (This was true.)

At the White House, I was ushered into Mr. Hopkins's tiny office. It contained, besides a most welcome air-conditioning unit, a table-desk, a swivel chair in which Mr. Hopkins sat, a letter file, a hat rack, and one other chair on the other side of the desk. These few pieces of furniture filled the tiny space. Hopkins looked thin and ill, and after greeting me, he sank back into his chair, whirling it around so that he sat with his back to me, rocking incessantly. Often, as I unfolded my plan, he whirled around sharply to question me, and afterwards he would again resume his backward rocking. His attitude seemed belligerent, and he often attacked my ideas. I became so incensed by his badgering that I rose indignantly. Mr. Hopkins whirled around again and with a relaxed smile begged me to sit down and continue. He explained that if my ideas were put into practice many military leaders would be angry, since the plan would draw personnel from *all* service branches. It might even provoke congressmen to question and attack. Mr. Hopkins wanted to be sure that I believed in what I said and that I would be able to defend myself in case the plan were put into practice. I understood and was ashamed of my indignation.

In a most friendly manner he thanked me for coming, asked me to type the plan myself, make no carbon copy for my files, and to deliver it personally into his hands at the White House as soon as possible. He added smilingly, "The navy snoops!"

I did as I was instructed, and when I delivered the plan, it was the last time I saw him, for only a short time later the president died. This was also the end of Mr. Hopkins.

I spent many evenings alone in my office composing for myself, after long days of composing for the navy. I wrote a symphonic work called *The Creation* (for narrator and orchestra); a sonata for cello and piano for Bernard Greenhouse, who at that time was in the Navy Symphony Orchestra; a concerto for viola and orchestra for Emanuel Vardi (also a member of the Navy Symphony); an overture; and a symphony, all of this in my nonnavy time awaiting the end of the war.

Many other evenings I left the station with Louis Palange, who would invite me to his apartment where his wife, Carmie, always managed to cook great Italian dishes.

Once in a while I was able to spend a weekend in New York. On one of these trips, I took Dame May Whitty to a performance of *Pygmalion* starring Gertrude Lawrence. The old lady seldom refrained from talking aloud as she watched. At first it was caused by the opening set (Covent Garden).

"Ben and I used to live just opposite" (pointing behind her).

As she had played Mrs. Higgins, she was supercritical of the actress in this production.

"All she does is write letters. She gives me writer's cramp. She ought to be pouring tea."

She could not bear Gertie's performance and seldom failed to point out its faults.

When the performance ended, I wanted only to get "Mamie" out of the theater quickly, but no! She was certain that Gertie knew we were there and would be offended if we failed to go backstage to see her. I knew that disaster was waiting, but I was powerless to prevent it. We knocked at the dressing room door, and Richard Aldrich (Gertie's husband) greeted us. He was an affable man and so invited us in and gave us scotch and soda. Gertie was in an adjoining room putting on her negligee.

In a moment she emerged and kissed both of us. Dame May began admiring the size of the room, then Gertie's negligee, and just everything, but she did not allude to the performance. I became increasingly embarrassed and was trying desperately to think of just any compliment I might make that the old lady would not dispute. Finally, I had an idea.

"Dick, I should think you'd be afraid to let Gertie do this part." All eyes were on me. "She's so beautiful [and she *was*] that I should think you'd be afraid of losing her."

I felt that I had triumphed. Dick and Gertie were pleased in that moment, but not for long. Dame May became instantly vocal: "Yes, you were quite lovely, Gertie—but you should have seen Mrs. Pat!" (Mrs. Patrick Campbell had created the role.)

The pressures of work in Washington were usually great, but they were not basically different from similar pressures I had always met. What *was* different was the idea of military life. While my life in the service was hardly military, I nevertheless felt constrained and began to experience unsettling sensations that translated themselves into a fear of fainting. This syndrome asserted itself with ever-increasing frequency and in a short time became a kind of nightmare. It was then that I came to know Dr. Zigmond Lebensohn, a psychiatrist and naval commander, without whom I think I could not have gone on.

During the hot summer of 1945 in Washington, where heat and humidity set records, I had a habit of tracing with colored crayons the war's progress on maps hanging on my walls. Suddenly, there were no lines. The bomb at Hiroshima annihilated them all and ended the world as we had come to know it. Then, there was only waiting for the inevitable, and at last it happened with the declaration of peace. There was much jubilation in Washington, as there was everywhere. Dance bands played in the streets. Buses did not run, nor taxicabs, nor streetcars, and I walked home that evening alone. No one was there. Outside everything was noisy and celebrative, ill-matched with my inner state. I wanted to talk with old friends or relatives, but it was not possible to telephone them: there was no service. I did not feel that it was a time of rejoicing, but only for sleep. And so at last I slept.

I recalled that on leaving Great Lakes, Max Epstein had given me a letter of introduction to Adlai Stevenson, assistant secretary of the navy. I had presented my letter to the gentleman, the most modest man I have ever met. There was nothing he could do for me (I suppose this was Max's purpose in writing the letter), and we had parted after a brief conversation, with admonitions from Mr. Stevenson to call on him if I ever needed anything.

The war had now ended, and the navy set up a system by which personnel could be separated from the service and returned to civilian life, provided they had enough points and their commanding officer was willing to part with them.

Although I had spent more time in the service than any of them, the members of my small division had enough points for release and my own were insufficient. The factors at work were length of service, marital status, and size of family; I was not married and had no children.

As our work had been completed during the first four months after the war's end, I released all of my personnel and found myself alone with nothing to do but play gin rummy with other officers still hanging about.

Since there was no longer any valid reason for me to be prevented from returning to my former life, I decided I would do just anything to be rid of the navy. Remembering my meeting two years earlier with Adlai Stevenson, I telephoned him, again found him accessible, and arranged to see him that afternoon.

I explained my predicament, and although Mr. Stevenson understood and sympathized, he wondered honestly what he could do to be of help. I was amazed at his so-slight self-regard and ventured to suggest that if he did not mind, he might call the separation center that had jurisdiction over me and *inquire* about my release under these circumstances. The call was made and to Mr. Stevenson's real astonishment and my joy, I was told to report next morning for discharge.

Like every single other experience in my life, the nearly four years I spent in the navy had taught me much. Until the concerts at Great Lakes, I had seldom conducted any "straight" instrumental music. (This was no secret from the men in my band.) When the navy sent me to Washington to work on film music, I had had no experience in that medium. Having been a theater composer and conductor, I had been using the ingredients. How music was put to a film—the actual technique—had been a mystery in the beginning. Since I had become an officer, I simply told everyone under me that I knew nothing and that I relied upon them to instruct me.

I also learned many things about people, some things that had formerly been frightening. Having lived alone from childhood and in a household of women, I had grown up to fear groups of men. At high school, where I first came into contact with crowds of boys who were strangers to me—bigger boys (for I was the youngest), boys accustomed to sports, boys brought up to know no fear (fears were my exclusive personal properties), secure healthy groups of Christian boys, as opposed to my sole small Jewishness—I was physically terrified. This terror—seldom the boys—had pursued me throughout four years of high school.

In the navy—my second experience with men en masse—I found an overall outgoingness, a general desire to be helpful, a genuine interest in the well-being of others. Without the navy, I might never have learned it.

And there were other things. In the service, people dressed alike, ate alike, slept alike, with little opportunity for any outer manifestation of personal tastes. And yet, if you were perceptive at all, the manifestations were always there. Each one betrayed himself in some way, and you knew what each was like. The tendency to sloppiness was still there (if it ever had been), little extremities of dress recalled the "zootiness" of the near past. At meals, the boys accustomed to better food usually ate everything and without comment, having grown to expect nothing very special of food under these extraordinary circumstances. The boys unaccustomed to much perpetually griped about the "chow."

Most interesting of all to me were those boys who eternally complained about the stupidity of their department heads, who registered unceasing complaints with their fellow workers about their own loss of opportunity by being in the service, who lauded their own superior talents and abilities which had not come in for proper recognition, and so on ad nauseum. There were many of these boys, and having seen a number of them again since the war days, I have had my observations corroborated. These boys still carry on bitterly in precisely the same way. They have merely substituted their new "boss" or "bad luck," and they still are not able to attribute their failures to themselves.

Uniforms change nothing basic in anybody: the people are the same. The opportunities of learning and experiencing are always present. One has only to be free enough inside to comprehend them.

II: Aftermath

Nᴇᴡ Yᴏʀᴋ ᴀꜰᴛᴇʀ the war was nothing like it had been before the war. Now it was a monstrous, overcrowded, overexpensive, traffic-ridden ugliness. The temporary overcrowding became the permanent crush.

Along with thousands of others, I had no place to live. For weeks I was shunted from hotel to hotel (residence for more than ten days was not allowed). From time to time I stayed with the Romes or the Wises. I had met the Wises (James Waterman Wise, son of Dr. Stephen S. Wise, married to Helen Brooks—until their marriage, an actress) through the Romes, and they were also to become close lifetime friends.

New York 1946 was the aftermath of a great storm. There was no finding one's place. And so, once again I began to run.

Harold Rome, still on the fringe of the army, with Arnold Auerbach, a fellow soldier, had written a revue, *Call Me Mister*. Harold's agent, Herman Levin, was affiliated with Melvyn Douglas as co-producer, and I was to conduct. As some of the money still had to be raised and it was December, I visited my family in Mississippi.

Still in my lieutenant's uniform and before leaving for Jackson, I was engaged by Jack Kapp, president of Decca Records, to write and conduct music for a children's album, *The Selfish Giant*, with Fredric March, and to conduct two records with Bing Crosby. When Crosby arrived in the studio, almost his only remark was,

Near the end of World War II, I conducted some Decca recordings with the always cooperative Bing Crosby (*left*).

"Now, Maestro, how do you want me to do these?" I was to learn in the making of hundreds of recordings that most people were to behave sincerely in this way, but with my little self-respect, I never expected it.

With the records done I went home, but before Christmas I was called back to begin *Call Me Mister*. My old Neighborhood Playhouse student Betty Garrett was the female star and Jules Munshin played opposite her. Maria Karnilova (recently of *Fiddler on the Roof* and *Zorba*) was prima ballerina, partnered by David Nillo. Dody Goodman was in the chorus. This was the happiest, most in-love-with-each-other theater family I have ever known.

Something simple but important to me happened on New Year's Eve in the Romes's apartment while I was staying with them for a couple of weeks. Although I was glad to be with old friends, I dread New Year's Eve parties. New York's noisiest din suddenly erupted: midnight. We were all holding glasses of champagne. The guests were married couples, and they gravitated toward one another. Florence and Harold saw instantly that I was alone, and without a second's hesitation, they came to me—one on each side—and kissed me.

The auditions and rehearsals of *Call Me Mister* were equaled only by the run for continuous fun, comradeship, peace, and pure joy. The whole experience was a quiet and beautiful love affair. And laughs. And empathy. And fun and games.

During rehearsals, the director and I believed the show was in need of a lively tune late in Act Two. Disagreeing, Harold argued. Finally, in desperation and fighting all the while, he brought out of his "trunk" something called "South America, Take It Away," which he reluctantly said could be used if anybody wanted it. This was the song that made the Hit Parade, and *Call Me Mister* became a big hit.

After having been tossed around in temporary living quarters for too long, I was told by Mrs. Lewis Isaacs one day that she could get me a permanent apartment. I did not need to see it: if it were to be mine there was no question of my wanting it. I have stayed on now for twenty-seven years and acquired an adjacent apartment in order to have sufficient space for my secretary and my ever-expanding library.

When I had time to spread out my things I found a quantity of music that I had composed during my nearly four years in the service. The service music—sketches (Palange had always orchestrated them)—filled four thick volumes. In addition, there were two sinfoniettas, two symphonies, the viola concerto, cello sonata, and *The Creation*.

I had long been familiar with the methods many of my composer-friends employed with their works, usually while the ink was still drying on the paper; they pursued conductors and other performers. Roy Harris in particular took understandable delight in running the gamut with distinguished listeners. He explained, played, exhorted, and sold. Eventually the new work was programmed. But Roy was by no means the exception. I was.

Since I wrote the cello sonata for Bernard Greenhouse and the viola concerto for Emanuel Vardi while we were still in Washington, I had the advantage of their advice relative to writing for their instruments. When we were reestablished as civilians, Bernie performed the sonata at his Town Hall recital, and it won the Society for the Publication of American Music Award, a sympathetic press, and publication.

Manny Vardi must not have liked the very difficult viola concerto because he never learned it and therefore never showed it to any maestro who might conceivably have performed it. Perhaps ten years later another violist, Olga Bloom, who usually played in the pit with me, asked to see a copy. She practiced hard and once played it for me and left me with the feeling she would "peddle" it to this and that conductor.

I conducted my *Creation* (related elsewhere) with the CBS Symphony, with Michael Redgrave as narrator. That score was subsequently published.

It is impossible for me to have any clear point of view about my music although by now, two decades later, I feel detached from all of these scores and remember little about them. Why did I never show them to conductors, pursue conductors with them—the habit of all other composers? Was it because I had no faith in my serious work? Did I entertain no wish or feel no need to hear it? I cannot say. But it is peculiar. These pieces in larger forms are neatly copied and bound, and they gather dust. I have no idea of their value or if indeed they have any value. But my own total lack of sponsorship seems strange even to me and wholly unaccountable.

And still on occasion, other work permitting, I go on writing. Usually I am published, and sometimes a royalty statement—especially for a chorus—tells me that performances in the recent past actually took place. Good. But why am I shy in this one area? Do I feel inadequate? I do not know and I am not disturbed for some unfathomable reason.

Many things happened quickly in getting started again, so that most of them will only bear listing. Virgil Thomson, then music critic on the New York *Herald Tribune*, asked me to conduct the American premier of some Poulenc choruses at a benefit concert for "France Forever." I composed a score for a navy film, conducted background music for three poems narrated by Walter Huston for Decca, made two albums with Conrad Thibault (both produced by Lois Moseley at Decca), and supervised the music for a swimming show called *Acquaretta*, which was the sole failure.

I also conducted a kind of "pop" concert with Grace Moore as soloist. Her actual performance was so unlike her single piano rehearsal with me that we might never have been introduced to each

The Creation, which I had composed during the war, had its premiere in 1949 with the CBS Symphony. I conducted; the narrator was my friend Michael Redgrave (*right*), not as yet knighted.

other. She refused to go on at the start of her section of the program until the management paid her in cash, a large part of which had to be gathered together in silver.

My mother in the audience was shushed by the people around her when she insisted on talking about me through my orchestral numbers. The last encore was *The Lord's Prayer*, at the end of which Miss Moore curtsied cutely and exited while I was still playing the closing "inspirational" bars. This was the last song she sang in America before she was killed in an airplane accident.

My social life was different from what it had been before the war. Working six nights a week in the theater made me ineligible for dinner parties, which usually begin at seven or eight. Instead there were unfashionable ones (my Anna was back). Two or three times weekly, with Anna's help, I invited four or five friends to dine with me. The hour was six, and it had to be punctual, for promptly at 7:30 I had to flee to the theater. I learned that this gave me precisely enough time for a "visit."

On Sundays during the season I attended Actors' Fund benefits, which enable people in the theater to see other shows. But in the summertime I often took a late Saturday night train after *Call Me Mister* and went to the Wises in the country. It was late when they picked me up at the Ridgefield station. The Romes were usually there, and we would play gin rummy until dawn. Not far away were the Shepard Traubes, the Paul Drapers, the Samuel Graftons, the Henry Wallaces, the Paul Osborns, the Jerry Chodorovs, the John Herseys, and many others. On Sunday nights we would go to one of their houses for a gay dinner, followed generally by cards, no matter what brilliant artist or conversationalist was present. Much of this seems to spell out antisociability, but it was really my cup of tea.

During the run of *Call Me Mister*, John Gielgud came to America in a brilliant production of *The Importance of Being Earnest*, which he had also directed. Frequently it was my good fortune to meet him at parties, and in time we became good friends. In the intervening quarter of a century I have been with him in New York, Toronto, Los Angeles, and London and always with the greatest of pleasure. Sometimes he wears a "social" facade—not an essential part of himself. In quieter surroundings he is a brilliant thinker and conversationalist.

On a visit to London I attended a performance of *The Potting Shed* in which John (by then "Sir John") starred. At the end of the play I was red-eyed, and I went backstage, as he was giving a supper party for me. I entered his dressing room, and he was all smiles and particularly "turned on" because my own mood was in such sharp contrast to his.

I said (pointing to my eyes), "Look what you've done to me."

To which he replied, rapier-like, "Oh, it's only an exercise, dear boy!"

During my earlier days in New York he invited me to lunch at the Ritz-Carlton, and he asked me afterward to accompany him somewhere (he would not say where). We went to Decca Records and entered a small studio. In the control booth there were two engineers who came out to meet us—me, actually, since we had previously worked together.

John removed his gloves and coat and put them neatly under his

Left to right: Sir John Gielgud, Anna Weissberger, L. E., and Milton Goldman, following lunch in London in 1972. *Photo by Arnold Weissberger*

hat and umbrella on the back of a piano. I introduced him to the men, who then retired into their booth.

John looked about the small empty studio and said rather sadly, "Who would have ever thought I'd have such a small audience at my farewell in *Hamlet*!"

He stood before a microphone and got a voice level. Then he began: "To be, or not to be. . . ."

He read it beautifully, then listened to a playback, which he thought was poor. When I left, perhaps an hour later, he was still recording the same soliloquy.

As John was playing *The Importance of Being Earnest* and I was conducting *Call Me Mister*, we had identical schedules. Two wealthy young men who owned a house in the East Fifties and worked at nothing invited John to dinner ("pot luck," he was told) on Sunday night and was told that I would be there. I was told that *he* would be there.

We arrived almost simultaneously, and our hosts took us to the living room on the second floor. When we asked for scotch and soda, we received a sermonette to the effect that anyone who liked scotch would be satisfied with water, and the hosts had figured out that by *not* serving soda they would save $7.84 a week!

Neither John nor I was happy. An hour and another drink later, we were invited to the kitchen to observe the hosts fixing "pot luck."

(This was the servants' night out.) The Frigidaire was opened and one by one a container of eggs, a package of bacon, a loaf of bread, a head of lettuce, and some tomatoes were brought out! John was furious and berated the boys for not understanding that this was the only night in the week when theater people could dine leisurely and well. There were echoes of "pot luck" as John haughtily invited me to be his guest at dinner and we went out.

I have often remembered John Gielgud's saying to me some time ago that acting is such a temporal thing. The actor may be "off" one night and not give a representative performance, causing someone seeing him for the first time to say, "Oh, I don't think he's such a splendid actor."

Of course, the same proposition applies to all performers. As I have so little time now to see so much, I generally do well to see someone or something even once. (I remember in earlier, more leisurely days seeing Nazimova's last five performances in *The Cherry Orchard*, John Gielgud five consecutive times play *Hamlet*, and Lotte Lehman as many times as possible in *Der Rosenkavalier*.)

The only time I ever saw Rudolf Nureyev, I was bitterly disappointed: he seemed to be sulking, not moving extraordinarily or with much energy. Unfortunately that is probably the only way I will ever remember him.

In the fall, with *Call Me Mister* still going vigorously, Peggy Webster made me part of the newly formed American Repertory Theatre, which she, Cheryl Crawford, and Eva Le Gallienne had organized. I wrote an elaborate score for Shakespeare's *Henry VIII*. Magnificently directed by Peggy, it was beautifully acted by Eva, Victor Jory, Walter Hampden, Richard Waring, Ernest Truex, June Duprez, Philip Bourneuf, Eli Wallach, and Peggy herself. There were five other productions, but none had any commercial success, and the American Repertory Theatre quickly ceased to exist.

I scored and conducted a children's album, *The Prettiest Song in the World*, in Hollywood with Peggy's mother, Dame May Whitty as narrator. At the recording sessions, which took place on two evenings because the old lady was making a film during the day, she sat at a table before the microphone and continued writing letters while I prepared the orchestra. Melvyn Douglas and the Gene Kellys entertained me. Julie Garfield drove me to his home and en route bought an enormous teddy bear wrapped in cellophane for his young son. Papa smiled as the child tore off the wrapping, only to be crushed when he began playing solely with the cellophane.

George Cukor, the director, invited me to dinner in his lovely home with Orson, an unkempt Rita, Ethel Barrymore, and several others. Two things impressed me. The first was the mixture of elegance of the place with the sloppiness of dress. The male guests (George and I excepted) were without ties and jackets (the weather was not uncomfortably warm), and Rita wore slacks thirty years before they became fashionable. The second surprise was Ethel Barrymore, the embodiment of elegance. She had charm and dignity, spoke beautifully, and was dressed in a manner appropriate to these qualities. She was silent, though pleasant, during much of the chitchat, until someone mentioned baseball. This brought her to life and volubility.

"Kapek made his fifth homer of the season. His batting average was 296 last year but if he continues it will go to 374. Caccino is the worst of all pitchers. If the Dodgers don't. . . ." In her voice, it was a song.

After dinner, George showed me his garden, in which there was an uphill path lined with Roman statues. At the top of the hill a small gazebo, perched perilously on the edge of a sharp precipice, looked out over a lighted Los Angeles far below. George pointed to a plane about to land. "That," he said with considerable nostalgia, "is coming in from New York."

Back in New York, with the rat race at top speed, I conducted a poor Rodgers and Hart album with Milton Berle and a very talented young man named Vic Damone and supervised the rehearsals of a road company of *Call Me Mister*, starring Betty Kean. In preparation for the latter, one afternoon at auditions a young man of twenty-one beguiled us with his charm and tap dancing. We were considering him for the role of the boy—played originally by Billy Calahan—who sang the title song. When we asked the boy to sing, he demurred and finally confessed that he was unable to carry a tune.

I have never believed this true of anyone, and as everyone liked the boy so much, I asked to be allowed to work with him. The job was not difficult. Chiefly the boy needed self-confidence. He got this job—his first in the theater. He was Bob Fosse and was to become one of our most imaginative choreographers, directors, and husband of Gwen Verdon. Carl Reiner, Buddy Hackett, and William Warfield were also in that company.

Nothing succeeds like whatever they say nothing succeeds like, and so I was asked to do Lerner and Loewe's *Brigadoon* and also Arthur Schwartz's projected *Park Avenue*. But as I had *Call Me Mister* to hang my hat on, I decided that I could not afford to leave a successful show for an unknown one. Now, most people are unaware that a musicians' union rule prevents a conductor or musician from returning to a show he has left for another one. (By the way, this rule is very fair.) Because I could not return if I found myself in trouble, there could be no question as to what I must do. The story is not complete, however, until the end.

Meanwhile producer Michael Myerberg engaged me to work on incidental music for *Dear Judas*, a verse play about Christ by Robinson Jeffers. I was to select Bach chorales and train a choir to sing them. I agreed to doing a week's tryout at Ogunquit, Maine, and then the New York opening between performances of *Call Me Mister*. My Bach choir drew rave notices. Finis.

Asked to "do" incidental music for *A Streetcar Named Desire*, I began work on it while still conducting *Call Me Mister* and preparing the Broadway opening of *Dear Judas*. In spite of the now well-known success of the Tennessee Williams play, it was not to be a happy experience for me.

I had known Tennessee slightly while he still lived in New Orleans. I knew Elia ("Gadge") Kazan, who was to direct, from the Group Theatre days. In my talks with Irene Selznick, the producer, I was surprised to learn that I was to *select* (not compose) New Orleans (Dixieland) jazz. As soon as I began choosing material, I was in trouble because Mrs. Selznick, Tennessee, and Kazan had specific though different ideas about what was wanted. Song titles, meaningless to me, were thrown at me and before rehearsals began I begged to be let out of my contract. Mrs. Selznick refused. Inasmuch as what was really required was a kind of "jam session," I needed to engage players experienced in this style. I consulted George Avakian (then of Columbia Records), who was well acquainted with these particular kinds of musicians, and Avakian was, unfortunately for himself, enthusiastic about helping me. He knew this music, I knew the theater. I made it clear to Avakian that I had no money to pay him out of my infinitesimally small and much-needed fee and that I did not, therefore, want him to do any work. (My original request was for names of players only.) He, on the other hand, suggested that he could be paid as agent for the musicians he would select. In my presence, the musicians agreed to pay him a commission. Avakian negotiated over-scale salaries for them, provided them with free living quarters with friends of his in New Haven (the men had no money), and lent them money and even overcoats, which a couple of them desperately needed.

After all the music was selected and agreed upon by the entire "board," Mrs. Selznick remembered that her father, L. B. Mayer, president of Metro-Goldwyn-Mayer, controlled several music publishing firms and that if the music were selected from *these* catalogs she could possibly save money. The work had to be done again, and Avakian again did the majority of it.

All the actors in *Streetcar* worked hard: Kazan infused them with vigor. Judging by the many rehearsals I watched, Kazan's biggest problem was with a talented and serious-minded young actor named Marlon Brando, who often stayed on to rehearse after the remainder of the cast had gone. Marlon worked relentlessly. Gadge was patient in trying to get the exact performance he intended.

The success of *Streetcar* is history, the musical contribution is not. The musicians refused to pay Avakian anything. They discovered a loophole: their friend Avakian had no agent's license, and they had no responsibility to pay him. Avakian took his claim to court. In view of his having no written contract, the judge threw out the case. I was filled with remorse for having gotten Avakian involved, although he always made light of it to me. I felt additional guilt because I was not doing my own thing.

The play succeeded for everyone else, and I greatly admired it, Gadge, and especially Tennessee, who was at the very peak of his talents.

Each of the subsequent projects or I was wrong. This difficult time was to last nearly four years. It was a period teeming with activities that were costly and frustrating. Besides, I had not even begun to settle my towering prewar and war debts, which fortunately seemed to bother only me. But me, it *did* bother. I had furnished an apartment, bought a wardrobe and a piano, but had no money left over.

The third show offered me (by that time *Call Me Mister* was weakening) was a musical revue, *Make Mine Manhattan*, which I was to conduct. I was neither impressed with it nor feeling well. After several weeks of auditioning, I withdrew, certain that *Make Mine Manhattan* could not succeed. (It did.)

Arthur Schwartz, the composer who had previously offered me *Park Avenue*, now offered me *Inside U.S.A.*, starring Beatrice Lillie. As I liked Schwartz and admired his music, I wanted to do *Inside U.S.A.*, but as there was no specific date set for it and *Call Me Mister* was nearing its end, I could not afford to wait. In an effort to keep *Inside U.S.A.* available I had an understanding with Schwartz that I would first open another show (*Bonanza Bound*), but I would leave it two weeks after its New York opening to do *Inside U.S.A.*, which would probably not be ready before that time.

Leaving *Call Me Mister* was much the same as saying good-bye to one's family, and it would have to be forever. We had grown close, all of us. We played backstage and onstage jokes (quite inadmissible). There was never any friction. We loved each other and the show, and the audience loved us. When I took my leave, the orchestra gave me a sapphire ring engraved, "With love."

Within a few weeks after my decision not to do *Make Mine Manhattan* and having left the dying *Call Me Mister*, I was in rehearsal for *Bonanza Bound*, which had amused me (I had read no script) at a brilliant audition given by its authors, Betty Comden and Adolph Green, with the composer Saul Chaplin at the piano.

Allyn McLerie and George Coulouris headed a large cast directed by Charles Friedman, with choreography by the brilliant, if difficult, Jack Cole. As I have often had occasion to discover since, the stage director is frequently deaf to the pleas of the musical director and composer for a proper share of rehearsal time. On the opening day of *Bonanza Bound* in Philadelphia, Charley Friedman was having a "clean-up" rehearsal. The entire cast was on stage in costume. The orchestra, bored, sat in the pit, seldom playing. The backstage crew stood by for scene changes that were never reached. The hours flew by while Friedman rehearsed and re-rehearsed the manner in which the villain was to throw the hero out of his saloon. The costs in merely waiting were mounting, but nobody could be dismissed because a large new musical cut, affecting both stage and orchestra, had been given me, and it was sufficiently complicated to need careful explaining to everyone and at least a single rehearsal.

I kept reminding Friedman that this musical change had to be gone through. He continued to delay with promises of "in another five minutes." By now it was seven o'clock (opening performance: 8:30.) Over and over again the villain tossed out the hero. Friedman did not like the way it was done. I was becoming frantic. The entire company had to eat and dress; I had to eat, shave, and put on evening clothes back at my hotel. Again Friedman was asked. Again Friedman continued to rehearse two men while an entire army waited around.

Finally, in despair, I threatened: If I did not have my chance at once (the entire rehearsal would have to end in a matter of minutes), I would go back to New York.

And still I was put off. I climbed over the orchestra railing into the theater, put on my overcoat and hat, and started up the aisle. Friedman asked me where I was going. "Since I can't rehearse, I won't conduct," I said. "*You* conduct. I'm going to New York."

He pleaded for a few minutes more. (This had gone on for hours. By now only five minutes remained.) I refused to go back into the pit unless he promised to stop instantly and turn what little remained of the rehearsal time over to me. He pleaded. I had to be firm. Friedman slumped into a seat. The company applauded.

Bonanza Bound was a bomb in Philadelphia. Its shortcomings were so obviously irreparable that within ten days it was abandoned. The closing, however, was not decided upon until days after an announcement appeared in the New York press to the effect that *Bonanza Bound* would stay out "on the road" for repairs and its New York opening would therefore be delayed for some time. This announcement caused Arthur Schwartz, by then ready to begin rehearsals of *Inside U.S.A.*, to engage another conductor.

I had put two hit shows out of my reach, for both *Inside U.S.A.* and *Make Mine Manhattan* were big successes, and *Bonanza Bound* melted away with the great blizzard of that year.

This entire cycle had been infinitely more disastrous to me than the shows themselves—success versus flop, for since I did not do *Brigadoon*, the conductor engaged to do it continued with authors Lerner and Loewe through the years into *Paint Your Wagon*, *My Fair Lady*, and *Camelot*. The conductor who did *Park Avenue* and *Inside U.S.A.* continued with Arthur Schwartz in subsequent shows and television. The conductor I suggested for *Make Mine Manhattan* graduated afterward with the show's director Max Liebman to television's successful "Show of Shows." These were positive dividends from which I had cut myself off. By choosing (at first) to do the little music in *A Streetcar Named Desire* and not being able this *one* time to extricate myself from it when I knew that I could not provide what was expected, I removed myself for all future time from two of the theater's most admirable artists, Tennessee Williams and Elia Kazan.

One extraordinary thing happened. When *Bonanza Bound* was announced to close, I asked Phil Adler, the company manager, whom I had known in *Call Me Mister*, to lend me a thousand dollars so that I could take a much-needed vacation. Without any questions, he wrote the check!

"There's No Business Like Show Business" was more than a song.

It is amazing how many more jobs tumbled along for me, how rapidly they came and piled up in an awkward precipitous succession of bewildering nothingness. A little nothing music for *Me and Molly*, sweet Gertrude Berg's theater failure; a little nothing circus music for Hal Welles's production of *The Temporary Island*, with Zorina and Ernest Truex; a little under-stage conducting of Michael Redgrave's short-lived *Macbeth*, directed by Norris Houghton and co-starring Flora Robson, with Julie Harris, whom I do not actually remember as the Second Witch.

My meeting with Michael again in *Macbeth* was both a result of his remembering me from his wartime visit to America and of my friendship with Norris Houghton. After its brief run, Michael stayed on in America for several months. During the summer, the CBS Symphony engaged me to conduct the premiere of my *Creation*, which Michael kindly agreed to narrate. Often he spent afternoons or evenings in my apartment while I was out working, playing the piano, listening to records, and reading.

Our friendship has continued now in the more than three decades since this time when we first came to know each other well.

Whenever I went to London, Michael always entertained me well. He was back in New York in 1955 playing in *Tiger at the Gates*, and he sang Macheath for me at a concert in Carnegie Hall.

He is a very tall man, gentle and sympathetic, somewhat like a large sheep dog. Michael is droll, shy, generous, and warm and is inordinately proud of the success of his children—Vanessa, Lynn, and Corin.

We have corresponded irregularly through the more than thirty years since we first met. Both of us almost invariably concluded our letters with "Love." Once, thoughtlessly, I concluded a letter to Michael with "Fondly." Since that time he has consistently addressed me as "Dear Fondly."

Shortly after *Macbeth* I began my first association with Gilbert and Sullivan through S. M. Chartok's company. Chartok was a unique mixture of incongruities. He assaulted me with his enthusiasm for Gilbert and Sullivan, which, coupled with an unquestioning certainty that his project must succeed, enabled him again and again to raise money. There was always a chewed cigar in the corner of his mouth, and his pockets bulged with pencil-written notes on dog-eared cards held together without order by rubber bands. He wrote down the answer to every question he asked anyone. He worried about money matters. He always seemed to have an "angle" about saving money, and when one of these led to limitation of rehearsal hours, I would scream, but to no avail.

Chartok engaged me as musical director of his company, although he knew that I had not only never conducted any Gilbert and Sullivan but that I had actually seen only one or two performances in my life. His eagerness was based on the need to have a fine singing chorus, and he knew of my experience in this field.

One of Chartok's erroneous beliefs was that he himself could perform personally and properly every service that is normally allocated to an army of people: producing, directing, booking, advertising, and everything else. In an effort to avoid the use of the regular booking services (and always to save money—both a necessity and a disease in his case), he personally arranged for the opening of the company in Atlantic City at a former burlesque theater that had been closed many seasons. After this we were to play a week each at the Academy of Music in Philadelphia and the Lyric Theatre in Baltimore.

On opening day an Atlantic City official condemned the theater as unsafe and forbade the sale of seats to students. Chartok had counted on a large student attendance. Also that week the weather was unseasonably cool, and the usual hordes of Atlantic City displaced persons were everywhere else. We had no attendance to speak of, but the Romes and the Chodorovs were there.

As we moved on to Philadelphia and Baltimore, the weather suddenly became so hot that people fled to Atlantic City, and so we closed permanently in the middle of the single Baltimore week. Poor Sam Chartok! Returning again to New York in mid-June, I was again without employment and facing the summer, which is never remunerative.

In twenty years the rate of my salary had been multiplied many times and with it my living habits, taxes, and new needs—unplanned—that swallowed up all I could earn. The hiatuses were ill-afforded, and a long one—a number of months—could end only in catastrophe. It was the insatiable financial need alone that truly accounted for the nearly unbroken line of musical shows that formed the outline of my life.

Conducting musical shows never fulfilled any deep desire within me. In the theater the show, after weeks of preparation, opens up for a run or abruptly eliminates the job. The opera and symphonic conductor rehearses different works constantly, performs a single one in the opera house six or seven times, or with the orchestra, two or three times during several seasons. In the theater it is always the same—eight times weekly or not at all. Make no mistake about it: there have been compensations in the theater but also constant mental, physical, and emotional expenditures besides the fulfillment of the contract.

The occasional compensations include the accomplishment of the show itself: putting it on, getting it satisfactorily set, making a chorus and an orchestra function as a unit, helping to create or present a star or a score in the best possible setting, piloting a suc-

cessful opening night through the nervousness of the other performers, and so on.

But the constant expenditures include not merely the standing up
night after night (twice on Wednesdays and Saturdays), the main-
taining of the tempo and dynamics, the overall quality (occasionally
improved during the run of a show), but communicating bright-
ness to stage performers (often against indifferent audience reactions), refreshing tired performances, keeping alive a too-relaxed
chorus and a bored orchestra, and more.

When I conducted, there was the star, not quite happy with a
drummer this evening or a "fluff" in the trumpets last night or the
dull response of an audience or the suddenly too loud brass, and
with each of these as I conducted—my eyes glued dutifully to her
long-memorized face—I detected the unhappiness, discontent, and
uneasiness directed at me personally as a disapproval that I could
do nothing to change.

If I was lucky and the show I was conducting succeeded, I was
blessed with a long run, which meant no hiatus in my income. All I
had to do was be able to stand in that eight-by-twenty-inch space
eight times a week, dressed and groomed neatly; smiling (for isn't it,
after all, a musical comedy?); sweating (I wish they'd turn off the
damned draft on the back of my wet neck); helping physically,
musically, mentally, and spiritually to make and sustain a performance as though *this* were its first; observing the fore-and-aft disapproval; plowing ahead in spite of them; and then? Be forever and
everlastingly bored, bored, bored! Of course, no one must suspect.
(What fun it must be!) And the discipline—stage and pit—must be
maintained, and I must be as proper as the rest.

God! The B-Minor Mass couldn't be fascinating to perform or to
hear eight times a week, week after week. So how much less fascinating can some of the nonsense be that does not even *pretend* to
have insides?

There was one satisfaction in feeling that people actually listened
to me, did as I directed, and sometimes even thanked me for it. This
was an undreamed-of and remarkable accomplishment and one that
earlier in my life I could never have thought possible. After all, the
scene boxes of my childhood and the actors in them had been only

paper and cardboard, but now they were real. Remember, I was always a child. I have never really changed. What thrilled or frightened me as a child remains equally effective today. The stars now, as in my youngest days, are still stars, untouchable, occupying their own great worlds. Imagine their listening to me! Imagine their actually *needing* me.

At the zenith of nothingness I received the script of *Mooncalf* by Alexander King from two young producers, Thomas Hammond and Jeff Bailey, who were eager for me to compose music for it. As this was not a play requiring incidental music (the kind usually sent to me) but a "musical show," I was sure the producers had made a ghastly error, but Hammond insisted that he, his partner, and Mary Hunter, who was to direct it, very much wanted me to do the score. I was interested in the play, a modern version of the biblical Joseph story, intended for an all-Negro cast; but since Hammond and Bailey had never produced anything, I was not willing to create so much music without some tangible proof that they might be able to proceed. To my amazement, they agreed to an advance of two thousand dollars. The summer ceased being a void, and I wrote the score quickly. Everybody was pleased with the music, and it remained for the producers to set up fund-raising auditions.

The author, Alex King, often came to my apartment for long afternoons of work on script revisions. I had known Alex slightly for several years as a friend of many of my friends. All of them warned me against lending him money. As I had none and Alex knew it, I was never asked.

He was a short man with the kind of light-colored hair and moustache that might have been blonde or gray. He looked twenty years younger than he was. He told endless amusing anecdotes, and more time was consumed in this way than with work. He was addicted to some kind of narcotic, and I was frequently appalled to see him remove a packet from his jacket, disappear into the bathroom, then return, apparently refreshed, to resume the conversation as if nothing at all had happened.

During this same summer, I wrote incidental music for an unsuccessful Connecticut tryout of Lynn Rigg's new play, *All the Way Home*, which Mary Hunter directed; furnished a little music for

Peggy's bus-and-truck productions of *Hamlet* and *Macbeth*; and for Norris Houghton's tryout of *Uniform of Flesh*, which reached Broadway months afterward as *Billy Budd*. And by mid-August I was torn between choosing to conduct Harold Rome's new musical, *That's the Ticket* and the Kurt Weill-Alan Jay Lerner *Love Life*, both of which were to rehearse simultaneously.

That's the Ticket, based on a book by Phil and Julie Epstein, was to be staged by Jerome Robbins, the extremely talented choreographer. *Love Life* was to be staged by Kazan. Kurt and Alan played *Love Life* for me. I found it novel and interesting. I had liked Harold's songs for *That's the Ticket* from their inception (his very best song, "I Shouldn't Love You," was among them). But I mistrusted the book.

By this time I had had such a long history of musical flops that I was fearful of casting my lot with *That's the Ticket*, which I did not feel would work. But friends, out of their very goodness and positive feeling that their decision *must* be the correct one for you as well as themselves, insist on your not standing in your own light. Harold Rome is such a friend and, as always, would only want to be helpful. Often in asking me to conduct his shows he was the most beneficent of benefactors. Twice, with the best will in the world, he was mistaken.

Harold's most persuasive argument was that Jerry Robbins obviously liked *That's the Ticket* since he was going to direct it. My feeling was that Jerry needed just such an opportunity to try his wings for the first time (how strong they have become in the subsequent years). In any case I knew that the script could not be made to work.

We began rehearsing *That's the Ticket* in mid-August 1948. Like *Bonanza Bound*, it opened lavishly in Philadelphia, where it closed in about two weeks without a Broadway viewing. *Love Life* opened a few days later on Broadway, where it ran throughout the season.

A few years later, while I was doing *Fanny*, Harold asked me to a "reading" of a new show, *Lady in Pink*, which he had been writing with Moss Hart. This audition, a small family affair, took place at Rhea and Jerry Chodorov's apartment with only the Chodorovs, Romes, Harts, and me present. Moss read the script aloud; Harold played and sang the songs.

Afterward we had supper and little was said of the show. The next morning I called Harold, who was a closer friend of mine than Moss, and expressed the opinion that the book would not work. Harold assured me politely that I was an idiot. He was sure that Moss knew what he was doing and that everything would proceed according to plan.

I left *Fanny* a few months before its end and after more than a year of its run, to do *Shangri-La*, which was to be an "interim" show. I had been aware of the unresolved problems that *Shangri-La* posed (in both libretto and music), but I had hopes that these might be taken care of. As *Shangri-La* was a late spring show and I was to do *Lady in Pink* in the early fall, I felt safe in the event of a disaster.

Before I left New York, Ethel Linder Reiner (producer) asked me to audition singers for her forthcoming *Candide*, by Lillian Hellman and Leonard Bernstein, which she also wanted me to conduct. As I had promised Harold to do *Lady in Pink* (in spite of my negative feelings), I asked Ethel to wait a couple of weeks for my definite reply. Ethel called me in New Haven to press me for my answer. I called Harold, and he could entertain no uncertainty whatsoever about *Lady in Pink*. I declined *Candide*. A month later when I was in Philadelphia—now positive beyond any doubt that *Shangri-La* could not succeed—Harold called to say that Moss had decided to shelve *Lady in Pink*!

I wrote incidental music to Maxwell Anderson's *Anne of the Thousand Days*, starring Rex Harrison and Joyce Redman. In Philadelphia, we changed directors and discarded many thousands of dollars worth of scenery in the back alley. Max Anderson was genial and was happy with my music. When scenes without music were being rehearsed, I generally played gin rummy in the theater lounge with Max's wife.

Again, I was without a job.

By the New Year—1949—backers' auditions for *Mooncalf* were held weekly in a private dining room in the Warwick Hotel. Prospective "angels" assembled at a stylish hour, and sat around tables drinking, as in a cabaret. I narrated the plot and three singers and a pianist performed the principal songs. Tom Hammond would describe the budget and invite investments. These auditions ground on month after month during which tens of thousands of dollars were pledged, but in the end there was not enough.

Simultaneously, Vernon ("April in Paris") Duke offered me his forthcoming musical, *He and She*. Here again backers' auditions were continuing month after month (on a more modest scale, however). Vernon was likable but strange. He had many people "hanging about": an orchestra contractor, a violinist, and several others were in constant attendance. Vernon liked being surrounded, and the others were longing for the pending job. Vernon took advantage of this all-too-obvious fact and used his entourage as messengers, as window dressing at auditions, but most of all as music copyists for other compositions of his own.

Since I was hanging around without remuneration or assurances that this show would materialize any more than my own, I needed to accept the first offer to conduct any definitely scheduled show for the earliest possible production. A revue called *Alive and Kicking* was it. *He and She* never happened. Nor—on Broadway—has *Mooncalf*.

My financial life had been saved intermittently on a small scale, at first by the Victor Company, which had me conduct records with Alfred Drake and Jane Pickens; then by RKO Pathé, which had me score two documentary films; and then by Columbia Records, through Goddard Lieberson.

I am Goddard's oldest friend in New York. He had come here—a tall, lean, handsome boy less than a year younger than I—nearly twenty years earlier and had telephoned me on arrival. (The why of this is somewhat vague but I seem to remember he had an introduction to me from a teacher.) Also there was something about a check that would come next week, and he had no place to stay.

Goddard was talented, and he wanted to be a composer. He won a scholarship at the Eastman School in Rochester, and when he went there, we exchanged letters. Shortly after I began work with the Madrigal Singers, Goddard sent me some choruses set to brief Chinese poems. Each was only several measures long (this was a sign of the times). I did not feel that I could perform them, and I *believe* he was miffed.

Time passed. Goddard was now living in New York. He had a job as librarian for Columbia Records. Then he became assistant to the

Listening to a playback at Columbia Records' studio about 1949, while Mary Martin was playing in *South Pacific*. *Left to right*: Mary; David Oppenheimer of the CBS staff, then married to Judy Holliday; L. E.; and Mary's husband, Richard Halliday. *Photo by Fred Plaut*

head of the Masterworks Department, and later vice-president. (This must have taken nearly twenty years.)

When I returned to New York after World War II, I met him at a cocktail party. He asked me to call him: he had an idea.

When we met, he asked me to conduct a recording with Mary Martin. This was to be the first of five albums with Mary. Goddard "produced" them, which is to say that he directed the sound, the style, and often the music itself.

Although these records did not do very well, Goddard—inordinately in love with musical theater—wanted to continue with a series of revivals, mostly shows which had never been recorded. (The idea of cast albums was just beginning and so was the LP.)

One reason the Mary Martin albums had not done well was that Mary sang all the good songs and left the dross to less important singers. The result was that she represented *nobody* in the show. She was everybody, and there was not only confusion for the listeners but an absence of drama. This was not Mary's fault, because in those beginning ventures none of us was quite certain about what we were doing. After those albums we *cast* the roles and allocated the songs accordingly.

Goddard always rode herd. We were fortunate in having Fred Plaut, a great engineer. Fred, Goddard, and I were long-suffering, for the atmosphere at these many sessions covering many years was always a little turbulent. Goddard had ideas—often brilliant ones— which he was not always at pains to explain clearly, and so Fred would be berated. Then, when I would try to say something from the studio, Goddard was usually talking through the too-loud speaker, and I could say very little. Then I would scream at God- dard. These contretemps seemed never to have left any mark. After- ward I would apologize to Goddard, but he would pretend that nothing had happened.

It was Goddard who persuaded CBS to do all of the financing for an upcoming musical called *My Fair Lady*. Afterwards he was made president of Columbia Records. Later he was appointed vice-presi- dent of CBS and is so high above the mere record section now that it hardly exists for him anymore.

But Goddard is unique. He has taste and charm. He has read everything and heard everything. Married for some time now to Brigitta—known as Vera Zorina when she danced—they have two grown sons. While Goddard knows everybody, the best part of this is that everybody *wants* to know him.

Back to the Mary Martin records: they were actually made with love. My then-current pianist (and often my assistant conductor), John Lesko, and I used to go to Mary's dressing room on matinee days during *South Pacific* between performances because Mary was in the country on most other days. At all rehearsals Mary's husband, Richard Halliday, was present, and all of us contributed interpretive ideas, which were discussed, used, or discarded, always in an at- mosphere of joy and love.

At one of these rehearsals I admired a shantung dressing gown Mary was wearing. I said that someday I would have a similar one of white shantung trimmed in slate-grey. Next day a package con- taining material for just such a robe arrived. An ingratiating note advised that Mary's seamstress would call to arrange a fitting. Some days later as the sewing lady snipped—her mouth full of pins—she inquired about Mrs. Halliday. What was she like? Was she pretty? I

ABOVE: L. E. (*left*) with Goddard Lieberson at the recording of *Porgy and Bess* for Columbia Records, 1951. *Photo by Fred Plaut*

RIGHT: Papa, Mama, and I, about 1950, during an intermission at the Starlight Operetta in Dallas, Texas. *Photo by Neal Lyons*

was astonished since the lady was Mary's very own seamstress! They had never met: Dick Halliday had delivered a dressmaker's form to the sewing-lady and had supervised all the fittings.

The first day at Columbia's studio Mary took me aside affectionately and handed me an envelope. At the close of the day I read the contents: an assignment of ten percent of Mary's royalties from these records. I called to thank her and protested that Columbia was already paying me a royalty. Her gift was her own expression of appreciation, she said. I must accept it.

In the late spring of the year I was offered through Gus Schirmer the musical directorship of the summer Starlight Operetta in Dallas, Texas. Charles Meeker, the managing director, was a man of enthusiasm. His immediate warmth toward me dispelled any fears I had about the new job and the faraway place, and I was agreeably surprised at the salary. My work was laid out for me, for I had eight shows to prepare for rehearsals in two months!

The Starlight Operetta, a branch of the State Fair of Texas, functions within Fair Park, and performances during my first two seasons took place seven nights a week in an open-air amphitheater.

We opened a new show each Monday evening. Tuesday we began rehearsing the newly arrived principals for the next Monday night's opening. On Sunday night, after the final performance of that week's show, the scenery was changed, one set of costumes packed up, another set laid out, and by 2:00 A.M. we started dress rehearsal of the new show. Generally we finished about 7:00 A.M. in the blinding, blistering sun. We had to race against sunrise (unsuccessfully) in order to judge the lights.

Somehow there were seldom any hitches. We performed *Up in Central Park* with Kenny Baker; *Rose Marie* with John Raitt and a little comedienne named Imogene Coca; *Bloomer Girl* with Avon Long and Nanette Fabray (who screamed to the front pages of every paper in the world when during her final performance a cricket lit on her chest); *Bittersweet* with Robert Rounseville and Ilona Massey; *Pal Joey* with Vivienne Segal (this was the beginning of the revival that was to delight New York three years later); *The Chocolate Soldier* with Polyna Stoska (who had sung in the chorus of *Within the Gates*), Elaine Malbin, and Robert Rounseville; and *Show Boat* with Carol Bruce and Hal LeRoy.

Occasionally there was rain. If it stopped by curtain time, we played, but then usually to a sparse audience. If rain began during a show, there was wild scampering: musicians (especially violinists) trying to protect instruments, performers dashing to offstage shelter, the audience racing to automobiles parked blocks away. If the rain was only a passing shower, performance was resumed.

I met many people and was constantly entertained. Some of these parties I enjoyed, but many of them seemed to be "public relations" duties. I was photographed everywhere on the least provocation, and the photographs were always published.

By the beginning of my second summer I was well known in Dallas and was bowed to incessantly by strangers everywhere I went. Charlie Meeker, the Dallas impresario and certainly my friend, arranged for me to buy a beautiful new Buick at a discount (I needed transportation during the three-month residence) and also arranged for a sale at the end of summer so that the entire transaction would cost me nothing.

During the preceding fall, an overhead drive had been completed, making it possible for me to enter it quite near my hotel in the residential section, bypass Dallas traffic, and drive off near Fair Park, where I worked.

The first day of the season I got off to a great start in my beautiful car, found the overhead drive, and sailed happily down it. I was certainly pleased by the number of drivers going in the opposite direction who continuously waved to me. Everybody seemed to recognize me. Suddenly I heard a siren behind me. A motorcycle cop edged by and cut me off, and I came to a stop. Off he came with his pad and pencil, did a double take as he looked at me, and said,

"Ain't you that fella that conducts them music shows in Fair Park?"

I quailed at the recognition and agreed that indeed I *was* that fellow.

Then he spoke as if confiding some state secret: "You know, you're on the wrong road. This 'un goes one way north and you ought to be on thet 'un over thataway that goes south. If you'll just folla me, I'll lead you outa this mess and onto the right 'un."

He began his siren, stopped traffic until I could turn around, and then led me triumphantly to the correct drive, where no one waved.

If I had had time to take stock of myself, it would have been clear that I had become a full-time conductor (much in demand) and a part-time composer. I had been meticulously prepared as a composer and little taught as a conductor. I had had only a few elementary class lessons in Cincinnati. The rest was experience. The major part germinated in the four Madrigal Singers years; afterward, I had to adjust gradually to the orchestra (as opposed to chorus) for the techniques are quite dissimilar. I came into the theater first as a conductor of my own music. In a brief time, I graduated to conducting the music of others, while my own music gradually disappeared.

Most valuable to me was the imposition of commercial time limits due to orchestral costliness. I was forced to conduct clearly, to acquire a vocabulary of physical gestures that would be instantly comprehensible to everyone. The vast number of records I made, shows I conducted, films I scored, and, to a lesser degree, the concerts I officiated at, all made invaluable contributions to my learning. The many different players and singers working with me for the one time only, the inflexible schedules that dictated how much had to be accomplished—allowing small margin for error—these did their best to educate me. I was further helped by the high quality of musicians that my contractor—from the very beginning, Morris Stonzek—invariably furnished me. These people who worked under me taught me whatever it is that I know. They helped to establish more firmly the fact of myself. The dream was my own private concern, as indeed I suppose it always is.

12: Strange Interlude

Ever since I can remember, there was talk of gambling at home. Papa played poker and shot craps. What I inherited from Papa was not money but his desire to gamble. My cup of tea is gin rummy or, in casinos, the equivalent, blackjack.

During my time with the navy at Great Lakes, I was everybody's pigeon. Lou Mindling and Lt. Bob Elson were my chief beneficiaries. When I was sent to Washington, Lou alerted his friend Ray Katz (now an important Hollywood agent), who inherited me. What was left was more evenly divided when I played with Collier Young, also from Hollywood.

Why gin rummy? The reasons seem clear to me. You have to concentrate hard to remember every card thrown, every one picked up by your opponent, and you have to reconstruct in your mind what you think he has and needs so that, if possible, you do not give it to him. For these reasons, it is next to impossible to think or talk about anything else during the game: the players are totally absorbed. The day's work has been finished, for good or ill. All of that has to be forgotten. And perhaps that's a good reason for gin rummy's being good for you. If you play, you must escape everything else. Or am I rationalizing?

Also, in my case, one of its attractions is that it is a busy game. You pick a card and throw it or put it in your hand and discard another. You never cease watching what your opponent does, and often you play breathlessly.

After the war the games took place almost entirely between Harold and Florence Rome, Jim Wise, and me. These were in New

York or on weekends at the Wises. Then the Wises moved to Europe, leaving Harold and me. Little by little we were joined by others. Melvyn Douglas played, and very occasionally Jerry Chodorov, Jules Irving, or Mollie Parnis. More frequently, for a time, the pool of the avid availables consisted of Harold; David Morgan; a delightful and successful Polish inventor, Arthur Kober; Paul Osborn; Kermit Bloomgarden; Diana Shumlin; and me. When Jim Wise would return to New York annually from Europe, we had what we liked to call "memorial" sessions. When Ira Steiner (Harold's brother-in-law) came from Hollywood, he was automatically a member.

This in no way means that all of us played together at any one time. Anyone finding himself free for an evening would call one of the others and a game involving two, three, or four developed. We have generally concluded that in any given year, we have each of us about broken even, although there are discouraging periods when it would seem that one or two people would never win again.

Now, after about twenty-five years since the war's end, we have developed little cliques within the group. As all of us play more or less equally well, the schisms are personal. Two are no longer friendly, so that a game involving both is out of the question.

Harold Rome plays very slowly and in trying to remember the cards taken by an opponent, chants them over and over aloud. Arthur is so unnerved by this that he refuses to play with Harold because he is afraid these irritations might destroy their friendship. Sometimes David irritates some of the others, because he is noisy and talks a great deal. I irritate Arthur because I am apt to remark about each card that's played—a nervous habit. Sometimes Diana is in the doghouse (as is Harold) for being too active in playing her partner's hand. (We "advise" but should seldom "insist.") And on and on.

The dialogue and measure of sound at these contests are best recorded. A game involving Diana, Arthur, Paul, Kermit and/or me is apt to be swift and silent (except, of course, for me). One with David, Harold, or Ira will be loud and full of acrimony. Each player has his own special dialogue.

Arthur: "I'm going to take that card if it's the first thing I do. . . . Your lips are moving."

In response to an innocent observation: "He's a philosopher as well as a jerk!" When someone loses a hand and remarks about how beautiful it was, he asks, "How'd you make out?"

David: "Sholom Aleichem! He took that card only because he needs it."

Paul: "Jesus!"

Kermit: "Shit!"

Ira: "Shit!"

Harold: [And if he is losing, he sings,] "Flaww-rence! You saw that hand. What could I do?!"

I hear someone say something—just anything—and it sets me off on a poetry (or Shakespearean) recital, which annoys everyone: (Someone, on picking up his newly dealt hand, says incredulously, "Is this a hand?" I continue: ". . . which I see before me?")

When the game ends (usually between 1:00 A.M. and 3:00 A.M.), there is the settling up. Most of us usually pay by check, and many times you are paid with your own check of last month or that of someone else who lost weeks ago. At these times most of us—win or lose—return to being ourselves, while others are apt to be morose. As in all games, the participants play to win. That's the ideal and the purpose. Sometimes this is erroneously translated to convey (to the loser) a sense of greed.

For me, I have heard all the *Walküre*'s, *Aïda*'s, *Lucia*'s and Franck, Mendelssohn, and Brahms symphonies I ever want to get dressed and travel to a concert hall to hear. If I *should* ever want to hear them again, I have an ample record library, which allows me to select a good performance and listen to it minus many hundreds of other people bringing their colds to me. I'll take gin rummy.

I have played the related blackjack in some casinos and have occasionally won. In any case, and of necessity, I have put a limit on my losses. I buy weekly lottery tickets and once won fifty dollars. In Cuba, in the dreamy past, I won twenty-five dollars on a twenty-five-cent ticket.

Once when I arrived at the Warwick Hotel in Philadelphia to prepare the opening of one of my shows, I was tackled by a lady as I raced through the lobby: Would I buy a ticket for some charity lottery for a quarter? Of course, I bought it, signed my name, and gave the Warwick Hotel as my address. Many months later I returned to Philadelphia to open another show. One morning my telephone rang: I had won the lottery, and an electric coffee pot, waffle iron, and toaster were delivered.

13: The Naked and the Dead

Aᴛʜᴇᴀᴛᴇʀ ᴄᴏɴꜱɪꜱᴛꜱ ᴏꜰ actors (and/or singers and dancers), orchestra, stagehands, and audience. Much has been written about performers, practically nothing about the audience. As I have observed
at close range more than eight million people in audiences, I feel it
is not presumptuous to make a few comments.

The audience is the family inquisitor, often thought of backstage
as a rich maiden aunt who needs to be pleased, is seldom loved or
lovely, and is often selfish and indiscriminating.

Audiences are more various and variable—even for the same
show—than any nontheater person can conceive. Some of what they
are is predictable, some incomprehensible. Opening nights, especially of a show that has a good advance reputation, is exciting.
Anticipation is so high that laughs precede laugh lines and applause
floods before the sluice gates are opened: reactions are prefabri-
cated. Nearly all the members of an opening-night audience have a
personal relationship to the show. There are the backers and their
guests; relatives and friends of the cast, authors, composers, and
producers, who are well-wishing with so much intensity—like ki-
bitzers at a dice table—that they almost burst; and, finally, agents
and ticket brokers, who are estimating their profits (or losses) on a
cinemascopic scale. The final verdict is with the quiet critics, and
so the next day after the reviews, this first-night audience relaxes
in happy concurrence or nurses a painful hangover-type malady.

The second-night audience wears a mood entirely conditioned by the press. The performance they see is tired and happy or tired and defiant or tired and despondent. The majority of the audience is unmindful of this, but either curses openly before curtain at having been "stuck" with long-purchased seats or is thrilled at having gotten in on the "ground floor."

For quite a long time (perhaps eight or ten weeks) most audiences are "benefit" subscribers, who will have paid two to ten times the box-office price for their tickets. The actors receive their ordinary salaries, but since seatholders have paid more, their attitude seems to be, "I dare you to make me like it!" Once at a benefit performance, during the overture, an irate man in the first row ordered me to sit down because he had paid fifty dollars for his ticket!

Benefit audiences usually arrive late, are more dressed up than the average, spend a great deal of time not looking at the stage but attempting to see and be seen by friends, seldom applaud or laugh, and except for waving at friends seem to be embalmed. Also they usually belong to a single racial, religious, or social group. Regardless of their affiliation, they are identical during superanimated intermissions and deadly unresponsive during the show.

When the show is a hit, when it has passed through the benefits wasteland, and if it is still winter (i.e., "the season"), audiences may usually be classified according to the calendar.

Monday's group is the most elegant, most theater-hungry, most cosmopolitan, most accustomed to going wherever it wants to go only because it wants to. Response is excellent and alive. The Tuesday and Wednesday evening contingents have elements of Monday's, but they respond less.

Wednesday's matinee is all-female, average age about sixty, noisy, and responsive to sentimentality about mother; otherwise, they are sleepy and asleep soon after they stop talking. What applause they intend is inaudible because of their gloves. They spring to life about half an hour before the show's end and knock each other down in a frantic effort to leave the theater ahead of anybody else.

Thursday usually draws a conglomerate. There are late shoppers with crinkling paper packages, small families, suburbanites (maid's day off, possibly), and the reaction to the show is mixed.

Friday night is a frankly expectant crowd. It's the event of the week for these people, and they are prepared to be enthusiastic. They are not dressy as a rule, and their intellectual perceptivity is usually apparent.

Saturday matinee is also expectant and holiday-happy. These people look like professors, schoolteachers, bright families: the cost is less than at night. Their response is warm and cordial. They are attentive in the extreme.

Saturday evening's crowd has leased the space as an after-dinner refuge or a pre-nightclub time-spending spa. It is slightly tipsy. It got seats to this particular show to demonstrate to its girlfriends that nothing in the world is too difficult or costly. The show is *not* the thing. Only the two hours and a half of sitting in the semidark, holding the hand of the one it loves matters. Response to the stage is bewildered, slow, and weak. Heart and mind belong to daddy. And a lethargic audience means a lethargic or angry performance. The relationship between auditorium and stage is always that of Echo and Narcissus.

In summer, the theater calendar I have devised is out of date, for there is no classifiable group at any time. Most people are out-of-towners and they come when they can get tickets—unfortunately, usually not difficult in summer. Many women overdress as if to lord it over all the others: the don't-try-to-tell-us-about-New York attitude. Others wear comfortable summer clothes without regard for who cares. This non-New York audience is in the presence of fame and is often predisposed in the show's favor. They like the broader and more decorative things best, miss many subtle jokes, applaud modestly, attend to everything.

In winter, the boxes sport royally dressed customers; in summer men are coatless and tieless.

Only in winter are there fashionable dinner-party guests arriving far into the first act. Six well-dressed people saunter leisurely down the aisle. Four seated people rise to allow them in the row. The hostess stands perfectly placidly, audibly deciding, directing and redirecting the seating order of her guests. While this bit of formal impoliteness transpires, nobody in the audience sees or can see anything else, and I have often observed performers trying to play against it forget their lines.

There are always celebrities in New York theater-hit audiences.

Once, after Truman was no longer president, when he entered a theater I worked in, the audience rose. Movie stars claim a great deal of attention, while visiting royalty often goes unrecognized. But the biggest (almost sexual) demonstration I have seen was when Ed Sullivan walked down the aisle. Most celebrated people (all celebrated people with taste) arrive for the beginning of the show and remain for the end. It is a responsibility to behave in this way since every flicker of each eyelash is studied by the rest of the audience for some reaction. Any reaction can be called gospel.

I am horribly self-conscious at every performance as I take my stand, partially concealing the stage from the two people immediately behind me in the first row. As I enter the pit I usually smile at them in the hope that they will understand that I am not committing a willfully malicious act and that I am apologizing in advance. Sometimes this works. There is, however, the occasional female who thinks I am flirting and reacts as though I had committed a terrible nuisance.

Once, when I came out to begin a performance of *Call Me Mister*, I recognized a very ancient and tiny lady I had long known, sitting in the first row immediately behind my podium. Before taking my stand, I reached through the iron railing to shake her hand.

"I'm sorry you are sitting behind me," I consoled.

"Oh, that's all right, Lehman. I've seen through you for years," she snapped.

In Boston at a performance of *Wonderful Town*, prior to the New York opening, there was an extremely hot early fall night when I perspired unusually heavily, even for me. My large handkerchief was so drenched that it was no longer of any use. A very dignified gentleman seated immediately behind me thrust his fresh handkerchief into my hand, and when he returned after intermission, he brought me a package of Kleenex.

My personal contact with the public is obviously sharper than the stage personnel's since I am so near that I hear what they have to say, and in those moments during a performance when I am not conducting, I am sitting among them, seeing them directly. Somehow it seldom occurs to people in the first several rows that the musicians and I are part of the show. The talk is loud throughout the overture, as though we were only playing to amuse ourselves.

The fortissimo brass is never quite loud enough to drown out the smallest talk. On the other hand, if my men and I gave the identical performance in Carnegie Hall, the same audience would be irate at such carryings-on by others. During the overture to one of my shows I became so irate at the audience's violent fortissimo that I cut off the orchestra in the middle of a phrase. The players were astonished. The stage manager peeped out of his corner of the stage expecting to view my prostrate body. I simply stood erect, my arms folded in what I felt was an attitude of defiance. In a matter of moments (the silence was far louder than the orchestra) I began to hear people "shh" each other. Their talking died out completely. Then I began again, and for the only time after an opening performance, the audience applauded. Masochists, anyone? In the theater the convention seems to be to pay us as little attention as possible. No breach of etiquette is involved. The candy wrappers are removed as noisily as if the seat-occupant were at home watching television with no thought of his fellow watchers in front of, behind, and next to him. This is, by comparison, a miniature nuisance since it affects a mere dozen or so others. But what about the flash-picture-takers who suddenly (and illegally) flood the entire theater with their little personal caprices, distracting the entire audience in that one selfish second, and often causing the performers to lose concentration and forget lines. Etiquette?

And there are many others within my sight and hearing. An elderly man, fascinated with the orchestra, "conducts" every number vigorously and offbeat. His wife fans herself noisily between *his* beats. Loud conversations are concerned with personal things (Sadie's new dress, fur, jewelry, hairdo) or how old the star looks or her costume or the perspiration or how much funnier she used to be on television.

Directly behind me disapproval asserts itself sometimes in harsh words, sometimes in persistent clicks of the tongue, moans, and even occasional taps on my back or tugs at my coattails: I'm blocking someone's view, or the orchestra is deliberately too loud for the comfort of someone sitting a foot away from three trumpets, three trombones, two drummers, and five saxophones.

Now, when I no longer want to be confined by the five uninterrupted weeks of rehearsal; the eight, nine, ten, or more weeks of pre-

Broadway touring; the two or three weeks of local preopening preparation with more rehearsing; previews; the opening itself; and recording; all of which preclude other activities, I would like to air a complaint which irks me and must continue to irk my colleagues, present and future: the ignominious position of the conductor in the theater. This catalogue of annoyances—talk, candy wrappers, disapproving clicks of the tongue, and so on—are, I believe, not the fault of the doers but of customs begun and perpetuated by theater management: the public has enormous respect for anyone, however unimportant, if it is told to. If that person is made nothing of, he simply does not exist. And that is how it is with theater conductors.

It does not occur to audiences that the little man drowning just inside the orchestra rail actually directed the star's performance musically, that he fashioned an orchestral ensemble out of a heterogeneous group of players, that he took a group of vocalists chosen at least partially for their pulchritude, good figures, and ability to move, and taught them to sing together. Who would even dream about such things unless they have been spelled out for him?

And how does or could this happen? Why, in the usual ways. By being given better billing, given a lighted entrance in a totally dark auditorium, and by publicity. The stars, authors, and directors get it; why not the musical directors and stage managers who together are responsible for so much?

Publicity. Recently at a performance of *Promenade*, a ghastly off-Broadway musical turned into a bonanza by several critics, I was horrified by the highly praised songs which lacked any unity of style and any relationship (except lyrically) to the present; it ought to be subtitled "A Dinner at Asti's," since every song is a watered-down aria from the French and Italian repertory. In the intermission I overheard a conversation between two gentlemen regarding the stylistic conglomeration. The older one observed. "I think this composer's hang-up is style. There is no unity."

The younger one replied in high dudgeon, annihilating his companion, "How can you say that? Why, he was on the Merv Griffin show!"

This is how it is with reputations.

In any case, conductors in the theater, unlike their confreres in all other media, are provided with *no* reputation. For audiences, the show commences only when the curtain rises. To change the status quo would cost much money. It will not be changed, because as David Merrick once quite rightly pointed out to me, no ticket-buyer will turn in his ticket because I or anybody else was not conducting, and that, Sonny Boy, is all that counts. As a matter of fact, things have gotten worse recently. I myself was the recipient of two Tony Awards (for three shows) and now the status of conductor has become so very unimportant that even that category has been abolished.

Whether audiences are dead or alive, rude or polite, groomed or unkempt, drunk or sober, pleased or disappointed, the theater family needs them. As long as they continue to attend in sufficient numbers, the theater family goes about its work without worry. The saddest sound is silence. The cruel specter of unoccupied rows in the vast auditorium is the beginning of the end. When this cancer gnaws deeply enough, there is no longer any backstage family. Each member must break away alone—no longer a part of the whole and once more in competition with every other family member, once again in search of the new, uncertain, temporary life.

14: Rat Race

Rᴇᴛᴜʀɴɪɴɢ ᴛᴏ Nᴇᴡ Yᴏʀᴋ after my first Dallas summer, I was to begin continuous work. Within five months I had conducted eight shows in Dallas and two operettas on Broadway (again *Mikado* and *Pirates of Penzance* on Chartok's shoestring); had written incidental music for Edward Chodorov's play, *Señor Chicago* (also unacceptable); recorded *Anything Goes* and *Bandwagon*, starring Mary Martin; and finally began rehearsals for *Alive and Kicking*. I was not to be out of rehearsal one single day for more than three years.

Alive and Kicking was produced by William Katzell, a businessman, and Ray Golden, a lyricist. Many composers* and sketchwriters** were involved. Jack Cole, whom I had first known as a dancer in Charles Weidman's group many, many years before and more recently as choreographer for *Bonanza Bound*, was the star of the show. Lenore Lonergan, the grown-up "Junior Miss," was the leading lady, and David Burns and Carl Reiner shared comic honors. Gwen Verdon, now a star, was one of Jack Cole's dancers.***

Alive and Kicking is a typical story of waste due to lack of knowledge and staggeringly bad taste. The revue form, at best, is a diffi-

---

* Hoagy Carmichael, Harold Rome, Sammy Fain, Sonny Burke, Irma Jurist, and others.
** Joseph Stein, Henry Morgan, and others.
*** Jack Cassidy, Rae Allen, Mickey Deems, and Bobby Van were in "support."

cult one and before opening in New Haven we knew we were in trouble. In Boston, Katzell and Golden became so frantic that they introduced some different vaudeville act at almost every performance. New performers arrived daily, rehearsed, went on, and departed. None of them worked out. When we reached Philadelphia, funds were running low, and almost daily one of the producers would turn up with a new investor. As the producers were by that time at loggerheads, the controlling hands shifted with each new investor. Directors were hired and fired; actors and material were replaced. We rehearsed incessantly with new songs, new orchestrations, new dancers, new actors. The hysteria was contagious. Probably no performer can be more difficult than Jack Cole, and in *Alive and Kicking* he ran the gamut. He would stamp his feet during performances to change tempi. His dancers wept. Once, in a fit of anger during a performance, he ran offstage in full costume and makeup and dashed out into the audience to scream at the producers who were standing in the back of the theater.

After two weeks in Philadelphia and the raising and spending of more and more money, we pushed on to Hershey, Pennsylvania, where it was hoped another week of work would salvage the show for Broadway. During that week we inhaled chocolate, bathed with Hershey soap, performed at the Hershey Theatre, walked down Cocoa Street, and went to sleep with the bearded face of Mr. Hershey glaring reprovingly from the walls of the Hotel Hershey. Nothing of the show was improved, and when we finally opened on Broadway, we received murderous notices. The show ran about four weeks, but immediately after it opened, I went into rehearsal for Gian-Carlo Menotti's opera *The Consul*, and simultanously I wrote music for Joshua Logan's *The Wisteria Trees*, starring Helen Hayes —a very kind lady. After three weeks of this terrible schedule the company gave me a gift and I left *Alive and Kicking* to a weeping Jack Cole.

Rehearsals for *The Consul* were a miracle of exactness. Menotti, who wrote both libretto and music, also orchestrated and staged it himself. Prior to my engagement Thomas Schippers, not quite twenty-one and a pianist of no small talent, had coached the singers. Before starting to work I asked Menotti to play the score for me so that I would know what he wanted. His reply was, "No, no, no. You

Gian-Carlo Menotti (*right*) with L. E. at a recording session of *The Consul* at the Decca Studios in 1950. *Photo by Warren Rothschild*

are the musical director. I am the stage director. I want you to make a performance. I will never interfere until after the first public performance, when I will give you criticism." As this was the reverse behavior of every composer I had ever worked for, I did not believe it. (This time I was wrong.)

I had not had sufficient time to learn the score, and so I asked permission to go to Puerto Rico for the entire third week of rehearsals where I might rest and study without interruption. Since Gian-Carlo needed as much extra time for stage directing and orchestrating as he could get, he was very willing for me to leave.

There were never any trial-and-error things in *The Consul*, unique in my experience. No music was ever changed or deleted, nor any words. The cast, headed by Patricia Neway, Marie Powers, Cornel MacNeil (now of the Metropolitan Opera), and Gloria Lane, was a beautiful one.

Pat Neway was no stranger to me. For one thing, years before she had sung (along with Eileen Farrell) in a chorus I had conducted at CBS. Now she was to become, for a while at least, a star. Marie Powers unintentionally terrified me. Gloria Lane was a young, sexy girl oozing with vocal and histrionic talent.

The first orchestra rehearsals went on for many days in Philadelphia in the auditorium of the Curtis Institute of Music. (The producers were Chandler Cowles, once of *Call Me Mister*, and Efrem Zimbalist, Jr., son of the famous violinist who was head of the Curtis Institute.) Mr. Zimbalist, Sr., and Gian-Carlo sat through every long day's rehearsal. I frequently had occasion to want to make small changes in the orchestration, and Gian-Carlo was invariably agreeable.

At the premiere in Philadelphia, *The Consul* was a triumph. Various "great" minds raced backstage to beg Gian-Carlo to cut out the final scene or to rewrite it. Everyone had a special finish in mind. Gian-Carlo listened to all of them patiently. In the end, he made only small choreographic and light alterations.

One day at a New York rehearsal a few days before opening I saw the orchestra members suddenly behave like statues. When I called an intermission, I asked the concert master the reason, and he pointed behind me to Toscanini, who, being deeply interested in Gian-Carlo, had come to hear the score. He had sat with his eyes closed, and when I called intermission, he greeted Gian-Carlo affectionately and was complimentary to me when I was introduced. He came to a number of rehearsals.

The opening in New York was exciting. Toscanini arrived half an hour early, and every important conductor in America was in the audience. The reception was fantastic.

The Consul was my first experience in years that had been somewhere within the frame of my dream. But *The Consul* was too little and too late, and I even had to leave it after only three weeks in New York. I left it to my assistant, Thomas Schippers—talented and personable—who went on with it and, with Gian-Carlo's help, to the Metropolitan Opera, the New York Philharmonic, and many other distinguished organizations.

During my three weeks with *The Consul* in New York, I emerged one evening from the stage door after a performance and was approached by a lady who had been standing in the shadows of the balcony fire-exits. As she drew nearer, I recognized Martha Graham: She was to go on a European tour and asked me to conduct it for her. Again, too late, because *The Liar* for one month and Dallas for three were already waiting offstage.

Seven years later, Chandler Cowles invited me to conduct a week's run of *The Consul* in Central Park. Patricia Neway, Gloria Lane, Cornel MacNeil, and Maria Marlo were to take their original roles again.

When I began to restudy the opera, I was shocked to discover that I could not remember a single note! It was a curious phenomenon, for after three days' work, and then quite suddenly, I recalled nearly everything. Then I played my original recording of it and was shocked that I disliked it. When I met the cast for the first rehearsal, I remarked about not liking the fast tempos on the recording. The singers reminded me that at the recording sessions Gian-Carlo had not wanted to make further cuts and had asked me to speed up the tempos!

We were rained out of four of seven scheduled performances. Once, just after the start of the opera, the pouring began suddenly and torrentially. Cornel MacNeil was under the stage waiting for an entrance through the trapdoor. There was no exit for him except through the trapdoor and a heavy chair rested on top of it. In everyone's rush to find shelter we forgot Cornel and it was not until a member of the also-fled audience inquired of him that he was rescued.

The day after the opening of *The Consul* on Broadway, I began rehearsals for *The Liar*, by Alfred Drake, Edward Eager, and John Mundy. (Walter Matthau was a walk-on.) It was not caprice on my part that I left *The Consul* after only three weeks: I had agreed a year earlier to open *The Liar* on Broadway, and in any case, I would have to leave a month later for Dallas. *The Liar* was a failure.

I departed for Dallas (second time) the morning after opening. Within a matter of days I was in rehearsal for eight more musical comedies! The summer whizzed by dizzily and happily and I was back again in New York hardly realizing that I had ever left.

Before starting rehearsals for Harold Rome's new revue, *Bless You All*, I recorded *Pal Joey* for Goddard Lieberson, with Vivienne Segal and Harold Lang. The enormous success of this album became the impetus for the revival of the show a couple of years later, and our choice of Lang got him the co-starring role in the revival.

Bless You All starred Pearl Bailey, Julie Munshin, Mary McCarty, and Valerie Bettis. This one fooled us. We got good out-of-town notices, sold out solidly in Philadelphia, and had the impression that we were a hit. In New York we closed after six weeks.

In Philadelphia at one matinee, in the middle of a song Pearl Bailey suddenly stopped singing and motioned me to stop the orchestra. She proceeded to the center of the stage and addressed me: "Mr. Engel, I don't like the way you're playing my music. I'm warning you—if you don't play my music right I'm going to tell my father and he'll write you a letter!" For a moment the audience and I were paralyzed. Suddenly everyone broke into laughter. It was the day President Truman's letter to the recalcitrant music critic (he had written a poor review of Margaret Truman's singing) had appeared in the papers.

During rehearsals and our short run Pearl used to invite me, as well as other friends, to her hotel where, with the help of another woman (not quite an employee, but perhaps), she took delight in cooking elaborate "Southern" dinners: fried chicken, "greasy" greens, black-eyed peas, corn bread, and much, much more. Pearl's pride and good humor permeated everything.

In the three months between the closing of the show and my third return to Dallas, I recorded four complete shows, a Renaissance choral album, and Christmas carols; put together music for Peggy's touring *Taming of the Shrew*; composed and conducted a score for a navy film; and prepared six shows for the Texas summer.

The first of the show albums was *Conversation Piece*, by and with Noël Coward and with Lily Pons. Coward was at all times easy to work with, amenable, and warm. We had our first meeting in his apartment at the Plaza one morning at eleven. When I arrived he asked, "What would you like to drink?" The idea appealed to me enormously because I was very tired, but I answered, "At this hour of the morning?" Coward said, "That is the rudest acceptance I have ever had. Now, what do you want?"

We began our recordings a few days later in Columbia's best studio on East Thirtieth Street. There was only an hour and a half between the morning and afternoon sessions for lunch. By the time I had taken off wet clothes and dressed in dry ones, an important part of the time had passed. Goddard, who also had not yet known Noël well, had ordered a limousine and invited me to go with them to lunch at the Plaza. While I wanted to be with them almost desperately, I knew there was not enough time: I was holding them up now and I must recommence on schedule with the orchestra (expensive not to) even if they had not returned.

Noël asked if there were not some eating place close by. I replied that at the corner there was a bar that smelled of stale beer and always had pigs' knuckles, sauerkraut, and boiled potatoes for lunch. (I think Goddard was shocked at the mere suggestion.) However, Noël suddenly waxed enthusiastic and could not see why we should not lunch in such a marvellous place. We did.

With Noël Coward (*right*) at a Columbia Records session in 1951, when we were making *Conversation Piece*, which starred Noël and Lily Pons. *Photo by Fred Plaut*

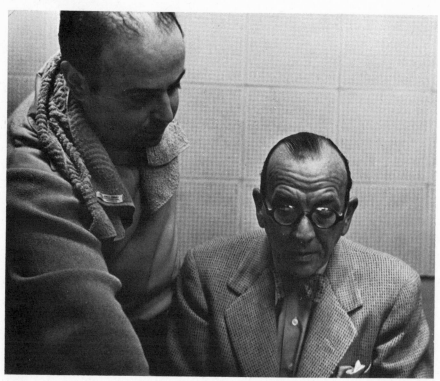

Lily Pons's husband, Andre Kostelanetz, went over the score with me days earlier because he could help by coaching his wife. We spent a long time getting a proper "take" of "I'll Follow My Secret Heart," and we were just finishing a satisfactory one when Miss Pons's alarm wristwatch went off, spoiling the take (this was before tapes were used)! She laughed like a canary. The next two recorded shows were Gershwin's *Girl Crazy* and Rodgers and Hart's *Babes in Arms*, both with Mary Martin.

Goddard and I made the most nearly complete recording of *Porgy and Bess* in existence: three LP's. I used many of the recitatives, cut as little as possible (mostly repetitions), and rehearsed principals and chorus three weeks prior to recording, which was completed in eight exhausting days. Much of what we did was not even included in the original production. I was also able to restore the original Gershwin orchestrations, and after pursuing many of the people who had participated in the premiere, we found out many directions Gershwin had given.

Two choral albums followed and then Dallas again.

In my third summer we moved indoors, into the newly air-conditioned auditorium. The great success of the season, for obvious reasons, was *Texas, Li'l Darlin'*, with Jack Carson. Dorothy Kirsten sang and looked beautiful in *The Merry Widow*.

For a long time I have been accustomed to having a drink of something alcoholic at theater intermissions. I find it relaxes me. I have never made a secret of it—my doctor approves. In Dallas, beginning with my second season, Charlie Meeker provided me with a refrigerator in my office, which he, in his usual opulent friendliness, stocked amply. Also, I always have a large thermos of ice water in the pit, which I resort to during performances.

Once, during the summer, Charlie made a hurricane tour of several other summer musical theaters. My Dallas job was the envy of musical directors in other theaters because my salary was better, and with a different schedule (a new show only every other week instead of every week), the Dallas job was a "plum." In one city on his tour, Charlie was invited to a supper party given in his honor by the musical director.

"Is it true, Mr. Meeker, that you allow Lehman Engel to drink gin in the pit?" queried the musical-director host.

"Of course, and we supply the gin. It's in his contract," replied Charlie.

In July of that summer I flew to New York to conduct a single concert at Lewisohn Stadium. Mrs. Guggenheimer ("Minnie," to her audiences) engaged me for a Gilbert and Sullivan evening because of my Broadway success with these gentlemen. The papers reported ten thousand people in the audience, but the concert from my point of view was not a success. It is too difficult to rehearse and routine twenty small pieces in two and a half hours on the morning of the concert. Stopping and starting is too time-consuming. The Ninth Symphony would be simpler.

During my last few days in Dallas, when I was at the end of my tether, I met one of the ensemble dancers, a tall, gawky Italian-American named Alberto Fiorella. After an entire summer of rehearsing, performing, and the ever-present heat, I needed laughter, and that's what Alberto supplied. He had been there all along, and we never happened to say hello. It was so near the end of the summer and in only a few days—just after the opening of the final show—I was to leave. But I had again made a friend for life.

After Dallas and ten days in Bermuda, I wrote and recorded incidental music for Peggy Webster's production of *Saint Joan*, starring Uta Hagen. I recall admiring Uta's performance. After the Boston opening, Peggy sent for me to make some musical adjustments. I arrived at the start of a matinee and stood in the back of the auditorium, where, to my amazed disappointment, I observed Uta give a terrible performance. Afterward, when I had to go backstage, as I passed her dressing room (the door was open), she called out, "Lehman! Please come in. I want you to meet my parents." The performance was then clearly understandable.

Next was *A Month of Sundays*, with music by Albert Selden, staged by Burt Shevelove, with Gene Lockhart and Nancy Walker. Just as it went into rehearsal I went to Jackson to conduct a concert of the Jackson Symphony Orchestra, chiefly because I would then be able to see my father, who was suffering with cancer. The auditorium was sold out. When I burst on stage, there was a long ovation. I recognized many of my old schoolteachers and friends I had not seen since my earliest days. In the orchestra, too, there were old music teachers, sitting side by side with college boys and girls.

When *A Month of Sundays* was rehearsing for opening in New Haven, I was up to my neck in small changes. Every hour the musicians were given their ten-minute intermission, but I was too busy fixing things in the score to go out myself. I was unaware that because of a plumbing mishap, there was no water. Intermission followed intermission, and I continued standing on my podium writing. During one of these, a stagehand whom I had never seen before and possibly never saw again, thrust a cold bottle of beer in my hand! I was too stunned to speak and very likely never even thanked him.

While *A Month of Sundays* was in Boston, by prior arrangement I flew to conduct the Dallas Symphony. I was nervous because this was a straight symphonic program, and my debut in that field. It was something I had always wanted to do, but having become typecast, I had had no such offer. When the manager of the orchestra called to engage me, he offered me four hundred dollars, out of which I had to pay travel and hotel expenses. As I was going to lose as much by being absent from *A Month of Sundays*, I could not afford to go and declined reluctantly. A few minutes after our conversation, the manager called again to say that José Iturbi and Bruno Walter were guest conductors for the two weeks preceding my proffered time, and they were coming for four hundred dollars, but what would my lowest fee be? After a moment's thought I replied, "One thousand dollars," to which he instantly agreed.

Not many months before this business with the symphony, George Dale, whom I had long known at Columbia Records and who lived within a few blocks of me, asked me to cocktails at his apartment. He had two roommates, Richard Foorman of San Francisco, then eager to become a part of the theater, and a young acting student from Mississippi, Wyatt Cooper. The three of us became quite good friends. We had much in common, and Wyatt and I especially had our native state, ways of talking, food, and general understanding.

Some weeks later I was in Dallas, where I enjoyed the luxury of five days of rehearsals prior to my concerts. So that I would not be alone, Wyatt did me a great favor by coming with me. On a Sunday afternoon I was sitting in my dressing room with him, nervous, an hour before the first concert. The manager came to visit me, and I asked what kind of audience he expected. He replied that Bruno Walter the previous Sunday had had half a house, so what did I expect? I was deeply depressed, especially since I was being paid two and a half times the sum he said he had paid Walter. I became increasingly agitated.

A moment before I was to make an entrance, the manager came running backstage and asked excitedly if I believed I would have a poor audience. Of course, I had; I had asked him, and he had informed me. Still panting from his sprint backstage, he laughed, reminding me that I had a "Dallas audience," that the house and standing room were sold out. A moment later I went on stage, where I received a standing ovation, but I was so unnerved that I could not recall what the program should begin with!

A Month of Sundays underwent drastic, but useless, surgery. It closed at the end of two Philadelphia weeks. This was my third experience in as many years with as many shows in Philadelphia.

Although I had no regular job, I continued to be busy. I was the behind-the-scenes director of my edition of *The Beggar's Opera*, produced by television's Columbia Workshop by Norris Houghton. On the same Sunday the New Friends of Music asked me to conduct in Town Hall a performance of Handel's opera *Il Pastor Fido*, which had never before been performed in America. I was allowed a budget that I had to distribute among five solo singers and members of the orchestra, and I broke exactly even. One hour after the *Beggar's Opera* performance went off the air, I stepped on the stage at Town Hall with Handel and accidentally unzipped trousers. Everyone received critical praise except Handel. That was my eighteenth-century Sunday.

Next day I recorded the Handel opera, then flew to Puerto Rico for a long-overdue vacation of two weeks. Returning, I embarked upon another large stint of record-making, which might also be record-breaking, for in two months I conducted nine albums: Rodgers and Hart's *On Your Toes*, the Handel opera, a set of Civil War songs for chorus, Jerome Kern's *Roberta*, an album of songs with the Negro baritone William Warfield, *Merry Widow* and *Student Prince* with Dorothy Kirsten and Robert Rounseville, and finally, *Oklahoma!* and *Desert Song* with Nelson Eddy, Virginia Haskins, and Doretta Morrow.

Nelson Eddy was a new experience. After greeting me warmly, he took me to a deserted corner of the large studio to say, "The one thing I want you to know is that you shouldn't follow me. Singers are pretty stupid, and you must conduct the music the way you feel it, and let me follow you." This I took with an entire barrel of salt. During the first song I watched and accompanied him. When the "take" was finished, we listened to the "playback," which was horrendous. Eddy sat quietly, and afterward he asked, "Do you like that?" I said it was too slow and that it got slower as it went on. He replied, "Now perhaps you'll believe me. Please don't follow me. Just conduct and I'll follow you." This is the way it was during all of the next days.

Immediately following this recording spree I went to Dallas for the fourth time. Once during that summer I flew up to New York to conduct a score I had written for an elaborate television show directed by Worthington Miner, starring his wife, Frances Fuller.

In the fall I began working for the third time with Sam Chartok on Gilbert and Sullivan. This time, Chartok had engaged Martyn Green and Ella Halman of the D'Oyly Carte Company, and I believed the project might succeed. However, in two weeks we tossed onto the stage in New Haven, preceded by disorganized dress rehearsals, *The Mikado* and *Pirates of Penzance*. By then we had only begun to study the remaining three operettas. As far as the staging was concerned nothing had been done. We moved on to Boston, and under the most difficult (money-saving) circumstances we played our first two bills, dress-rehearsed *Trial by Jury* with *Pinafore* and began studying *Iolanthe* musically. No performer was able to go through his dialogue without terrifying omissions. Music was sung with appalling inaccuracies. Costumes were decades old and ill-fitting with ill-fitting wigs. No rehearsal schedules were ever adhered to, and within the three weeks prior to the Boston opening we had only rehearsed thirteen days (from scratch) and only previously performed two out of the four bills. Yet Elliott Norton, dean of Boston critics, gave us rave reviews!

In New York we drew notices that were not bad but certainly not

Taking a bow at the Shubert Theatre in Boston in 1957. *Photo by Will Rapport*

good. Martyn Green received personal accolades, and my own notices were so unusually good that my name was hurriedly put up in lights on the marquee. If *that* was intended to stimulate business, it failed.

We went on to Philadelphia, where the signs in front of the Shubert Theatre (again Chartok's budget) looked as though I had written them in longhand. Business was terrible. I opened the week's stand in Baltimore, then flew to Bermuda for a week's rest, as I was not only exhausted but had many other projects racing ahead for me. In Bermuda there was nothing but rain, so I not unnaturally passed the time composing a score for an underwater documentary film about Honduras.

I had promised to conduct the Washington opening of Gilbert and Sullivan, and I took off from Bermuda by plane in plenty of time. A short way out, we encountered engine trouble and had to turn back. There was no other plane, and so I arrived in Washington the day after the opening (of *The Mikado*), which was a disaster. The critics made sport of my nonappearance as though I somehow equated conducting in Washington with slumming.

I had to do the second-night performance of *Trial by Jury* with *Pinafore* and without an orchestra rehearsal. And imagine my shock when the curtain went up and I discovered a chorus of almost fifty percent new faces. There had been discontent, many people had resigned, and new singers in many cases had had only one day's rehearsal on stage. (Jeanette Scovotti of the Metropolitan Opera and the Hamburg State Opera was in the chorus.) The seeds of disintegration were blossoming rapidly. In spite of this, I received great personal notices and the only favorable ones during the company's two weeks' Washington stand. I did not continue on to Chicago, where the project collapsed.

Back in New York, I began a series of successes and more than a year's employment with *Wonderful Town*. Robert Fryer, the producer (with Lawrence Carr), engaged Jerome Chodorov and Joseph Fields, old friends of mine, to adapt their play *My Sister Eileen* as a musical. George Abbott, the veteran stage director, was to preside. At the brink of rehearsals Mr. Abbott decided against the composer and lyricist on the grounds that what they had created was not for the theater. With the approval of the other powers, he called in Leonard Bernstein (music) and Betty Comden and Adolph Green (lyrics).

Although I already had a contract to conduct, I felt that I ought not (probably insincerely) bind Lenny to accepting me. I did feel that he would want me. I telephoned him and said rather tentatively that I did not want him to feel bound by my contract. At first he assured me that he was delighted but went on to add, well, did I understand anything about the music of the thirties? This did it. I not only felt that I did but that (a) Lenny would compose (how could he help it?) Lenny's own music with perhaps a flavor of the thirties, and (b) it would be a show and why not me? I was suddenly positive. Lenny demurred. I stood where my contract allowed me to stand.

When I first heard the opening number I said that it would not work, because it was complicated, argumentative, and too "special" for so simple a comedy as *Wonderful Town*.* Mr. Abbott violently disagreed, and the number required most of the total rehearsal time allotted the singers, further complicated by daily lyric changes.

---

* I have long since concluded that opening numbers of musical shows should be written *last* since it is only after a show has been completed that the writers can tell what is most essential for the start.

There was an excellent and complex jazz piece that Lenny had composed earlier that was to serve as a ballet for the opening of Act Two. Its libretto was set in a jail, and it dealt with dope addicts and prostitutes. This I also felt was wrong for a second-act opening to so light a play. Again Mr. Abbott firmly disagreed. The dancers spent three-quarters of all their rehearsal time with choreographer Donald Saddler learning it, and hours of orchestra rehearsals (one conducted by Lenny himself) also were given over to its complexities.

After the very first performance in New Haven, two important things happened: the second-act ballet was dropped and Rosalind Russell had such a violent case of laryngitis that she was unable to appear during the rest of the week.

By Boston, it was obvious that the first act was failing to get its quota of laughs and the complex angry opening number was eyed suspiciously. Roz felt so strongly about the opening that she delivered an ultimatum: either it or she would go.

For a few seemingly interminable days we seemed to be treading water trying to determine some course of action. Although we worked daily, we knew that what we rehearsed was no answer to what was needed. I recall Mr. Abbott in the lounge of our Boston theater, practicing the vignettes in Act One that already worked well. Joe Fields, the coauthor, was pacing behind him chain-smoking and becoming increasingly impatient. Periodically, Mr. Abbott would chuckle at him and change something inconsequential. At these times, he would turn to Joe, smile, and ask his agreement.

In these farcical vignettes, one line recurred many times: "It would be the clean fine thing to do."

Feeling that Mr. Abbott was wasting time, Joe, when asked for his agreement again, replied in disgust: "Why don't you go take a clean fine shit for yourself, George. It would be the clean fine thing to do."

And he left.

In the meanwhile the all-talented Jerome Robbins had been called in to help both Mr. Abbott and Donald Saddler. Lenny, Betty, Adolph, and Jerry put their talented collective heads together, came up with a great opening number, "Christopher Street," and after its introduction into the show in Philadelphia the entire act glowed.

Although everything about *Wonderful Town* was brilliant, a large measure of its success was owing to George Abbott, with whom I had never previously worked. He was even then an old man, tall, erect, distinguished looking. He always wore a necktie and never removed his jacket at rehearsal. What he said was absolute and positive. (Nobody ever called him "George," not because he himself ever required it, but his manner, pleasant as it was, always seemed to forbid it.) At meals, the food he ate seemed simple to the point of austerity. He drank when someone else was the host. His sense of timing, speed, and scene-to-scene continuity never allowed the audience time to ponder any element of the show. It was a smash.

Roz was fun. She worked harder and for longer hours than anyone else. After theater she was a bundle of jokes. Because she was tall, had an unusually long neck, and was no longer thirty, she seemed to suffer (unnecessarily, I thought, and in silence) because of the length of her neck. This was not as evident as she apparently thought, judging by the efforts she made to conceal it. There were always multitudinous strands of beads, high collars, and so on.

Meanwhile, my father was slowly, laboriously, and painfully dying. Everything was done to keep him hopelessly alive; his suffering was increasing and absorbing my mother's life. I made as many trips to Jackson as I could. My father, especially with the passing of time, had grown very dear to me. After a frontal lobotomy, which was intended only (so far as I knew) to relieve the suffering, he became a vegetable. He never again addressed my mother, who was in constant attendance. When I would arrive at the hospital on one of my visits, he always looked up out of his private world and uttered a feeble, "Hello, Brother." Then he was gone again to pick at a pajama button or to stare uncomprehendingly at a newspaper, his lips moving silently in the shape of the words, his mind still.

One day during *Wonderful Town* my mother telephoned. I should come home. I was met at the Jackson airport at nearly midnight by my mother, my cousins, and my aunts. My father was asleep. There was no point in our going to the hospital. We talked together for several hours and finally my cousins left us and we too slept. It was late.

At six in the morning I awakened suddenly and sat upright in bed.

It was a startled awakening. I sat wide-eyed. In a minute or two the telephone rang. The nurse said we should come. When we arrived, it was to find what I had already known.

As *Wonderful Town* ran on, Bobby Griffith and Hal Prince, the stage managers, were planning their producing debut in association with Frederick Brisson, Roz's husband, with *The Pajama Game*. This had a score by Richard Adler, my old friend Clarence's son, with Jerry Ross, and was to be directed by George Abbott. Bobby and Hal asked me to conduct.

I read the script and became extremely jittery at the thought of leaving a hit for anything as flimsy as this: there was no second act at all. I declined. Again I had done it, for *Pajama Game* was a big hit. Hal Hastings, who conducted it, went along with Griffith and Prince to *Damn Yankees, New Girl in Town, Fiorello, Tenderloin, Cabaret*, and *Zorba*. No one was more surprised by *Pajama Game*'s reception than I. When I finally saw it, it still had no book, a usual cause for failure. It certainly had no second act. But Abbott moved it so swiftly that it bothered nobody. Mister George Abbott rode again!

A month before *Wonderful Town* took off for its tour, a short two-character opera I composed called *Malady of Love*—"a sham in one act"—was performed at the Columbia University Centennial Festival. Lewis Allan wrote a libretto that made singing in English as free of problems as in any other language. (The helpful pianist was John Kander, later the composer of *Cabaret; Flora, the Red Menace; The Happy Time*; and *Zorba*.) Critical reception was largely favorable, though I am constantly struck by the confusion that a "light" piece (this was a mere bonbon) creates in the minds of many reviewers. It is as though the light character of the work has some deprecating effect upon its artistic seriousness.

I scored a documentary film and recorded *The Boys from Syracuse* and *Bitter Sweet* (never released) for Columbia and six abbreviated show albums for Victor. Then I helped to replace and rehearse the largely new *Wonderful Town* cast (starring Carol Channing) for its tour, which I opened in Chicago.

During perhaps five years when I was very tired, I went to Varedero Beach, Cuba, in the straits of Florida, one of the most unspoilt and quiet places I have ever known. With its long white beach and gentle, clear blue water, continuous sunshine, and nontouristy hotels, it became my personal place of refuge.

I always stayed at a small unpretentious hotel, Dos Mares, opposite the beach and was regarded by the personnel as a member of the family. Often I took writing or composing along with me so that I could rest and not become bored. Between sundown and dinner I was to be found at the tiny bar opposite the dining room. Often a trio of musicians passed by, stood in the barroom, and sang Cuban songs. The trio consisted of men—all singers—the outer two playing guitars and the center one with claves or maracas.

One evening a song they sang reminded me of "Mack the Knife," and I was just mellow and foolish enough to teach them the Weill song. Although I could remember none of the lyrics, I succeeded in setting the melody and the harmonies, and it would be hard to say who was the prouder of this achievement, the men or I. Afterward, nightly, the trio returned and always included "my" song.

Perhaps six months later, I came back on another visit to Varedero. Getting out of the car that brought me from the little airport, I called, "Humberto!" (the general factotum of the hotel and nephew of its enormously fat owner). Instantly all eight employees came running to the porch. They shook my hands warmly and then assumed a ceremonious air. One of them approached their newest gadget unsuitably set on the front porch: an elaborate multicolored juke box. He deposited a nickel. There was a musical introduction, then a voice unmistakably singing "Mack the Knife" in English!

The assemblage eyed me as they might have regarded God, and it suddenly occurred to me that they thought *I* had composed this song. I protested with a wave of the index finger, metronome style (my most nearly perfect Spanish expression), but this did no good. They chuckled smugly, and I was never able to dissuade them: I *was* the composer of what was by this time their favorite song.

On my return from Varedero I usually spent a night and day in Havana. On one of these trips I went as usual to an excellent restaurant named La Florida, referred to by habitués as "Floridita." The daiquiri was invented there.

At Floridita, I left my name with the maitre d'hotel for a table, then returned to the crowded bar area, and sat at a tiny, remote bar table. As I waited, I began listening to some very gay, boisterous music coming from one end of the bar. Two Cubans were playing guitars, and between them, laughing and singing, was the familiar face of Ernest Hemingway.

The songs were infectious. The mood of the place was high. As I drank on alone, I became aware that Hemingway seemed to be smiling at and singing to me. I returned the smile, which I was probably already wearing.

Finally, after four or five songs, Hemingway—red-cheeked and happily drunk—came through the labyrinth of tables and approached me. I arose, and we shook hands. He remarked that he was glad to see me again, whereupon I assured him that if we ever *had* met, I would have been the first not to have forgotten it.

Hemingway was in no way put off but embraced me cheerily: "You have the happiest smile I've ever seen. Adios, amigo."

And he returned to the bar.

15: All for Nothing

For a long time the jobs ground on. I did them the best way I knew how, but nothing ever led to anything else and every contract was a separate entity that expired with conclusion of that project. Except for the reputation that I accumulated they led specifically nowhere. No obligation to anyone the week after closing. No future guarantee. No more if it was a hit (longer, but not more). Sudden full stop if it was a failure. All in the nature of things. If the show reaches New York and has a run, the schedule is ostensibly set: eight performances a week. But don't count on it. One's free time is subject to change without notice.

There are of course no free weekends because of two Saturday performances and a Monday evening one. The times I tried going away at midnight on Saturday discouraged me from even entertaining the idea any longer.

Holidays? Of course not. Since the management can raise the price of tickets for "special" holiday matinees, we have these on every conceivable one, usually in lieu of the Wednesday matinee.

Illness? Not if you can help it. First of all, it is "unprofessional" to miss a performance for anything as human as an illness. (A television appearance is different. One is in demand.) Also I was not paid for any performance I did not conduct.

Salary? Not to be computed annually in advance. The show may not last three months or two weeks or might not even open on Broadway.

It seems likely that everybody who has ever had any success has had to endure—again and again—two wasteful things. The first and the lesser has to do with money. It is assumed by too many people that as soon as your name appears in print you are in the chips. Strangers write letters asking for money for just anything. Julie Garfield told me about a man who came to his dressing room claiming that they had gone to grade school together and now his wife needed an operation. Couldn't "Johnny" (the name that only *strangers* to Julie called him) lend him two thousand dollars?

I have had "touches" outside stage doors by former (but actual) friends—now alcoholics. I acquiesced once or twice and then realized that I had unintentionally put someone on my payroll, and rather painfully, I had to stop it. Others have claimed kinship with people in my hometown I had never heard of, and they have asked me to cash checks at 11:15 P.M. for two or three hundred dollars: their mothers were dying, they had to catch a plane, and so on.

On one occasion I went across the street to Sardi's and called Aunt Flo in Jackson to ask about one such young man. She said he existed only by passing worthless checks and that she had seen his mother that very day in the supermarket.

These money tales are endless, and no one who has ever worked in the theater has been spared the embarrassment. Also I have been "stuck," but I hope my olfactory nerves have developed sufficiently since those days.

Another kind of waste results from the well-intentioned approach of someone who may be somewhat known to you. What this person does can happen only in relation to theater since theater employment is noncontinuous. The theater person does not exist who is not hopeful of doing something he is not presently doing, or something following what he is now engaged in, or something else tempting either artistically or financially.

One published proof of this is the list of projects announced for next season. Just compare that list at the season's end with what actually materialized and you will be amazed or aghast.

These announcements do not necessarily hurt anybody except unemployed actors, who may rush to be auditioned. But it is even more outrageous when the producer or author comes to you with a "sure thing" and takes lots of your time going over budgets, your ideas, your schedule, which *has* to be altered, and so on. Then, after countless meetings and discussions, the project evaporates.

A well-known composer hired me to conduct three of his shows. Three. I was asked to be present innumerable times as "window dressing" for money-raising auditions. I went over the scores with the composer. None of these shows was ever produced. So it goes.

And then there was my version of *The Beggar's Opera*, which I had hopes of producing and directing, but World War II suddenly erupted and my time was chalked up to loss. And *Mooncalf*, a musical with libretto by Alexander King, which I was paid two thousand dollars to compose. After dozens of not-quite-successful backers' auditions, rewrites by Lewis Allan and Joanna Roos, and a tryout in Cleveland, nothing ever did, or will, come of it. And *Serena*, a musical based on S. N. Behrman's readaptation of his play *Serena Blandish*, which Leonard Sillman wanted to produce. I was paid several "advances" according to contract (fifteen hundred dollars in all, I believe) as stage director because Behrman wanted me to do it. I was enthusiastic. I spent a great deal of time adapting the original play so that Sam would have a "dummy" to make his work easier. I worked with the composer and lyricist. All of us talked a lot. Then there were difficulties between author and producer and again—finis.

Chartok worked years on a plan for making movies of all the Gilbert and Sullivan operettas. I worked with him on budgets, timing, and casting ideas. I went to union meetings with Chartok and Morris Stonzek (my orchestra contractor) to ask for concessions based on the educational, noncommercial aspects of the project. This went on for five or six years. Chartok was always just about to line up the last million. Over and over again it was in the bag. Once he called to tell me that it was all signed. I telegraphed congratulations. Nothing.

There have been recording budgets and meetings, but the projects failed to happen. A star lost interest or the budget was too high or the schedule of future releases was too crowded.

I conducted a test broadcast with Lucille Ball for a series based on *My Sister Eileen*. I wrote the music. Nothing.

I did the same for a projected series with Gertrude Lawrence. I remember this one vividly because I had a ghastly cold and Gertie forced me to use *her* dressing room at intermission so that I could rest. That was the prime result of this undertaking.

I taped a television pilot with Pinza for an NBC series that was never sold.

I was urged by three reputable theater people to produce a musical show myself. After lengthy searches involving the reading of dozens of plays and novels, I found one, *The Spirit of the Chase*, which I thought had possibilities. I got John Roberts and Larry Kasha, two stalwart partners, to help. We bought options and submitted the book to every well-known author we knew for adaptation. One by one, they turned it down. (Our time and money were running out.)

Finally, we made an arrangement with Ronald Alexander to do an adaptation, and we found in a small Village nightclub a talented young man named Jerry Herman, who sang and played his own lyrics and music and who was delighted to undertake the score. Every director turned down the adaptation, and every director loved the score and lyrics. There were no other available and likely adaptors we could find, and with the money and the time lost, this too was abandoned.

These are only a very few of the very many long, involved, time-consuming, frustrating tales that are not to be listed in my précis. Similar ones happened and continue to happen in one form or another to everyone—the unsuccessful as well as the successful. I feel that they are unavoidable in the main and are an integral part of "free-lancing." They have no public cast of characters, no curtain up or down, no salary, and no holiday.

All in a day's work? For us, yes.

I was nearly always employed on numerous simultaneous projects, which, when I was lucky, created simultaneous incomes. Composing and writing started with breakfast and continued on between phone calls; meetings outlining future projects were the catsup over lunch and dinner; recordings dotted the afternoons; preparations went on in all the hours preceding performances. More meetings, and occasionally, meetings with friends, bridged the gap between nightly performances and bed. (There were always Joe and Mildred, Harold and Florence, Gerry, Chuck, Alberto, Sally Ann, and many more.)

Somewhere along the line the need for a secretary evolved—a few hours a few days a week at first, then for whole days, then every day and weekends and many evenings, and finally incessantly.

All of this, of course, costs money, and I could just afford it. In the end I had nothing left. And so it was essential, as always, to remain busy.

The saturation point of being busy that Robert Bishop—my secretary, factotum, and friend—and I reached long ago is, however, not by any means because of the work I do. The unbroken chain of activity in my life (and in the lives of most other people like me) is forged by just everybody and anybody else who wants just any little old thing of me ("Brother, it won't take but a minute"). These "little things" began compelling me a great many years ago. After all, was I not taught that it was rude to say no to anyone and that anyone's wishes were a command to a polite "little man"?

At first the requests were from friends. These were never outrageous. As I became more prominent, they came from anyone, sometimes one-time acquaintances, often friends or acquaintances of my family or friends of friends. Sometimes they came from strangers who had merely read my name in a newspaper. The requests fall into only a few oft-repeated categories: interviews or auditions for opinions, advice, jobs, recommendations, and such; social appointments; public services; but most of all, requests for theater tickets. Each of these—even just the requests—consume several hours and interrupt and finally shatter all attempts at continued concentration.

The social invitations have very little in common with one's personal life. The latter is private, quiet, and generally *a piacere*. Invitations from friends are as acceptable as time permits. Since I am publicly busy, invitations from acquaintances are usually not too difficult to dispose of, except when a telephone-call follow-up says, "We want you to come to dinner. We are free any night at all. We know you have to dine at six and that you are on a diet. When can you come and what can you eat?" (I never can frame an adequate refusal for this.) It is followed with a promise of quiet adherence to the prescribed diet (simple, unseasoned, high proteins) and punctuality.

When I have been put in the awkward position of accepting such invitations, I have almost invariably found that I have to expend extra time traveling far out of my way; that I am the "glamorous" guest at a gathering of some six to twelve people at a dinner party at which I am obliged to "perform" (personality stories about stars are acceptable); that dinner is announced at 7:15 because of the stylishly late arrival of other guests (I must leave at 7:30); and that the part of the dinner I have time to sample is calorically "fancy" and in disregard of my diet.

I arrive finally at my work harassed, overliquified, and either underfed or overcalorized. In any case, I am irritated with myself for having walked into a trap.

From my earliest days I can remember only too vividly what it was like when we were to have "company to supper" (in Mississippi, but called "dinner" nearly everywhere else). We were to eat in the dining room rather than in the more familiar breakfast room. The best linens were dug out of drawers, the best silver was polished until the monograms engraved at the time of my parents' marriage had become almost invisible, crystal was carefully lifted down from the pantry shelves and washed again, and I was given a list of do's and don't's. Altogether the evening was to be a time of discomfort and boredom.

Times have not changed. I have lived now in quite a different world, in which the linen, silver, and crystal are in everyday use. Nobody except myself fills me with big or little terrors. But dinner parties are still for me the "terror of the pampas," and I avoid large ones whenever I possibly can.

In my own apartment, where I have Kitty Spence, an excellent cook from Jamaica (Anna died some years ago), I like to tell the friends I invite to dinner that I would like them to come about 6:30 for cocktails and that we will dine at 7:00 and that I think an hour and a half with friends is enough at one time and that I hope they will leave early so that I can read, write, or sleep. They nearly always do and do not appear to feel offended.

I enjoy Florence Rome's parties the most. The menu (she calls it "delicatessen") is nearly always buffet and consists of smoked white-fish; smoked salmon; hot knackwurst; hot baked beans; a platter of cold cuts; pickles, a salad bowl; an assortment of cheeses, pastry, and fruit; and wine, beer, and coffee. The guests sit where, and with whom, they wish. Dinner is nearly always early, and the guests are usually people with interests in common. There are no formalities. Conversation afterward is usually carried on in groups of two, three, or four. Anyone is free to leave when he wishes without making any excuse.

Roz Russell once told me that when she planned an important formal dinner party, she had the extra servants come to her house the night before. The cook prepared the menu she had ordered for the party and all waiters performed their duties as though all of the prospective guests were present; so, although Roz dined alone, she gave herself the opportunity of approving the food and the service in advance!

But it is my feeling that sit-down dinner parties in houses where one is invited two or three times a year and at which the twenty or so guests are heterogeneous are a carry-over from a barbarous custom that probably flowered in the eighteenth century. Travel over distances—especially by carriage—was time-consuming, and when guests went to the trouble of attending, they had nothing else to do but go home, and they expected, and in the best homes got, an evening's entertainment. The Esterhazys of Vienna, for example, engaged Haydn to provide the after-dinner music.

The average dinner party today is given for the pleasure of the host (who can afford it) or in an effort to repay past favors or to stimulate social or business contacts. Sometimes it is given in order to see lots of people at once and have done with it. Sometimes there is a chef d'oeuvre in the person of a celebrity, the aftereffects of which—within that particular social circle—would dwarf the most celebrated doings of Mount Etna.

What specifically am I objecting to? Well, now that I have asked I am prepared to answer.

First of all, there is the intentional erroneousness of the time when festivities are to begin. The hostess says on the telephone in a practiced cadenza, "Oh, come about eight." It takes quite a number of years to admit to yourself that such a lovely lady is a barefaced liar! And so I come at 8:00, or at 8:05 at the latest, being afraid that she is sincere. But no! The host and hostess have not quite finished dressing. You feel guilty. You are alone in a large drawing room, but not quite alone because a maid is eyeing you with suspicion. She approaches you with half-concealed contempt and asks you haughtily what you would like to drink.

After ten or fifteen minutes the hosts appear; the lady, diaphanously coy, is apologizing for their tardiness. Within half an hour a few others have gathered. As it is long past my usual dinner hour, I am getting drunk, so that when a waiter tries to race past me with a tray of hors d'oeuvres I make a dive for them; this has the effect of making him stop lest he drop the entire tray.

By 9:00 people are pouring in, in couples, and by 9:30 the hostess whispers orders to a servant, which is tantamount to "Well, everybody's here, so let's go into dinner." The double doors to the dining room creak open, the candles lit, everybody saunters in as nonchalantly as if they actually lived there. Then there is a general reaching inside pockets and bags for eyeglasses because there are place cards, and everyone wanders about in an unchoreographed tangle to the giddy refrain, "Oh—here I am!"

The false hour and the overdrinking are the first two of my objections. Now comes the third. Oh, joy! Between whom are you sitting? Usually I look at their place cards for a clue. The lady on my right is simply remarkable for ninety, and she tells you apologetically that she forgot to put a new battery in her hearing aid but that she will be able to hear you anyhow if you will just speak up.

The lady on your left is really charming at seventy, but she keeps dropping her napkin, and after picking it up several times, you try to ignore it; but she nudges you, and you lunge down there for it again.

Both ladies talk to you simultaneously and both want to know what you do. If you tell them honestly, they become so profoundly interested that they regale you with the names of all the shows they have seen and how they hate so-and-so and love so-and-so and, oh, what a fascinating this and that.

I recall accompanying Helen Gahagan to a dinner party years ago when she was at the height of her (star) acting career. A lady gushed at her, "My dear, you're *so* lovely. You ought to go on the stage!"

Since the basic idea of dinner parties (next to the guest list) is the "party" aspect, the food will be wildly extravagant, too rich, too much, and too many hours in progress, what with "seconds" and the etiquette of clearing a single plate at a time. (These are my fourth and fifth objections.)

Afterward the ladies adjourn to go about some little ladylike mischief, leaving the men together; it then becomes necessary to enter into conversation with actually "new" people, most of whose names you do not know. Brandy and cigars may be heaven, but they do not really compensate for this sixth uncomfortable dilemma, which invariably includes listening to jokes you have always heard years before (and of course laughing on cue) and discussions of the stock market and politics that you would sooner throw up at than begin to argue about.

The ladies flutter into the drawing room, and you play musical chairs again. There is at least an hour to go before you can possibly excuse yourself. So you finally reach home, stuffed, with an headache due to the wild mixture of too many cocktails, a variety of wines in bottomless glasses, and cognac. You just thank God that it is over, and you go to bed. It is after 1:00 A.M., but you cannnot sleep. Two Alka Seltzers later and the clearing up of a variety of chores *may* get you to sleep by 3:00. And what was it all for, and whom did it please? Not me, certainly.

One of the most celebrated dinner-party-goers in history was Marcel Proust. Lucky man with his asthma and all, he had to stay enclosed in a room, and during the last years of his life, when Paris was cool and its air less filled with pollen, he went to his clubs and restaurants very late at night and dined alone with a waiter or a doorman who had really good tales to tell him about the night's parties: who was present, what they said, and so on. Proust ate when he arrived. He dined with one or two really *interesting* people, and left when he wished. That is precisely the way I like it.

The so-called public-service requests involve a kind of do-gooding that everyone, it is thought, will *want* to do, and at first, one feels rather flattered at being asked. Also, the causes are nearly always worthy ones.

Within a very brief time I accepted six simultaneous requests to serve on boards of worthy organizations. One had its meetings on Wednesday afternoons, when for years I conducted matinees. My name continued to be used (after all, the stationery was printed), but I never was able to attend a single meeting after the first.

A second group elected me its president. I presided at a meeting about every six weeks for two years, on Sunday afternoons—my day off—but otherwise, I was never able to do any work for the organization. I tried several times to resign. After two years, I insisted upon it, and when I had made it clear that I was irrevocably determined, there was only perfunctory objection. Sweet irreplaceable me.

The third group's board meets only twice annually. As a board, nothing ever is accomplished for its organization. Once only was I able to accomplish something on my own.

I lent my name to two other groups representing "good works" and send regretful telegrams when meetings are called. Although I was asked merely to lend my name in the beginning, I tried to resist, feeling that I could not be helpful. I acceded to the requests ultimately and am certain that I am cursed for continuous absence.

But the sporadic phone calls persist. "Can you come to a meeting on the twenty-fourth?" "Can you sell twenty tickets at fifty dollars each?" "Do you know how we can get a donation of a piano?"

Now—tickets!

I do not exaggerate when I calculate receiving seven hundred requests annually. The sources and the number of the requests, and the methods and manners of those making them, are nearly incredible to me and entirely unimaginable to anyone else.

I alternate in my theater contracts between being guaranteed a pair of "house seats" for each performance and declining to ask for such assurances. There is much to be said on both sides. Having them (one definite pair of choice seats reserved for each performance to be paid for at box-office prices) is like turning on a neon sign. Word gets about. A variety of cohorts call me for their use. This method, first off, insures my having them whenever *I* need them, but it necessitates fancy bookkeeping: For what nights have I issued them? Have I paid for them myself? if so, who owes me the money for them (current market value, thirty dollars per pair), and have they paid me? There is an awful lot of phone-answering in any case.

If I do not have house seats provided in my contract, I can occasionally say no to a request: I simply do not have any. But most people are not so easily discouraged, feeling that it is impossible that I lack contacts. Indeed, it is impossible, and I am truly, if silently, annoyed with myself for acquiescing, again nearly always unable to refuse.

The requests (telephone calls) usually begin stealthily with what is supposed to be a casual inquiring after my health and a sympathetic observation as to how I work too hard. (This sort of conversation is never thought to be an additional part of my doing "too much.") It is difficult to get the caller to come to the point. Finally, after much time-wasting, it emerges in all its hideous nakedness.

I then call the producer's office. The lines are busy. I continue to call. Eventually after a wasting of some ten to fifteen minutes, the phone rings through. The keeper of the ticket charts is out, but I can call back in two hours. As the requestee is awaiting my return call, I oblige, explaining that I cannot give any answer until I am able to reach the proper person. Then I must remember, in the face of work, to call the office at the proper time. Again, there is the period of busy lines, the final breakthrough, then the call again to the requestee, who is probably out. This sort of thing—the answer to what is thought of as a "simple favor"—involves nearly always and daily an identical routine. Finally, the seat order, a slip, arrives in my mail. I address and mail an envelope to the requestee, who calls then to thank me and to insist on dinner before the show or a drink afterward. Failing to set up either date, the "friend" will call up the day following the performance to thank me again or to offer unwanted praise or criticism. This is the usual, simple, garden-variety request involving from five to ten phone calls—every one of them disturbing, harassing, enervating interferences with work or rest.

The exceptions to the norm can assume fantastic shapes and proportions. There are the requests for tickets to shows *other* than the one I am conducting. This type invariably originates from people who are distinctly *not* friends (how could they be?), and they concern shows that are impossible to procure seats for except from dishonest brokers. Still I am *supposed* to obligate myself for them with producers or managers with whom I should only become involved if my problem is important personally to me.

More frequent exceptions involve the people for whom I succeed in procuring a seat order, who then call to change the date or ask for an additional *adjacent* pair (and at the last minute—usually when I am at dinner), or ask me to pay for the seats myself so that they will not have to come to the box office before performance time.

In this latter group, the subgroupings are legion. Let it be understood immediately that I always *do* pay when I am asked to. Then at performance time I am telephoned backstage to cancel the seats; the day before I am called to exchange them for another date; or I am not reimbursed, and embarrassed, I must try and try again to retrieve my investment of thirty dollars. Even more shocking, I get tickets for people who think the tickets are free, who either become embarrassed or belligerent (thinking that I am asking for money under false pretenses) or tell me that they cannot possibly afford such a price for tickets; I must take them back, leaving me with the guilty feeling that I *ought* to pay for them myself. And sometimes I have.

Perhaps the strangest single-ticket experience I ever had was related to a most innocent-seeming request. A chorus singer in the City Center revival of *Wonderful Town* (which I conducted briefly during the run of *Jamaica*) came to me at a rehearsal to ask me to exchange for a future date two *Jamaica* tickets that she had already bought. I told her that I would not mind doing it. I suggested that she let me know what date she wanted, after the close of *Wonderful Town*, and meanwhile, I took her tickets to return them to the *Jamaica* box office.

About a week later, as I was putting on a jacket I had worn at this latter rehearsal, I discovered the tickets still in my pocket. They were dated for the performance of the preceding evening. There was nothing I could do about them. When the girl called two weeks later, I simply bought her a pair of seats for $16.70.

So much for tickets.

I doubt that I have ever forgotten the helpful things many people did for me when I first ventured to New York. I remember them all so well that I cannot complain when new or unfortunate people come to see me by appointment with letters of introduction. Of course, there is some purpose in making the introduction (there was when I was the presenter), and the hope is that I will be able to make some contribution, provided that I really can and that in being able to, it will not become necessary for me to dedicate my life to the deed or the person.

There have been many people with such letters. I have been able to be useful to some of them, and just as often I have been impotent. My being able to be helpful somewhat depends upon the circumstances of the times and my own appraisal of the qualifications of the person.

I am afraid that I can never forget one letter that figures here. During the run of *Call Me Mister* when I felt free of the navy and I was flying with an authentic hit, Ginny Davis (Meyer Davis's daughter and a very old friend) called to enlist my interest in a recently arrived refugee from Europe. (German, I think.) He was a young (thirty-five or so) conductor without a job. He came to call on me and he possessed the usual social graces. He described his background and experience and asked me fervently to help him find a job as conductor. (He had a family, I think.)

It goes without saying that such jobs do not turn up by the gross, nor is it advisable to recommend someone whose work you have never seen. However, in good faith, I said I would do what I could.

Once or twice after that only meeting, he wrote me a note of reminder, to which I replied. One afternoon my telephone rang, and a man identified himself as a police sergeant: would I please oblige him by coming at once to such-and-such a station? Without knowing any reason for it I became frightened, and I tore out of my apartment into a taxi, arriving very shortly at the station.

The officer was expecting me, and thanked me for coming so quickly. As we strode inside, he held my arm especially tightly and apologized for asking me to identify someone. I was totally unprepared for the horror I was to encounter. The nearly unrecognizable mutilated face of a body lying on a bench was uncovered: Did I know this man?

The sergeant gave me physical support. I stammered that I thought it was—what was his name? The officer produced my last letter to the refugee conductor, and we read his name as I had addressed it. The police had sought me because my engraved return address was all that was recognizable on the man. He had leaped from a high floor of the Chanin Building.

The sergeant thrust a glass of whiskey in my hand and deposited me in a taxi. For weeks, I could not sleep in darkness: the glimpsed face reappeared then, like Jesus' face on Veronica's veil.

The phone still rings whether the call benefits me or merely wafts the continuing gentle voices of requests. One morning as I sat composing a score for Peggy for the Old Vic in London (*Measure for Measure*), I made a record of the telephone interruptions within the space of two hours. All of the callers were known to me: an author wanted information about making a contract with a producer; a composer wanted an appointment to play me his newest score; a lawyer wanted tickets for my current show; a vocal coach asked me to hear his pupil's popular version of *La Boheme*; a lady asked me which among a list of new operas she ought to buy tickets for; a television producer's office wanted to know what songs Edie Adams had sung in *Wonderful Town* four years ago; an orchestra contractor called to relay gossip about another conductor; a producer wanted information about a budget item in connection with a show he was contemplating; a conducting teacher asked me to advise two of his students; and a gentleman asked for a date convenient to me when he might call a meeting of an advisory board of which I am a member.

God biess Alexander Graham Bell.

16: The David Merrick Era

Fanny was David Merrick's first solo production, and it was to be the start of a prolific and unique career. It was my first connection with Merrick (through Harold Rome), and I was to work almost continuously for him in eight shows during many years.

We first met at the Plaza Hotel one morning for breakfast. He was slightly taller and slightly younger than myself, with sharp eyes and a small moustache. He seemed shy and spoke ingratiatingly, and I was charmed by him. We discussed business, and he was agreeable to everything. I said I would have MCA (Music Corporation of America) draw up the agreement.

A week later my MCA agent told me he had tried unsuccessfully to get Merrick on the telephone all week, and when he did finally reach him, Merrick had said, "Let's forget it." I called Josh Logan, the agent was called, and the contract was signed by Merrick.

I do not know why this happened, but it has become a pattern with new Merrick employees. In a different and more violent way, it happened to my orchestra contractor, Morris Stonzek, who was so upset that he did not want to accept the job. It is my opinion that David *intends* to upset people in order to show authority. It is *his* way.

David becomes disturbed by unexpected things. He rails. His eyes flash. He tells authors, directors, or choreographers extravagantly terrible things about their work—often out of proportion to its real faults. This is David's method of getting changes made, and he employs it effectively with nearly everyone.

He questions every usual procedure and frequently finds new, less expensive, and more effective ways of accomplishing things.

He leans heavily on exploitation and has proven often that by gambling upon it he can get a lengthy run out of a show—good or bad—that has drawn anything but favorable press notices.

He enjoys a high average for his taste in plays, directors, and players, and is active in every production. He does not fool himself about the true quality of his shows and often falls in love sincerely (and rightly) with some of his "ugly ducklings."

He is loyal to a staff of workers that he tries to keep with him continuously: stagehands, electricians, stage managers, and others.

I am fond of David Merrick, am sometimes embarrassed by him, often disapprove of his methods, but believe implicitly in his sincerity and his dedication to an ideal of theater. He makes mistakes, but he paints a broad, vigorous, courageous canvas. He operates bravely and holds to his convictions, and I truly believe his motivation is not money but achievement. He works at this twenty-five hours out of every day.

Having been engaged to conduct *Fanny*, I began hearing auditions of several thousand singers with Joshua Logan, Harold Rome, S. N. (Sam) Behrman, and David. These auditions were in many respects like all the others I had experienced, but they differed in one important respect: Joshua Logan.

Josh is tall, inclined to stoutness (already making a common bond with me), and usually wears a small white moustache. Nedda (Mrs. Logan) is also tall and a raving beauty. I remember her when I first came to New York as a glamorous actress, Nedda Harrigan, the daughter of Ned Harrigan (of Harrigan and Hart). She is no less lovely today.

I used to go in summer—for the day or for a party—to their lovely home near Stamford, Connecticut, where there were very special flowers. I remember the hanging baskets of highly cultivated begonias that had grown to look like roses and were unusual colors of orange and red and yellow. There were lovely daytime parties out of doors, and swimming.

Before we went into rehearsal for *Fanny*, the Logans, the Romes, Sam Behrman, and I were invited to a Sunday dinner at the country house of Fleur and Gardner Cowles, who were charming hosts. The only "outsider" was Irene Selznick, who when she saw me said, "Don't speak to me!" That had to have been somehow connected with *A Streetcar Named Desire*, which she had produced, but I cannot recall any reason for such hostility. Anyhow that's the way it was.

At dinner, Irene was seated next to Sam, who, at it turned out, was the reason for her being there. She never stopped talking to the poor man for a second. She wanted to enlist his aid in trying to get her son into Harvard. She made the point and pounded at it, although Sam had said at the outset that he would be happy to do whatever he could.

After dinner, we adjourned to a sitting room where there was a grand piano. Josh said that he would like to sing (he does not sing but then almost nobody who is interesting really *sings*) some songs from *Fanny* and that Harold Rome would accompany him.

Everyone showed quiet interest (and politeness), except Irene, who continued to talk to Sam. Several songs went by under this deplorable condition until Harold, I think it was, barked at her, and Irene rose—regally, though not embarrassed—and left.

Josh came to all of the chorus auditions for *Fanny*, unique for a stage director in my experience. It was usual for me to screen the two or three thousand auditionees and then present two or three times as many of the best ones as we needed at a final audition that was always attended by director, composer, choreographer, and such—all of whom express preferences.

But Josh was there always, and his behavior was amazing. He heard every person and spoke to each one—sometimes at length. He would lean over to me after one of his typical audible exhalations that seemed to indicate he was having a problem and say, "Don't you think she's fascinating?"

As a rule I did not, because I knew she could not sing as we needed her to. But Josh was sincerely taken in one way or another with them all, and as a result, we had interminable auditions. When I went about Broadway the next day—before final decisions—I discovered that *everybody* thought he himself surely would be hired for *Fanny*.

The rehearsals for *Fanny*, starring Walter Slezak and Ezio Pinza, were easy and pleasant. Josh was approachable at all times, and he and I worked together harmoniously.

Premieres of new shows anywhere, but particularly away from New York, provide many kinds of object lessons. At the opening performance of *Fanny*, "To My Wife," sung by Walter Slezak, got no applause, although throughout rehearsals (everyone take note and beware!) the cast had always been much affected by it. At the production meeting following the show, there was as always a general move toward cutting and discarding—both often essential when considered judiciously. "To My Wife" was to become a victim. It was my opinion that one verse and one chorus failed to expose the song strongly enough, so I begged for a reprieve: let the orchestra *play* a second chorus while Walter (Panisse) spoke a sentimental toast; then let Walter *sing* the final eight bars.

This was arranged and tried the very next night with the result that the song then worked, and so it remained in the show.

Once in Boston at the Shubert Theatre when we had come together just before 10:00 A.M.—the company milling about the stage and Josh and I happening to meet somewhere in the auditorium—I said that I had given a lot of thought to a short scene that he had been unhappy about. He had staged and restaged it and seemed a little frantic about what to do next. I ventured to say that I had an idea to present to him and to my horror, while I was in the middle of telling it to him, he walked away quickly, raised his voice to the stage, and announced, "Lehman has a good idea for this scene, and I'd like him to stage it!"

I could only think that I had offended him but this was not the case. He said he could see that the idea was a good one, and why shouldn't I do it myself?

Fanny was a success. After the opening performance in New York, the Cowleses had asked us to a party, at the Pierre, I think. I remember going for a while but leaving early enough to meet a group of old friends who also wanted to celebrate with me.

At the party, I was introduced to Ali Khan, and as we heard each other's names, we had identical reactions. Each stared hard at the other's face as we shook hands. Then we began to speak rapidly at the same time. It seems that each of us had had identical experiences over several years. For myself, many people wherever I went —on planes, in foreign countries, on the streets of New York— would stop to address me as Ali Khan and ask for my autograph. Initially, I protested, but as no one believed me I did the easiest thing: I would sign Ali Khan's name. This happened also to Ali Khan, except that the people who mistook him for me simply paused to greet him.

During the long time I stayed with *Fanny* and vice versa, I felt acutely the need to have someone drive me to my apartment after performances. I have always dressed at home in order to have freshly laundered and pressed clothes next day, and so, after performances, always wet with perspiration, I needed to return home quickly, especially in winter.

Taxis were hard to come by after the show break (especially after matinees), and when I finally succeeded in getting one, I would inquire as to the possibility of the driver's picking me up eight times a week. I promised an attractive tip. Each time I asked, the answer was the same: "Sure. I'll be there tomorrow night."

Tomorrow night never came.

One night I was luckier, and the driver said, "Well, I don't know, but I'll give it a try."

He did meet me the next night and during the next twenty years since then, Benedict Pollio has been an indispensable part of my life, without whom I could not do so many things. He takes me to airports and meets me when I return. Aside from the convenience this affords, I am also given the special feeling of being welcomed home, as though by a part of my family. He takes me wherever I am to go and does many errands I could not otherwise do. "Mister P," as I call him, is an indispensable part of my life pattern.

I wrote some music for Josh's play *The Wisteria Trees*, already alluded to, and we worked on Paddy Chayefsky's *Middle of the Night*, with Edward G. Robinson. I have always found Josh willing to listen to a score by a new composer (someone at work in my BMI

Workshop), and I think he has often been truly interested. He has never been impolite.

My memory next latches on to the opening in Philadelphia (prior to Broadway) of a musical that Josh directed. I was in Philadelphia at the same time with *I Can Get It for You Wholesale*, and my only free evening coincided with the opening of Josh's *All American*. My dear friend Eileen Herlie was the female star and Ray Bolger, by then a too-frequent performer, was the male star. Anticipation.

I hated the show and was embarrassed by the things Eileen was doing in it. Afterward I went backstage to see her and would have happily avoided Josh. Not at all—I ran smack into him! He cornered me with the force of opening-night anxiety to ask what I thought. The first meaningless thing that came to mind was that "it needed cutting." Knowing my passionate enthusiasm for anything I really liked or felt that I would eventually like, Josh grunted and left me without another word. Oh, dear. . . .

I saw Eileen, told her my reaction to her performance, and was not surprised by her full agreement.

I returned to the Warwick Hotel and slept uneasily, thinking of Josh and his worries and regretting his irritation with me. At eight the next morning my phone rang, and it was Josh. He was living in the penthouse of the same hotel. He was sure I had specific criticisms. Could he come down at once and have coffee with me?

In a matter of minutes he was at my door. He looked as if he had not slept, and I felt sorry for him. He alternated between pacing and sitting and made frequent notes. I made specific criticisms, and I think Josh was in agreement and grateful.

The rest of my relationship with Josh and Nedda has been purely social. Out of a mass of cocktail parties and dinners, I recall two special small dinner parties. One was touching, the other embarrassing.

The first occurred about a week after the death of Moss Hart, and it was given for his beautiful widow, Kitty (Carlisle). I think there were perhaps eight of us including the Bennett Cerfs; Gloria Vanderbilt and her then-husband, director Sidney Lumet; perhaps Arlene Francis and Martin Gabel; and others whose names time has erased. However, everyone had known Moss, and the party became a long series of humorous stories about him. Kitty laughed a great deal, and there were no tears. It was bright and sensitive of Josh and Nedda to have planned the evening that way.

The other dinner party occurred on a Sunday night and rather early because Bennett Cerf had to appear later on television on "What's My Line?" The guests, besides Bennett and his wife, included Mary Martin and her husband, Richard Halliday; Goddard Lieberson, who had left Brigitta at home not feeling well; Molly Williams, the very relaxed wife of playwright-actor Emlyn Williams; and myself.

Just before we went in to dinner, Josh made a little announcement that, in the absence of their cook, who was on vacation, they were able to have another who was Marseillais.

The main course was cassoulet, a casserole of highly seasoned goose, pork, and whatever, with white beans. Bennett took a large forkful, opened his mouth and began fanning it with a childlike, "Bring out the fire engines! Bring out the fire engines!"

Phyllis had another objection. Mary said Richard couldn't eat it (he had been ill and was looking cadaverous), Molly (I think it was) said she was allergic to garlic. Only Goddard, the Logans, and I ate and enjoyed. Then there was a green salad, several cheeses, and more objections. A dessert brought more complaints, by which time Josh and Nedda looked defeated.

We adjourned to the living room, with its red-rose carpeting, for coffee. Bennett would have to go to the television station soon. As soon as he left, his wife Phyllis said that she and the other spouses of the regular television panel were to be the "mystery" guests on "What's My Line," so she had to leave. Goddard said he would drive her, and although Nedda asked them both to return, Phyllis was uncertain and Goddard said he ought to go home to his ailing wife.

Mary Martin, looking out of the window, saw several snowflakes fall and said she had to take Richard home before the weather got worse. They lived directly across the street from the Logans.

That left Molly and me. Molly reminded Nedda that she had a morning flight to London the next day and had not as yet packed. She then asked me to take her home. As the elevator door closed, we saw Josh and Nedda alone, and it was still early evening.

This is New York and friends—especially those who know everybody. For twenty years the Logans and I have been friends and that fact I believe is unerasable.

With the start of rehearsals for *Fanny*, I began to know Sam Behrman, a warm, witty man who wrote with elegance, laughed without restraint, and never hesitated to express his enthusiasm for whatever he truly admired.

One of his characteristics that I became aware of early in our relationship was his treatment of himself as an old and ailing man, which in 1954 he was not. When we were in Boston with *Fanny*, I heard that Sam had disagreed about something that Josh wanted to change. He took to his bed, and I believe he honestly thought he was ill. Subsequently, he went off to Europe. He was a Jewish leprechaun.

Sam and I in a curious way developed a unique kind of friendship. I certainly enjoyed the lunches we had together from time to time, and it was not for about a year after we first came to know one another that I first heard about or met his wife, Elsa (Jascha Heifetz's sister), and their son.

The last time I saw Sam was probably four years ago, when he and Elsa invited the Atkinsons and me to dinner. It was an uproarious evening. Since that time his health had been poor, and although he wrote me once and wrote a wonderful critique of my book, *Words with Music*, he has never let me call on him. Recently, he passed away.

For years he never answered the telephone. When he had a secretary, the calls left with the answering service were returned by her in the afternoon, and occasionally Sam himself would speak. For years he had unpredictably (to me) disappeared to Europe. Postcards would reach me from many places. Then he would be back and silent.

Mind you, this in-and-out of his was not peculiar to my relationship with him. Somerset Maugham had been a lifelong friend of his, and on Sam's piano, among a group of photographs, there was one of Maugham looking up. The inscription, as nearly as I can remember, said, "This is a photograph of Willy Maugham asking the God of the Hebrews whatever happened to his old friend, Sam Behrman."

When *Fanny* had been rehearsing only a few days, Sam (whom I knew only slightly at that time) admired the aroma of a cigar I was smoking and asked where I had bought it. Several hours later he returned from lunch with the *New Yorker*'s Lillian Ross, and proudly handed me a box of the same kind of cigars. I was stunned. He turned to the singers and said, "When I told Miss Ross I wanted to buy Mr. Engel a gift, she asked me what he was like. I thought a minute and said, 'I don't know!' She asked, 'Then why do you want to buy him a gift?' I thought again for a moment and could only say, 'Because he exists!' "

That was Sam Behrman.

By the time of *Fanny* I had become a fixture in Florence and Harold Rome's lives. When you know people as intimately as I know the Romes, it is most difficult to write about them. A large part of my career in the theater has been spent with Harold. After meeting him during the run of *Pins and Needles*, I was asked to do all of his other shows. I actually did conduct them all except *Wish You Were Here*, which I had to decline because of a prior commitment in Dallas. In all, I conducted eight, covering a span of nearly thirty years.

Harold has an endearing disposition, which on a few occasions becomes explosive: a mounting irritation. He is loyal and lovable. He and Florence behave like newlyweds.

Harold is enthusiastic about his own shows, but deep down he is anxious. This anxiety takes many forms: overeating, overshopping, and being overactive in general, though not necessarily with the show being rehearsed. He has always said that all of his shows were going to turn out successfully and has not nearly always been correct. He is honest with others and generous to a fault.

For a while after we first met, he studied composition with me and later on with Meyer Kupferman.

Florence writes. She began life writing advertising copy at Ruthrauff and Ryan, later with Young and Rubicam and after the premiere of *Scarlett* (*Gone with the Wind*, which I conducted in Tokyo), she wrote a witty book called *The Scarlett Letters*.

Harold paints a great deal in a small studio on the Lower East Side. He also collects African art, which he seems to have learned a lot about. Their Fifth Avenue apartment has more African pieces than the Cairo Museum has mummies. Between shows, he is like an unemployed panther and is apt to fall into periods of depression.

The Romes sincerely love to entertain and be entertained. In their apartment it was never unusual to find at buffet Moss and Kitty Hart, Dick and Dorothy Rodgers, Ben and Melanie (Kahane) Grauer, Mollie Parnis, Arthur Kober, the Burton Lanes, Paul and Millicent Osborn, Harold Taylor, Sam and Edith Grafton, Arthur and Mary Schwartz, Fritz Loewe, Walter and Jean Kerr, Billy Rose, Chaim Gross, Josh and Nedda Logan, and many, many others.

One of the stars of *Fanny* was Walter Slezak.

Where does one begin or end with Walter Slezak? There is so much of him that meets the eye and so much more that does not. Despite his considerable girth, he reminds one of Til Eulenspiegel or Puck. Although his career classifies him as an actor, his chief love (next to his beautiful Dutch wife, Johanna, called Kaasi, or "cheesehead") has always been music. This is not an altogether profound mystery since his father, Leo, was the most celebrated tenor of his time, and Walter adored his father.

We first met when Walter played Menelaus in an Experimental Theatre production of *The Trojan Women* directed by Peggy Webster. Although we met here and there as people do in New York, it was not until fourteen years later, during the run of *Fanny*, that we became close friends. He *invited* me to hang my hat and coat nightly in his dressing room and his quiet dresser, Bob Moss (somebody had to be quiet), kept us in scotch and soda, which Walter and I paid for alternately.

The Slezaks lived at that time in Larchmont with their three children. (I think I first met Walter and Jean Kerr at one of their parties.) Walter has an enormous and valuable collection of musical manuscripts and letters written by all the greats. These are, next to his children (now grown) and Kaasi, his joys in life. And eating.

The Slezaks have lived for some years now in a small Swiss town that becomes Italian as it marches through a modest arch. They are in semiretirement, which Walter professes to like—but only until he receives a lucrative offer to do a film. Kaasi has begun working in

Walter Slezak (*left*) and I at a backstage Christmas party during *Fanny* (1954). Note the wilted soft collar worn with tails. Ezio Pinza suggested this costume, which then began to have a vogue.

ceramics, and Walter counts among his blessings the fact that their house has not as yet burned down. They drive to special musical performances—chiefly opera—all over Europe, and I doubt that there is a single repertory opera that Walter does not know intimately.

He and I are faithful correspondents, and his letters are bawdy and hilariously funny. In these letters I address him as "Waltraute" (usually the fattest of the Walküre riders), and as this is all pure camp, he addresses me as "Tink," from the well-known Barrie character in whom we all believe.

Walter's co-star was the celebrated bass-baritone Ezio Pinza. In spite of Pinza's consummate artistry, his great *Don Giovanni*, Verdi *Requiem*, the father in *Louise*, the Ninth Symphony, and many other great works in which he literally dazzled listeners, he was unable to read a single note of music! Everything had to be taught him by rote, over and over and over again.

When we first met, I conducted some recordings with him (neither distinguished nor successful) and a television pilot that was never sold. He was pleasant to work with but hardly more than that. He was businesslike, did what he was asked to do, and never made comments, and it was quite impossible to know what, if anything, went on inside his head. He was tall, with almost totally gray hair and a ruddy complexion, and was apt to "clear" his throat noisily quite often.

In *Fanny* I came as close to knowing him as possible. He was noncommittally pleasant. He never complained about rehearsing, and after we had opened in New York, he settled himself in a small two-room suite of dressing rooms, where he had a television set that was usually tuned to sports, to baseball in particular, and he was profoundly interested in the stock market. He was always in costume and makeup at least half an hour before curtain time.

In *Fanny*, one of the songs was a simple waltz, "Love Is a Very Light Thing," which he learned without undo strain. He did it perfectly during rehearsals, the pre-Broadway tour, and for a few weeks after our opening. At one performance, however, he did a most irregular and unmusical thing: he omitted one bar, which destroyed the easy waltz pattern. (It would have been most difficult for a more "musical" person to do this, but Ezio managed.)

After the performance, he was waiting for me. "What I do wrong?" he asked.

I told him, and I sang it for him correctly. He said he understood.

At the next performance the same omission occurred. Again we spoke. When it had happened a third time, I suggested that we have a little rehearsal next day, and Ezio was agreeable. Meanwhile, I had mapped out a solution to the problem: at the end of the first phrase, after singing "Love is a very light thing," he should say "wait" on the next beat and *then* begin the second phrase. We rehearsed it that way. At the performance that night, he spoke "wait" quite proudly at the proper spot in the song!

One Saturday afternoon just before starting a matinee, I was sitting as usual in Walter Slezak's dressing room, and the radio was on. We were listening to the Metropolitan Opera broadcast. Ezio was pacing back and forth in the hall outside, dressed for the show, his hands clasped behind his back. Suddenly he stopped and looked inquisitively at us.

"W'at that?" he asked.

It was *Don Giovanni*, in which he had registered one of his greatest successes!

Following a matinee at another time, Ezio invited me to dinner between the shows. I understood at once that he was trying to say, as he did to his play-son, "I like you." It was difficult for him, and I truly dreaded being alone with him through dinner: I wondered what we could talk about, but I accepted his invitation.

His dresser went out into the street and stopped a cab, which waited until Ezio had gathered himself together, and we drove to Capri, a small unpretentious Italian cafe in the theater district. When we got out, he paid the driver and tipped him only ten cents, which nearly caused the driver to have a stroke.

The maitre d'hotel recognized Ezio, and we were seated at once. Ezio wanted me to have only the best, and he set about ordering in Italian, which none of the waiters or captains could understand. In the end, I did the ordering in English.

We were then reduced to waiting and trying to make conversation. I decided that a discussion about Toscanini would work and so I began, "It must have been wonderful doing all the things you did with Toscanini."

There was a pause while the waiter served the appetizer. Then a reply: "Very int'resting."

After eating a bit, I felt it absolutely essential that I return to Toscanini.

"But you did so many things with him—concert, oratorio, and opera."

"Very int'resting," he insisted.

Again I tried.

"Didn't you *enjoy* working with him?"

Now he put down his knife and fork as if to deliver a speech.

"I tell you. This man make you sing avry note, avry word exactly as written!" A long pause in which to consider. "Very int'resting," he concluded, and so did I.

A few months before its end and after more than a year of its run, I left *Fanny* to do *Shangri-La*, which was to be an "interim" show.

Shangri-La, however, was messy. Stars were changed in midstream (Dennis King for Lew Ayres, Shirley Yamagouchi for Susan Cabot), as were directors. The authors, Lawrence and Lee, reluctantly agreed to allow changes to be made in the script, but these did not save the show, for the biggest fault lay in the undramatic idea (for the stage) of the original book. Harry Warren, the composer, who was not primarily a theater man, returned to Hollywood in disgust, feeling abused. Shirley Yamagouchi, the petite Japanese singing actress, understood all directions she agreed with and found English incomprehensible at disagreeable moments. Boston in early May was cold; Shirley wore only Japanese kimonos and went around clutching a hot-water bottle to her middle.

Although *Shangri-La* opened on Broadway to a uniformly bad press and closed within three weeks, and *Lady in Pink* (a Moss Hart–Harold Rome musical) was no longer a prospect, Michael Kidd out of the blue asked me to conduct *Li'l Abner*: rehearsals would commence in August.

This was most important for me. I had conducted uninterruptedly, made recordings (*Carousel* with Robert Merrill and Pat Munsel; *Show Boat* with Merrill, Munsel, and Risë Stevens), written and conducted music for Hallmark's television *Taming of the Shrew*, starring Maurice Evans and Lilli Palmer (directed by George Schaefer, whom I had first worked with in Dallas), and I was just then in a position to pay every single debt, even though nothing would be left afterward. With *Li'l Abner* settled, there were no longer any problems, so I went to Varadero Beach for a brief vacation before rehearsals.

The authors of *Li'l Abner* discovered their hero on a U.S. Army section of "The Ed Sullivan Show." Peter Palmer—tall, well built (ex-football player)—had a fine voice (but as yet far from well produced) and was guileless and sweet. Edith Adams, who had been in *Wonderful Town*, was Daisy Mae but unfortunately had only a cardboard role with which to work.

The energetic performances of Michael Kidd's dancers were the show's chief quality. Michael's boyishness often made the work seem less difficult. As in *Fanny* and *Shangri-La*, the book problems

ABOVE: Recording *Carousel* for RCA Victor in 1955. Robert Merrill (*right*) looks happily surprised. BELOW: At the *Carousel* recording, listening to a playback in the studio, I am anxious, but Gloria Lane (*left rear*) and Patrice Munsel (*right rear*) are amused.

were never completely resolved, but the spirit of the choreography was so contagious that audiences overlooked many of the imperfections.

The opening of *Abner* in Washington was filled with a special kind of confusion, despite which it was well received. Since the musical about Dogpatch, U.S.A., followed the Al Capp comic strip, there had to be animals, including fowl. These are provided in the theater by special trainers who see that the animals do what the director wishes. Early in the Washington first night, the trainer was making a "crossover" on stage, prodding some half dozen geese along in front of him with a long forked stick. It was probably because of a combination of orchestral sound and blinding lights, but whatever, as the geese reached stage center, they spread their wings, quacking furiously, and "took off." One landed in the middle of my music, another clutched at the bald head of a violinist, and the others lit here and there among the customers.

While we worked at a Sunday afternoon rehearsal in Boston, a Negro valet (dresser) I had known in other shows came to see me at the Shubert Theatre as emissary from Fredric March, who was dress-rehearsing at the Wilbur in O'Neill's *Long Day's Journey into Night*, scheduled to open (world premiere) the following evening. Mr. March, remembering me from many years earlier when we had recorded together, was inviting me to the final dress rehearsal of the O'Neill play. I was flattered and delighted but asked if an audience would be desirable, in which case I would invite the entire cast of *Li'l Abner*. The dresser shuffled back across the street and returned with "No, sir, but you can bring a guest if you wish."

Promptly at seven, my pianist and I entered the Wilbur, where there were no people other than the actors' agents; Jose Quintero, the director; and the lighting man. I expected a stop-and-start kind of rehearsal but was thrilled to find we were seeing a complete and full-out performance.

I was so moved by the play and the performance that afterward I felt it was impossible to speak to the Marches, but when I returned to the Ritz-Carlton where we were both staying, I wrote a letter of thanks and sent it down to Mr. March's box. The next day—opening day of the play—I found a lengthy, handwritten letter of thanks in *my* box, in gratitude for my words of encouragement!

Li'l Abner opened on Broadway and fared better than I had thought possible. Peter Palmer suddenly found himself a Broadway star without personal identity. Peter Palmer? At present he is touring in *Lorelei*.

During the year prior to *Abner*, I had been at work on an opera, *The Soldier*, based on a horror story by Roald Dahl, made for me into a libretto by Lewis Allan. Also I had been asked by Harry Friedgut to accept the presidency of the Concert Artists' Guild, Inc., an organization dedicated to the promotion of the careers of young concert artists.

Friedgut conceived the idea of having the Guild present my opera in concert form in Carnegie Hall: he thought that as a premiere it would attract critical and audience attention, that tickets should be sold cheaply, and that the Guild would gain prestige.

Although I was naturally desirous of giving the opera and of conducting it myself, I was reluctant to go ahead. First, I felt that *because* I was president of the Guild it might appear that I was using the organization to promote myself; second, I was not at all certain that Friedgut was not "railroading" this idea through without the backing of the entire executive board. I expressed these objections at a board meeting, and I was assured that no one opposed it.

I began rehearsals of my opera immediately with Warren Galjour; Valerie Bettis, the dancer (the principal female role only speaks); Brenda Lewis; and John Reardon, since the performance was scheduled only ten days after *Abner*'s New York premiere.

As my opera lasted only fifty-five minutes, I preceded it with songs from *The Beggar's Opera* with Michael Redgrave, Brenda Lewis, John Reardon, and Martyn Green. The press reception was favorable and the audience was amazingly warm.

In spite of the fact that not nearly all of the members of the Concert Artists' Guild board (I later discovered) favored the performance, Carnegie Hall was sold out. The price scale was so low, however, that there was a small loss.

During the run of *Li'l Abner* I wrote a book, *Planning and Producing the Musical Show,** which received a good press; recorded

---

* New York: Crown, 1957.

At the RCA Victor Studios in 1959, Jeanette MacDonald (*left*) and Nelson Eddy (*right*) look worried as they listen to a playback of a duet; I (*back to camera*) continue conducting what we are hearing.

Oh, Kay! and *Li'l Abner* for Columbia; taught a weekly singer's "clinic" for the American Theatre Wing; conducted a concert of the Goldman Band and a Texaco television show with a large roster of stars; worked with Sam Behrman on the projected musicalized *Serena Blandish*; recorded *Desert Song* with Georgio Tozzi for RCA; wrote and conducted music for George Schaefer's television production of *Twelfth Night*, starring Maurice Evans, for Hallmark; and bought an option on *The Spirit of the Chase*, about which I have already spoken.

While *Li'l Abner* was still going strong, I also conducted an album of duets with Jeanette MacDonald and Nelson Eddy for RCA, duets which they, symbolizing the world's most romantic lovers, had made famous twenty years earlier. Working with Nelson was no new experience for me, but I had never before encountered the "Iron Butterfly." Miss MacDonald was pleasant, plain but gave off an obviously staged flavor of delicacy, and fluttered her eye-lashes excessively.

At the first recording session, when we came to fermatas (notes held longer than precisely indicated) in their duets, I allowed a tasteful amount of time, then led the two singers and orchestra on. At the first take, Eddy, the orchestra, and I proceeded together (after the held note), but the take was spoiled because Madame continued to hold her note after we had gone ahead.

Nelson took me aside to explain that she had *always* done this in the celebrated movies they had made until the conductor, in des-peration, had complained. The truth was that as she held such notes, she closed her eyes rather "soulfully" and could therefore not see the conductor go ahead.

Although I complained, we made several other "takes" with iden-tical results and for the same reasons. Finally, I took Miss Mac-Donald aside and explained that if she continued to sing without watching, her voice would be worn out long before we completed everything that was scheduled. I think she became frightened. In any case, we never again had this difficulty.

Life had transformed me into a whirling dervish. I came to know dozens of people, and in remembering them, I can conceive no real connection between some of them and me.

One of these, Billy Rose, was a little man and remarkable in a number of ways. I often ran into him at other people's parties, where he gravitated to me and sat speaking softly, nervously, but seldom glanced in my direction.

He had a beautiful house on East Ninety-first Street that was filled with important art works and decorated in the grand manner.

There are just three incidents with him that belong exclusively to me. Once at a theater opening, during the intermission, I went to the men's room. The little man standing next to me was Billy Rose. He said hello and in the same moment said he had forgotten to put his money in his pocket: could I lend him two dollars—all he would need, since his chauffeur would be picking him up? I insisted that he take ten, which he never remembered to repay.

Several years and many parties later I spent a Christmas vacation in Jamaica at Sunset Beach Lodge. There was to be a New Year's Eve party at this most unlikely tropical place, and I wanted only to avoid it. Since I was alone, the owners insisted that I attend and sit at their table. We sat outdoors near the beach on a roofless dance floor, and there was the usual noise-making, overdone gaiety, and bad dance music. Unscheduled excitement was created by sudden showers that came and passed on quickly. During these intervals, the elegantly gowned ladies and evening-suited gentlemen (many of them British and titled) ran to shelter but returned when waiters and busboys had dried off their chairs.

In one of these hasty excursions, I ran into Billy, who asked me to his table for a drink. He was with his sister Polly, her husband, and a pretty young actress. He seemed genuinely glad to see me and asked me to his house next day for lunch. He would send his car for me.

His house, decorated by Melanie Kahane, was stunning and original. Billy took great pride in showing me around. Melanie had done a surprising thing that came off beautifully: she had papered the upstairs bedrooms with extravagant floral designs, had used large decorative bird cages filled with artificial flowers, and all of this on a tropical island where the real McCoy was everywhere evident! It was courageous, and it worked. In the sitting room on the first floor she had festooned the walls at intervals with clumps of musical instruments, most of them archaic.

The five of us had a happy lunch. Billy talked about his courtship of Fanny Brice. I told many stories too. When lunch was over, Billy asked, "Will you do me a great favor?"

"Of course. What is it?"

"I'm having about twenty to dinner this evening. Will you stay for dinner?"

I explained that as I had nothing planned I would be happy to come to dinner, but I wanted to return to my hotel for a nap. Billy offered me his own bedroom but saw at once that I really wanted to leave, and so he sent me back and had me picked up again at eight.

About six months later I read in the newspapers that Billy had undergone surgery in a Texas hospital. I wrote a brief note wishing him a quick recovery. One day soon afterward he telephoned me.

He was disproportionately overwhelmed with gratitude for my note; reminded me of the pleasant time we had had in Jamaica, where he was going next day; and asked if I would come to dinner as soon as he returned to New York.

A day or so later I read of his death in Jamaica.

At a small after-theater supper party* in New York I met the distinguished English actress Dame Sybil Thorndike, who was then eighty years old and full of enormous vitality. She was tall and elegant and spoke deliberately and beautifully without any identifiable accent. Aside from her many fascinating stories, she won my admiration because of her sheer spunk.

The hostess—a wealthy lady, now dead—had been born and reared in Brooklyn but affected an accent far more British than any Dame Sybil, or even Queen Elizabeth, ever dreamt of. During supper the hostess said, "I say, Dame Sybil, when are you and Sir Lewis returning to London?"

The grand dame, busily eating, replied, "About the end of May."

"Oh, bully! I'll be going to London at just about that time."

To which she never received any reply. While there are certainly two ways of evaluating this, I felt admiration for Dame Sybil, who was making it perfectly clear ("no entangling foreign alliances") that she did not wish to be bothered.

When the party broke up at perhaps 2:00 A.M., I asked Dame Sybil if I might see her to her hotel. (She was playing in *The Potting Shed*.) When we were on our way in a taxi, I asked if she and Sir Lewis Casson (her slightly older husband, who was playing in her company) would allow me to take them to supper or if, I suggested rather idly, she might like to meet some American theater people at a small party in my apartment. Much to my surprise, she preferred the latter, and we set a date.

It was raining the night of the party, and although I had limited my invitations to about sixteen fairly distinguished people (actors, writers, directors, composers), I was nervous about the possibility of Dame Sybil's not coming. This was gratuitous because after my

* Other guests were Myrna Loy, her husband, and Ben Washer, a publicist distantly related to me.

Abner performance, when I stopped backstage for her with a taxi, she was ready to leave and only apologized that "Sir Lewis was an *old* man and needed to go to bed," so would I forgive him.

As we went along, I explained that she would probably know most of the people I had invited except an actress who had recently "made a success in a Tennessee Williams play."

When we reached my apartment no one else had as yet arrived, but I had no sooner settled Dame Sybil on a couch than the doorbell rang.

The first person to arrive was Rosalind Russell, who was stylishly dressed in a multicolored sequin gown that extended from her chin to her ankles: miles and miles. I brought her over and introduced her quite clearly. In response the old lady said:

"How do you do, my dear. I believe you are having quite a success in a Tennessee Williams play!"

"No," answered Roz, "I'm not in the Williams play."

"Oh, then you are not playing this season."

"Yes," persisted Roz, and very modestly added, "I'm in *Auntie Mame*."

"What is *that*?" queried the Dame.

We were partially saved by the front-door bell. Others arrived in small groups, and the two stars were no longer obliged to continue sparring.

As the evening went on, each of them was surrounded by admirers and each outdid the other with anecdotes. At one point, Roz summoned me with a rapidly flexing index finger.

"Who does that old bag think she is? She's only running because of the people who can't get tickets to *Auntie Mame*" (a partial truth).

Next day was matinee day for all of us. On my way to the theater, I bought a small bouquet and stopped by Roz's stage door. The doorman knew there was no need to announce me, but I asked him to take the flowers to Miss Russell (I had enclosed a card that read "Love, Dame Sybil") and not to say who had brought them; I would wait in her outer room where I would be able to hear her plainly.

The flowers were delivered. I heard the rustle of the paper in the box. After a short pause, there was a loud scream of "You dirty son-of-a-bitch," followed by violent laughter. Roz was waiting for me, for as I entered her dressing room I found a sign over her mirror: *DAME SYBIL THORNDIKE.*

These were the fifties when shameful and destructive things were happening.

Paul Draper proves that despite the laws of gravity it is possible for a man to be turned upside down: one minute his fabulous feet were earning him a high income as they pattered rhythmically on the earth and in the very next, they were in the air making no sound at all. It is a true story, unfortunately not unique, a preposterously sad one, but there is somehow a happy ending.

Before Paul was in my life I knew his mother, Muriel, who was a strange, colorful, and somewhat celebrated lady in the world of artists. Paul's father was an internationally acclaimed concert singer who had died. His aunt was the unique Ruth Draper, whose monologues were thought highly of by theatergoers everywhere.

Muriel wrote a rather "smart" book—autobiographical, and at the time thought to be somewhat risqué—called *Music at Midnight.* She knew all creative people, as well as everyone she wished to know socially. She was also connected with all artistic and political causes. I probably met her first among the composers who were usually to be seen at "smart" parties.

Muriel would have been called unflatteringly in her time "a free soul." When I knew her she lived in a garish house on lower Lexington Avenue. She spoke in a guttural voice, and her speech was as elegant as her fingernails were otherwise.

It was inevitable that Paul's and my paths would at some point merge. Without being sarcastic, let me say sincerely that there was scarcely anything about which Paul failed to know more than anyone else. He was incredibly successful as a tap dancer with a style of his own, which embodied elements of ballet and many other techniques. His execution was impeccable. He preferred to dance to classical music, and to Bach in particular. He shared many a concert tour with Larry Adler, an artist on the harmonica, who also adapted the musical classics to his instrument. Both made a good deal of money.

Paul is slight, well developed but slim, with red hair and freckles and withal—one of the world's greatest snobs. However in Paul's case his superior knowledge of many things, his taste in food, wine, perfume, and clothes makes the term "snob" a respectful epithet. He would wince at the sound of a piano fractionally out of tune. In restaurants he might order venison but would have to be assured of its proper period of hanging—however long that is supposed to be. His friends often played jokes on him with wines by filling a bottle labeled one way with a wine of a different locale and vintage. Paul could always name the general location of the vineyard (often the precise one) and invariably its correct year. He would argue about art, music, dance, and literature, and seldom was convinced of the truth of someone else's opposing view. Despite all of this and more, Paul Draper always remained a truly simple, beguiling, and lovable man.

When I conducted Harold Rome's *The Little Dog Laughed*, Paul had the male lead. He enchanted the audiences despite his unfortunate stammering, which never seemed to embarrass him.

He lived in a handsome duplex apartment on Sixty-sixth Street, just east of Lexington Avenue, with his charming wife Heidi Vosseler, who had enjoyed a successful career in the American Ballet, and they had three beautiful daughters. There, the Drapers gave exquisite parties for hordes of (usually) celebrated people. The food was superior to the food anywhere else. It was there that I first tasted fresh caviar and smoked turkey—delicacies that I never even knew existed. Everything was the best and the most expensive.

Paul dressed meticulously but never garishly. He had a small bijou of a limousine driven by a somewhat older liveried white chauffeur who addressed his boss courteously as "Paul," and in return Paul preceded his driver's name with a courteous "Mister." All of this somehow seemed perfectly natural.

Along came Senator Joseph McCarthy and his famed "subversive" hearings. Everyone now knows in retrospect—but unfortunately not everyone realized it at the time—that it was not necessary for the senator to *prove* any of his charges—they needed only to be hinted at. And they ruined many a career.

Paul was one of the accused. He—if I remember correctly—was "guilty by association" (with alleged Communists); the accusation was supported insofar as it could be (but never proved conclusively) by the nature of Paul's mother's political activities, by some of the benefit performances* that Paul and Larry gave, and by his friendship with some intellectuals who were either proven Communists or thought to have been.

Paul fought back. The charges were absurd. The results were undreamed of. Paul used up all of his resources to clear his name. Meanwhile, his professional engagements were canceled, and he was left with nothing—nowhere.

For a decade or more Paul rented studios by the hour and gave lessons when there were willing students. The apartment and all else were gone. They died with the McCarthy era. Finally, after what was for me—a spectator-friend—a heartbreaking effort to survive, he was engaged for the faculty of the Drama School at the Carnegie Institute of Technology at Pittsburgh.

Paul and Heidi have changed very little in any way. Certainly I never knew them to be embittered. I have never heard them refer to the "old days." They must remember them. In case they do not, I do.

After nearly a year *Li'l Abner* was still playing to capacity. The tourists loved it, and it promised to go on for a long time. In spite of this security I had been listening for some time to David Merrick, who wanted me to conduct *Jamaica*, starring Lena Horne and Ricardo Montalban. It was to begin practicing in August, but as that time grew nearer, I still had received no firm offer. Meanwhile I was told that in the composer Harold Arlen's contract, David had agreed to engage Harold's brother as conductor. I also learned that in Lena's contract she was given the right of approval of musical director. Before the terms of the Arlen contract became known, Bobby Lewis (director), Jack Cole (choreographer), and Lena said they wanted me as musical director. Only two or three weeks prior to rehearsals, the matter came into the open and there was war. Lena refused Jerry Arlen; Harold Arlen was emotionally distraught, and while he was still in this state, Bobby Lewis, Jack Cole, and Lena each separately asked him to approve me. His refusal was as logical under the circumstances as it was positive: they might engage *anyone except me*. Or so I was told.

* Peggy Webster was constantly stalked for the same reason.

In many ways I was relieved. I had nothing to gain by a shift in jobs. Besides, I had only once met Harold Arlen, and although I always admired his music, I had no desire to work for him under duress. Finally, Jay Blackton, whom I respected, was engaged to conduct, and so he took his leave of Ethel Merman and *Happy Hunting*—not a success—to begin rehearsals.

All, however, was not by any means settled on the *Jamaica* front. There were incessant repercussions of the original discontent, and these never failed to reach my ears. Shortly after the opening in Philadelphia, I began to hear again from David Merrick, who inquired of my quick availability in case he could offer me the job. I had not read the script nor heard the score nor seen the show, and I was not happy at the thought of becoming embroiled in a sticky personal mess.

The Philadelphia telephone calls for help became more frequent. Michael Kidd, who had directed *Li'l Abner*, was contacted for permission to release me. Overnight I gave Dogpatch, U.S.A., to my assistant, and the very next day entered the hotter clime of *Jamaica* in Philadelphia.

On my way to the theater before Wednesday matinee, I ran into Blackton, who had not been informed of my engagement (though gossip had burned the insulation off telephone wires between New York and Philadelphia). In an attitude of "help" I had agreed to open *Jamaica* in Boston the next Tuesday. I was seeing it for the first time this preceding Wednesday!

During that half week I suffered unique horrors. I met with Jay twice that first day. On my very entrance into the theater I met E. Y. "Yip" Harburg, the lyricist, who welcomed me wildly and said that after the matinee I was to come to a meeting in Arlen's suite at the hotel. Just inside the theater I ran into Bobby Lewis, who wanted to see me after the matinee, but in Lena's suite! When I said that I thought we were all meeting together in Arlen's place, he warned me that by going there at all I would be committing a fatal error.

I saw the show, attempting to soak it up. (It was not very good.) When it was over, I visited both camps briefly. The authors saw in me the messiah who would save the show, and the others seemed to take it for granted that I had *already* "saved" it. I was, at once, all things to all people.

We moved to Boston, and considering the circumstances, I opened the show incredibly smoothly, having also written and inserted all new incidental music. Before the passing of many days, Ricardo and Lena requested an after-show meeting of authors, producer, director, choreographer, and conductor. It occurred in Arlen's suite (I think) at the Ritz, and it was the most hideous affair I have ever witnessed.

Since the authors' lawyer was to be present, Lena brought along her personal manager. We sat about awaiting a tornado, which was not long in developing.

The authors—except for Harburg—were pained by their recent exclusion from rehearsals and conferences, but their spirit at the meeting was conciliatory. (Legally, the authors have everything to say and performers and directors must listen. A star may quit if she is at odds with them, providing her contract allows her to.)

Harburg, however, was seething, and in no time he erupted. (Arlen; Fred Saidy, the book writer; and their lawyer threatened to evict him, but to little avail.) He continued to erupt, saying that the show had been taken out of their hands, that they were experienced, creative people, and that on any basis they had a right to a voice in all matters: inarguable.

Harburg's anger was suddenly topped by Lena's. She said she would leave the show unless Mr. Lewis (Bobby), whose taste she admired, were left alone (by the authors) to make whatever changes he wished (with the aid of another approved author).

David Merrick asked Bobby to outline his plan. He carefully changed his spectacles, opened a leather folio and, looking even more like a Buddha in glasses, he began to read.

His first sentence was barely out when Harburg again erupted. Turmoil Two. Bobby again changed spectacles and closed his book. What followed is not remembered in any orderly way. I know that Lena's manager said, "I don't like anybody in this room." At another time St. Ricardo asked why we could not all work peacefully together and offered to resign. Bobby said it was difficult to work when you heard constantly that you were being fired. Harburg erupted again at this, wounded by such unthinkable nonsense. Bobby laughed and said, "Yipper, you might learn to close your transom because I heard you say it yourself as I passed your room in

Philadelphia." Jack Cole voiced a similar story. My sole remark was that we had exactly forty-five more rehearsal hours from that moment until the New York opening. This statement of fact seemed to have a sobering effect.

The results were tabulated, and no one had to guess what they added up to. The authors were dismissed (this was shocking to me) because the only alternative was to have no show at all. Lena knighted Bobby, and henceforth he was in full command. The called-in author made a few helpful deletions. Jack rehearsed his dancers hard. (Alvin Ailey was one of them.)

Jamaica opened on Broadway. The reviews were "mixed." Lena got almost unanimous acclaim for her beauty and her singing. The theater was sold out many months in advance through the efforts of the always industrious Merrick. The look of success was there.

After a few more intermittently turbulent months during which I recorded a complete *Chocolate Soldier* with Risë Stevens, Bob Merrill, Jo Sullivan, and Peter Palmer, I resigned from *Jamaica*, but not without a firm assurance that I had another show in just one month.

I went to Europe.

17: Going Away

MOST PEOPLE DREAM of travel. In my own case I believe two particular factors stimulated this dream.

Ever since I can remember, my mother longed to go to Havana. It was her life's ambition. Although Jackson is no distance from New Orleans, which, even before air travel, was only a short distance by boat to Cuba, it never occurred to my parents that the Havana dream could quite simply have been made a reality. (Many years later it was my own thinking of doing the impossible that took me to Greece for the first time.)

Then too the condition that prevented my spending weekends or occasional nights during my childhood with friends had set a pattern of isolation, which became strongest at bedtime. I have never outgrown this, although its cause faded from my life more than forty years ago. It always seemed desirable for me to decline invitations to the country homes of my friends—and both the homes and the friends grew to enormous proportions through the years.

Only now, as I write this, do I realize that my vigorous negative decision was caused by the earlier pattern of my life, but being unaware of this I invented excuses and reasons that in the end were really not so irrelevant: What if I awoke at 5:00 A.M.? could I make coffee without disturbing the entire household? If, being overtired, I slept until 10:30 would the whole ménage be inconvenienced? Besides, if I were committed to a host and hostess—particular friends

—for this weekend, wouldn't I be unhappy when *their* friends (known or unknown to me) simply dropped in at just any time? (What a carry-over this is from my childhood in Jackson!) This whole line of reasoning and feeling, plus oft-repeated tales of ghastly traffic congestions leaving and returning to New York, made *any* invitation for the weekend or even longer less and less palatable, so I almost invariably declined.

The exceptions have been few. I went for many weekends to the Wises near Ridgefield, Connecticut, and years later to their houses, first in Geneva and finally near Tourrettes in the Alpes Maritimes. Both Helen and Jim were close friends and schedules were unknown in their lives: I *could* find coffee at six or sleep half the morning with no feeling of disturbance or inconvenience. At Ridgefield, where the Romes visited as often as I did (gin rummy was one magic lure), there were the many drop-ins but I was seldom bothered, knowing that the interrupted game was a solemn warning to unexpected guests to get the hell out soon.

In Geneva and at Tourrettes, Jim discouraged the conversion of neighbors into friends, and so, with the exception of gardener or postman, nobody unlisted on the program ever invaded our privacies or nonplans.

Once I stayed with the Romes, and at another time with Thomas Hammond, both on Fire Island, and this miniscule list thoroughly completes my "guesting" anywhere in more than forty years.

On the other hand, I have traveled often, mostly for pleasure, a few times because of work, and all but two weeks of two trips alone. All but two of these trips many years ago were by plane. I escaped the weekend auto traffic and was lifted completely out of this environment.

On all of these occasions I stayed at comfortable, often distinguished hotels where my privacy was assured and reasonable orders were carried out to my liking. I was able to plan what I wanted, was not imposing on profferred hospitality, and paid for what I received. (God was in my heaven.)

For both pleasure and work I have often been to London (never anywhere else in the British Isles), my favorite city: polite and civilized, and the home of several of my closest theater friends.

Paris has become for me a city where I spend a maximum of two days, chiefly to see the relatives of Grandpa Lehman, who are warm, tasteful, and bright. Although Paris may very likely be the most beautiful city in the world, it is unfriendly, money-grabbing (this is all too evident), and enormously overpriced.

Rome contains much that is marvellous to see, but tourists, and I believe Americans in particular, have converted it into a kind of international Forty-second Street, where whores and pimps of all persuasions are obnoxiously aggressive and servants are disproportionately obsequious.

I loved Florence. Venice made me feel nostalgic.

On one of my excursions to Sicily, I drove almost everywhere, loved the land, the rich rolling hills, and stood in awe of the great monuments left by the Greeks, the Normans, the Romans, and the Carthaginians.

Portugal and Spain were delights: especially the great El Grecos at Toledo and the Moorish leavings in south Spain.

I was lucky in having seen something of Egypt just prior to the 1967 war: Cairo, Luxor, and Aswan, where the poverty and filth of the majority of the inheritors is incongruous, considering the sublime glory of the heritage.

I think life in Israel is admirable, and those who have worked hard to create a garden in a desert deserve full credit and admiration, but I would be no happier to become a part of it than I was with barracks life in the navy. Community existence is something I never learned to like.

Cyprus is beautiful. Each of the Greek Isles is different from the others, and each offers a wide variety of extant ancient culture coupled with unforgettable natural loveliness.

I have been to Greece often. While I enjoyed everything I saw and did, several personal experiences are worth relating.

I engaged a car with a guide—a young female archaeologist—and after spending some days in Athens, we set out for other parts of the Peloponnesus.

We arrived in Delphi just before sundown and went directly to the ruins of Apollo's temple situated at the top of a rapidly descending hill. Directly above it, lost in mist and cloud, was the precipitous black Mount Parnassus.

The temple itself was now only a kind of floor plan—semipartitions in the ground. A few columns stood and others lay in segments on the grass.

As we stood quite alone in the stillness of the sunset (my grandmother's garden was not far away), I gazed far down the long hill and saw what appeared to be a silver sea (but in fact a large olive grove), and then beyond it a blue one—the Gulf of Corinth.

Suddenly there was a magical sound resembling nothing I had ever before heard—a bit like the pipes of Pan, but too strange to be related to anything I had ever known. I was rooted to the spot.

"That is a nightingale," the lady archaeologist said. "It has three hundred and forty-seven notes and is. . . ." I menaced her with a clenched fist. She was instantly silent, and we heard the balance of this private concert, which ended as the sun finally disappeared.

Next day we boarded a ferry in the Gulf of Corinth, on which we rode—car and all—several hours before continuing on to Olympia. On the boat there was incongruous recorded music blaring through a hoarse loudspeaker. Suddenly there was my MacDonald-Eddy album, every last duet of it!

At Olympia there was Praxiteles' great *Hermes*.

During five days I toured a number of Aegean Islands by boat.

On Mykonos, midday, hot, I sat at a table in a sidewalk cafe (I was the sole customer) facing the sea. A man emerged from the dark interior and it was obvious that he spoke no English. I was then limited to ordering ouzo.

He retired most politely, returned quickly with a glass of ouzo, a small bowl of ice, and a bowl of fresh, warm, crisp potato chips. When I had finished, as I could not find the man who had served me, I consulted a menu where the price of ouzo was listed at two drachma (about four cents), and so I left a five-drachma piece and walked on slowly down the street.

Presently I heard an excited voice behind me and turned to find the man who had served me, breathless, holding out three drachmas change. I gestured protest: he should keep them. He politely but firmly refused. I assumed that he must be the proprietor. His dignity was overwhelming. I accepted the coins, and we both bowed.

Before landing on hilly Patmos, the ship's guide warned that when we passengers reached the dock (via tender), we would be greeted by children who would present each of us with a flower and that on no acount were we to tip them: they would be offended. I was among perhaps sixteen passengers in the first tender. One by one we climbed to the dock, where we were confronted by about thirty silent children. Until all of us had arrived, they made no move at all. Then one by one, each of them singled out one passenger—a little girl of about twelve chose me. She came forward smiling demurely, a long-stemmed red rose in her hand. She curtsied and extended the flower to me. I took it, bowed silently, impotent to do more than receive it. I think most of us were shattered by this giving that would take no reward. And always the dignity.

In Turkey, Istanbul is an exciting city. Ankara contains nothing of interest.

I cannot imagine why I have not as yet been to Russia or Poland, unless it is that I fear the same feeling of lack of independence that I dread when I am invited to other people's houses. I do not willingly choose subjection to the restrictions spoken of by everyone I have known who has visited Russia.

On the other hand, Yugoslavia—especially the Dalmatian coast—is one of the world's jewels, and no restrictions are imposed there.

Something else occurs here that ties in with the preceding remarks, my traveling observations, and my childhood upbringing: the food. I was brought up to eat everything. I recall a feeling of revulsion when as a child I first encountered spaghetti: I thought it was a plate of worms. I learned to love it, but first I had to have tasted it, and this was done solely because of my mother's insistence. In later life I vowed I would eat anything that other people ate. It was in manhood that I faced escargots (snails) on a dish; as a boy, I frequently saw them slowly slithering up wooden fences, leaving their thin silvery traces behind them, not unlike the vapor lines that high-flying jets deposit in the air. In accord with my earlier vow, I was resolved to eat them but not before I had drunk four martinis. After that, there was no problem.

And so, in all my travels, I have asked maitres d'hotel everywhere to serve me their specialties, often without learning what I was to eat until afterward. But I have too often been disgusted at the spectacle of my fellow countrymen in other lands who almost invariably mistrust and eschew all foods they have not encountered daily at home. In the end, whether it is the best restaurant in Paris, Lisbon,

Athens, Cairo, Tokyo, Hong Kong, or anywhere else, they miss half the fun of *not* being at home, and most often I have observed their patent order: cream of tomato soup, steak with "French fried" potatoes and peas, Coca-Cola, ice cream, and iced tea. I heard an American lady at the finest restaurant in Madrid sneer at the very *idea* of gazpacho, which she had never tasted. I heard a man burst a gut laughing at a waiter in Rome who displayed a bowl of *fraises des bois*, remarking that *our* strawberries were ten times as big. Which indeed they are. But he would not taste one of these tiny special delicacies.

I enjoy the going even though as time goes on the packing, unpacking, standing in lines through passport and customs, and finally settling into another strange but lovely hotel room becomes increasingly difficult. But while I am wherever it is, I give myself to it because I know that in that way I will enjoy whatever special something exists only there, and perhaps nowhere else.

One ruin does not look like another to me, nor one painting, nor one cathedral.

Besides, I always carry along some work, which provides me with the biggest supplement to my whole life wherever I am.

Arriving in Florence, I telephoned Villa I Tatti. Miss Nicky spoke brightly but firmly: Mr. Berenson was ninety-three and in bed with a painful back ailment, but I could see the house, the gardens, and the pictures the following morning.

Although it was only May, the next day was hot. Clouds of dust flew behind the car. I brought an enormous bouquet of pink peonies to Miss Nicky (coals to Newcastle) and felt foolish half-hidden behind them.

Miss Nicky—secretary and devoted friend of the old man—was tailored and crisp, solid, gracious, and keenly knowledgeable. After welcoming me, she introduced me to a young Englishman who in turn introduced me—one by one—to the Sienese pictures, to the old furniture, to room after room made dark against the sun's heat. The semidarkness made even the gilded pictures difficult to see. Saints, angels, apostles, and crucifixes mingled in one faded labyrinth that began to whirl and then cancel itself out. At length we abandoned the antique darkness and emerged onto a flagstone terrace. There were enormous azalias of blinding intense color, and beyond, a limitless vista of garden framed by tall, nearly classical cypress trees. I breathed again.

We walked down into the formal garden. Everything was meticulously manicured: clean, green, and perfect but alive. A maid came running. She spoke rapidly. The young Englishman explained that Mr. Berenson was feeling better and wanted to see me.

It was Miss Nicky, waiting indoors, who took me to see him. The bedroom was comparatively small, and with drawn blinds, it was dark. In a canopied bed lay a tiny ancient man with strong, bony, dark-veined hands, which were extended to grasp mine. Miss Nicky placed a chair close to him, as he had difficulty in seeing and hearing; then she withdrew, perhaps into the shadows of the ever-so-dark room, perhaps out of it altogether. One small, powerful reading lamp restricted its light to a special circle on the bed. Beside Berenson, in linen and lace, there was a gigantic stack of international periodicals.

As Eudora had warned me, he fired questions at me. How did I spell my name? Where were my parents born? Wasn't I Jewish? (I was jolly and spirited, he observed.) How was Miss Welty? How was Sam? Did I know Mr. Cole Porter?

I told him that both Eudora and Sam had observed (and quite differently) that he and I had much in common. What? Eudora said that we both lived by the clock, that we were punctual, that we filled out time with parcels of work, people, activities. Bernard Berenson said that was true of him. What had Sam said?

I had once told Sam that my life was a failure in spite of some obvious success. Yes, Bernard Berenson said. This was also true of him. He had done nothing. Nothing perhaps except the collecting of a library of which he was proud. This was a personal achievement and the only one. Had he not discovered Sienese art, someone else would have. He was pained that he had not done more. I joked that he had lived long, but he would take no credit for this. He sighed, looked appraisingly at me. It was true that we had much in common. It seemed then that we talked forever. Miss Nicky emerged from the darkness; I must not tire Mr. Berenson. As I left, he said that he felt he had met his oldest friend for the first time and was now saying good-bye for the last time.

It was a shattering experience. Miss Nicky put her firm arms around my shoulders and led me from the room. I felt dazed, and it was hot as it always had been in Mississippi. And there was the garden and the heavy odor of roses, peonies, and wisteria.

I had promised Berenson that I would not leave without seeing his library. Miss Nicky led me there, and it seemed to occupy an enormous, newly made wing. There were several librarians and the book stalls extended from floor to ceiling, with shelves back to back in all directions. I looked at it bewildered. For the first time I realized that it is impossible to *see* a library—only a mass of books. I urged Miss Nicky to convey my congratulations to Mr. Berenson and left hurriedly.

18: Hors D'oeuvre *Varié I*

On my return from Europe I was involved with Bob Whitehead, who was producing his first musical, *Goldilocks*, by Jean and Walter Kerr, with music by Leroy Anderson, to be directed by Walter Kerr.

We went into rehearsal with Elaine Stritch (who is talented but cold) playing the heroine, who was supposed to be talented (an actress) but cold. (The wrong was being compounded.) Barry Sullivan was her hero, and I never met a warmer man. Russell Nype, Pat Stanley, Margaret Hamilton, and Nat Frey were featured. Agnes de Mille was the choreographer.

The script problems were never resolved. The music was pretty, but it was nontheatrical. Agnes's dances were not "top-drawer" Agnes. After several painful out-of-town weeks, when the notices were poor and Barry Sullivan had been replaced (at his own request) by Don Ameche (hardly the epitome of warmth in an already cold role), I believe Walter wanted to call in another director. Alas, no one was available.

Bob Whitehead asked me to have a look at the orchestra pit in the new Lunt-Fontanne Theatre before the pre-Broadway tour, since *Goldilocks* was to be its first musical. We were accompanied by the man responsible for the renovations that had restored a dowdy movie house to an attractive theater. Murals on the ceiling were being filled-in by several painters, including George Maharis, an unemployed actor.

The miniscule orchestra pit was enclosed by a wrought-iron rail-ing, and I could tell at a glance that it could not possibly contain even half of our twenty-five men, much less their instruments, music stands, chairs, and adequate space for playing.

The gentleman who accompanied us argued. I suggested that he borrow a dozen music stands and chairs from the theater across the street. When these were simply set in the pit, they occupied every inch of space!

During the ensuing weeks the front carpeting had to be taken up. A row of seats was removed. The brick wall at the back of the pit had to be knocked out and rebuilt several feet farther back. The cement floor of the auditorium had to be dug out for a foot or so, along with both ends of the pit—extending these to the walls of the auditorium. All of this because nontheater people design theaters without consultation with working personnel. (The Forrest Theatre in Philadelphia was completed without dressing rooms and the Music Box Theater in New York had no box office!)

Finally *Goldilocks* reached New York. I believe there was a hope that because of Walter Kerr's position as critic, the reviewers would be lenient. They were not.

A week or two before *Goldilocks* closed I was in rehearsal again— this time for *Destry Rides Again*, by Leonard Gershe and Harold Rome, directed by Michael Kidd, produced by—who else?—David Merrick, starring Andy Griffith and Dolores Gray.

Again there were book problems, and Michael, an experienced choreographer but an inexperienced director, failed to put Humpty Dumpty together. His dances were brilliant, but it seems inevitable that because you can create brilliant dances—proven—there must be other fields for conquest. And so it was with Michael.

The casting was far from ideal, because *Destry* is a romance about a cowboy and a nightclub lady in which the duo ought to be inordinately attractive. Andy is a charming but plain-as-an-old-shoe character actor. Dolores has a great voice and a marvelous figure. Period.

Out of town was about par for the course. But Michael had some-how changed since *Li'l Abner* days. He wanted no suggestions, no consultations. I would show up for a rehearsal, and he would say genially, "Ole Lehm, isn't there some movie you'd like to see?" (Yak

yak.) Meanwhile, he discussed his problems not with the author, the composer, or me, but with assistant choreographers (dancers) whose experience consisted of moving precisely according to direction. Even musical problems were discussed only with the pianist.

In Boston, Michael had a famous fight with Dolores Gray, who unfortunately already had a reputation for fighting. However it happened, it was messy, and Michael slapped her face. Nothing very creative was accomplished by it at a time when creativity was definitely necessary.

Destry opened on Broadway to a mixed press, and David Merrick made nearly everything "come up roses."

Someday *Destry* may ride again (as it was, it lasted about a year), and with a romantic pair in the principal roles, and some revision of the book, and Harold Rome's score, I think there might be a lovable show.

During my tenure at *Destry*, I made a sentimental journey to Jackson, where I conducted two performances of my opera *The Soldier* (the first staged ones), along with *Malady of Love*. All seats were sold. The governor made me a colonel. There was a public luncheon at which the mayor (who had proclaimed "Lehman Engel Day") made a touching speech and the Jackson Opera Guild struck off a gold medal in honor of the occasion.

While I was there, I resolved an unhappy problem. Several years before, I had offered to the Jackson Municipal Library a gift (a small part of it to be sent from time to time, and the balance on my death) of letters, books, music, manuscripts (my own and many from composer-friends), records, and pictures. These were offered as a collection, and would comprise a fairly large and unusual assortment of items. I wanted the young people growing up in my hometown to enjoy some of the advantages I had lacked as a boy.

The library readily accepted my offer, and I, in turn, sent a number of items (several large packing cases) immediately. When I spoke to the library board, I mentioned our signing a contract. My intentions were not clear to me at the time, but I was bothered by intangibles that I wanted clarified.

At length I realized what I had in mind, and I sent a contract embodying several points of paramount importance to me. Roughly, they included acceptance of *every* item I sent; the keeping of everything together in a single section so that the integrity of my collection as such would be preserved; and right of access by all persons regardless of creed, color, or religion.

My contract was unacceptable to the board. Being in Jackson for my opera, I offered my collection to Millsaps College. All conditions were found agreeable, and the items previously sent to the Municipal Library were transferred.

While *Destry* continued, I recorded the lovely score of *Brigadoon*, with Shirley Jones, Jack Cassidy, and Frank Poretta; and conducted a television "spectacular" and a second recording of *Wonderful Town*, again with Rosalind Russell.

David Merrick meanwhile asked me to leave *Destry* (I had been with it nearly a year) to conduct *Take Me Along*, a musical based on O'Neill's *Ah, Wilderness!*, with music and lyrics by Robert Merrill, starring Jackie Gleason, Eileen Herlie, Walter Pidgeon, Robert Morse, and Una Merkel.

Far ahead of the general rehearsals, Peter Glenville, the gifted English director, began work with Eileen Herlie, who had never before sung in public. As most British actors have some vocal technique, Eileen's initial efforts were not those of a novice. (What she lacked chiefly was confidence.) She has a lovely light soprano voice and is a beautiful woman and an actress of considerable distinction.

Bob Merrill, the composer-lyricist of *Take Me Along*, had been successful with pop songs such as "Doggie in the Window" and had written *New Girl in Town*—an unsuccessful show based on *Anna Christie*. He is shy, likable, and well educated, but knows little about music. He "picks out" tunes on a toy xylophone, on each note of which is pasted a numbered label. A musical "secretary" then commits the notes to paper. Bob sings the tunes (usually snapping his fingers to establish the rhythm) and listens to harmonies until he identifies what he has in mind.

Walter Pidgeon is musical, has a fairly good voice, and, like Eileen Herlie, needed confidence more than anything else. Una Merkel is a dear, dear lady, and Robert Morse, as the young Richard (actually the principal role), is enormously talented and sometimes appallingly lacking in discipline—Puck in sheep's clothing.

Now—Jackie Gleason. His obesity and his alcoholic exploits are legendary. He is able to sleep little, goes to bed very late, and is up again in a few hours. At rehearsal he was pleasant but positive, without benefit of questions or permissions, as to when he would be present or absent.

In Boston we received a marvellous press (unequalled later in New York), but some drastic things occurred. David Merrick was again riding herd, and he was opposed to Onna White's dances. He ordered the large second-act ballet deleted the night before opening, found that the second act would not work without the ballet, and restored it for the opening. (In Philadelphia three weeks later he called in another choreographer—who did new dances with new costumes, music, and so on—and then recalled Onna to restore the original ones).

A disconsolate Bobby Morse telephoned me late one night at the Ritz to weep because David had threatened to fire him. (A few years later David was to threaten Barbra Streisand). I promised to help Bobby and to speak to Glenville about it next morning. As Bobby was one of the show's chief assets, he was not fired.

In New York things began smoothly enough but became more agitated with time. I think that once Jackie had had his triumph at the opening of the show, continuing with it no longer interested him. In a variety of ways he was frequently and really incapacitated. At such times he failed to appear. Audiences were disappointed. A Merrick-Gleason feud flourished. Poor Eileen played all of her scenes with Jackie, and she was fond of him. When he had been drinking he was inaudible and his tempi (scenes as well as songs) became slower and slower and overly articulated. Eileen was at first frightened, then sympathetic, then numb. (Once he fell on stage, and Eileen literally picked him up.)

In his famous soft-shoe duet with Walter Pidgeon, Jackie, when in good condition, would push the tempo not only faster than it should have been but to an impossible degree for Walter, who was hardly terpsichorean by nature.

Jackie was a theatrical law unto himself. He arrived at the theater, made up, just before overture time. He would rush in quickly to evade autograph hunters. After the bows at the end he raced into his overcoat (costume and makeup still on) and into his waiting limousine.

He is a kind and talented man, lonely and sad. He seems to have

Rosalind Russell with L. E. at a Columbia recording session of *Wonderful Town* (1958), in connection with the TV production five years after the show's Broadway run. *Photo by Fred Plaut*

Backstage, just after the final curtain on opening night of *Take Me Along* (1959). *Left to right*: L. E., Eileen Herlie, Walter Pidgeon, and Jackie Gleason ("The One").

everything, but needs something indefinable that he has no prayer of ever having. He adores his children and takes pride in entertaining. When he remembered causing me any trouble, he invariably sent me a gift next day—a uniquely generous giver among stars in my experience.

At the end of his year's contract—champing at the bit—Jackie departed *Take Me Along* (I left for Merrick's *Do Re Mi* a few weeks earlier), and *Take Me Along*, starring William Bendix, collapsed shortly thereafter.

During the run of *Take Me Along*, Eileen and I often went about together on Sunday evenings. She could not drink: two and she was flying, which is why she never drank before a performance. One Sunday we planned to see an off-Broadway show, and I bought tickets. That day Eileen called to ask me to Lucia Victor's apartment across the street from mine for cocktails before dinner and theater (uh-oh . . .). Lucia was our very capable stage manager.

I went. I had my cocktails and Eileen had her two, and I found myself tugging at her to come out to dinner so that we could make the theater on time. As it was quite a while before we finally left, it was obvious that the play would not have us in its audience.

Once outside, I suggested that we go to the St. Regis for dinner. Okay. For those unfamiliar with the St. Regis Oak Room, it is small, quiet, and elegant. Eileen opened the menu and her eyes lit immediately on the first item—fresh beluga caviar—which she wanted. (I was glad that I had a charge account. Eat *now* and pay *later*.) And so I also ordered caviar. Eileen wanted champagne, then filet mignon and a salad, and it was all deliberately spelled out, albeit with a certain amount of difficulty.

When the captain rolled the serving table to us he carefully measured out the prescribed level tablespoonful of caviar for madame's plate. (That's why it says "$8.25 p.p.," which I have always taken to mean "per portion.") But Madame was belligerent at the size of her portion and demanded more and more. (I think she was reliving Gertrude in *Hamlet*). The captain happily obliged. The champagne was served but not tasted. (I myself dislike champagne.) Then Madame decided after caviar, when the filets and salad were served, that she was no longer hungry and would have only coffee.

When the bill was given me, I gulped at the $86 but signed it, plus tip, plus captain, and all. Madame caught sight of the check and began screaming "Robbers! Robbers! I'll never come in *this* place again." And we exited haughtily, but to no applause.

Next day three bottles of rare wine were delivered to me with a sober and profound apology.

Whenever Eileen dines out, she dines on this story embellished with roulades of laughter that only she can produce.

While I still worked at *Take Me Along*, I composed and conducted a television score for *The Tempest*, starring Maurice Evans, Richard Burton, Lee Remick, Roddy McDowall, Tom Poston, and Dennis King, and directed by George Schaefer. God bless the Welsh, with their beautiful voices, and the English, who prepare their actors for almost anything. For I had written quite difficult songs for Caliban and had fully expected Richard Burton to refuse or be unable to learn them. To the contrary, they were duck soup to him. He seemed to like them and learned very quickly and accurately.

I also recorded "Ballets on Broadway" for RCA and held auditions for a new musical, *Mad Ave.*, for which I was paid, although the show failed to materialize.

The album "Ballets on Broadway" has a curious history. Original-cast albums seldom if ever include the ballet music composed for shows. This is true generally because the dance music is composed by so-called dance arrangers who base their work on themes by the show's composer. The show's composer will want as much of his own score on the record as possible, and he will not be at all opposed to dropping the music he did not write.

Because of this, I took the idea to George R. Marek, the president of RCA Victor, who thought it an excellent one and gave me the green light to proceed. The playbacks that we heard seemed quite good and with some satisfaction, I wrote notes for the album jacket.

A few weeks later Marek called to explain that because of a reorganization at Victor, no department head (mostly new ones) wanted to be saddled with the cost of my album and that it therefore would not be released. I found the logic difficult to follow but could only accept it as fact.

However, in 1970 I began to hear tales here and there around the country that so-and-so had my "Ballets on Broadway" and *loved* it. At first, I thought it was an error until I began to hear more of the same. Then in California I heard through a member of my workshop that a collector he knew had a copy. The owner was obliging: there it was—RCA Victor LPM 1865, released in 1959 with my credit, notes, and all!

Finally I called the Victor Company and was treated most cordially; but at this writing, no one has located a copy of the album. No one seems to know how or where it was released or why I have never received a royalty statement! Unique? I'll say. We'll see. . . .

I appeared several times on the Ed Sullivan Show because of the stars I conducted for. Every time I worked on the Sullivan show I was amazed at the host's behavior. It was a foregone conclusion that being on that telecast was an invaluable aid to the run of any show and especially an ailing one. The national audience was immense, and Broadway shows literally fought to be represented.

As conductor for Gleason or Pinza or some other star, it was necessary for me to be in the theater (studio) on Broadway and Fifty-third Street at about 11:00 A.M. Sunday morning. I awaited my turn with Ray Block (whose orchestra played the show), distributed the music that I had brought along, explained it, and "read" it with the players. This gotten out of the way, I had to wait for my star or ensemble's rehearsal, and then we did it again (often again and again) for lights, cameras, and so on. (This was on Sunday— our day off!)

There would be a run-through of the show. All of this was *without* Sullivan. Then he himself—not a motion picture—would arrive at about 5:00 or 5:30. (He is a very short man.) He usually greeted no one, and he seemed not to want to be disturbed. His staff would discuss things with him. His "script" appeared on a teleprompter machine, so that he had to memorize nothing. Sometimes he would inquire humorlessly how a name was pronounced. I always felt that he was disassociated from the show, if not from all mankind. If by some act of God someone were introduced to him, he would extend a lame hand while being otherwise occupied.

There was a dress rehearsal, and then the show itself took place before an avid and worshipful audience. Then and only then did Ed Sullivan *seem* at all involved with people. In my own case, I never knew beforehand whether he might speak my name or even actually introduce me. When he did either of these things, he made me sound not only very important but like a very old friend—first name and all.

Somewhere in the fading shadow of the once-great Judy Garland in the 1960s, there was her daughter Liza Minelli, who was beginning to be heard of as a singer. Most beginnings have a way of being a little tentative but this one had to have been more so than most. Like the Son of Rin-Tin-Tin.

One of my former Madrigal Singers, Simon Rady, had become important at Capitol Records, and one day he asked me a favor: Liza Minelli had made an album for them (her first, I believe), and he was worried because the results left something to be desired in the matter of pitch. It seems that Liza had sung flat in attempting high notes.

What Simon wanted me to do I had not only never done but had never even imagined possible: Would I come to his studio, let the engineer play back the isolated orchestra track, and help Liza to sing more accurately, then re-record the faulty phrases that had occurred here and there throughout! How could I do this? Hypnosis? Black magic? Or how could it be done by *anyone*? Not having even met or heard Liza, how might I go about trying to get her to sing beyond what must have been her normal limits?

Foolishly enough I agreed to try. The very next afternoon I went to the Capitol studio, where I met a frightened waif of a girl. She seemed so alone and somehow so pitiful that I relied on this impression to supply me with some clue for working with her.

The two of us went into the recording studio, facing Simon, with various engineers seated behind their glass partition. They played back the first song and indeed I heard quite clearly the here-and-there faulty note. Liza looked more frightened than ever. The orchestra track was played again minus the voice, and when the questionable phrase came, Liza, trembling, sang it. The tension was horrible. You heard the inevitable rhythmic approach of the spot, you knew the voice had to make an entrance (here it is!) come hell or high water. And how could it ever be bettered under conditions that were bound to *tighten* the voice, rather than relax it and hopefully extend it by a matter of a quarter tone?

I was "cueing" and conducting Liza—poor little girl. Repeated failures made matters more difficult by erecting more and higher barriers, without any idea on my part as to what to do to lower them. I took Liza by the arm, put my arms around her, and quite naturally seated her in my lap in front of the microphone. We made another try: the miracle began to happen.

We continued throughout the album and by the end of the afternoon all of the corrections had been made: the little girl in my lap, my arms around her, singing with increasing security.

I have never again seen Liza during the intervening decade in which she has become a big star.

19: Hors D'oeuvre *Varié II*

I HAVE ALWAYS FELT that had I lived at an earlier time I would not have cared to work with, or know, either Beethoven or Wagner. The fact that they had superior talents and even genius would not have compensated for their tantrums, abuses, and lack of consideration.

Something of this was built into the production of *Do Re Mi*, which constituted the grimmest period of my professional life, despite the show's qualified success and my involvement with many people of genuine and distinguished talent.

Rehearsals began peacefully enough in October of 1960. The author-director was Garson Kanin; the composer, Jules Styne; the lyricists, Betty Comden and Adolph Green; and the choreographers, Marc Breaux and Deedee Wood. I had known Gar and Julie over many, many years but had never worked with them. Comden and Green were old fellow workers of mine in *Wonderful Town* and the ill-fated *Bonanza Bound*. Marc and Deedee were old friends and had danced in *Li'l Abner*, and Marc had been in *Destry Rides Again*. David Merrick was the producer and by this time a fixture in my life. The production stage manager was Neil Hartley—now a successful film producer. The setup seemed ideal.

"Seemed" is a photographer's filter.

Rehearsals began normally enough. By the third day Garson announced that we would do a run-through of the entire show! Although this was unusual, it would be interesting, nerve-wracking, and possibly instructive. Most of the text had been memorized, but

the staging was only sketchy, the songs and lyrics were as yet inac-
curately learned, and there had been no time allowed for staging the
innumerable musical numbers. All fine for three days' time, *but* we
were informed that there would be a run-through (lasting four
hours) *each* day. This would leave only three working rehearsal
hours daily.

Although run-throughs were finally given more seldom, the loss
of preparatory time had already done considerable damage. Because
of insufficient individual musical work, numbers were given to the
orchestrator (of necessity) without certainty of key or routine.
Then, when numbers were finally staged and completely learned,
many of the keys turned out to be incorrect and many musical routines were no longer valid. (This created pandemonium in the
arranging-copying department and resulted in unnecessarily high
costs.) Several songs were orchestrated and copied and then dropped
from the show at least two weeks in advance of the Philadelphia
opening. More work and waste of time and money.

Then there was the matter of Garson's schedule, which was
demoralizing: the entire company was always called every day at
the same time. There was no schedule. Everybody was there. Obviously everyone cannot be dealt with simultaneously. The sitting-
around was endless. Garson's wife Ruth Gordon, the actress, also
sat around and at every rehearsal, every day, without exception.

Then there was the matter of Julie Styne. His talent is large. He is
a compulsive worker who never lets up. He is short, excitable, talks
like a machine gun, is usually positive on all points, and rarely
listens. His reputation for screaming is historic. I had been warned.
I had heard in detail about his "scenes" in *Gypsy* (his preceding
show), but since I had seldom had difficulty with anyone, it did not
occur to me that I would experience what I did experience and that
I would be able to behave as I did.

Julie is nervous and intense. No one was exempt from his screams,
but he screamed at me only once. It came as such a shock that I
responded in shock. I did not yell back (as I might have expected)
nor did I cringe (as he might have expected). I did something
unusual for me. It happened at a rehearsal in New York when I was
trying to conduct a run-through with a new pianist (whom I had

never before seen or met) of Julie's choosing (he had been violently unhappy about the one of my choosing) who was seeing the jumble of music for the first time, had never played for a conductor (he had performed at a bar), and was nervous. When the second number failed to do anything that either Julie or I wanted it to do (because I had no control over the pianist), Julie ran down the aisle of the Martin Beck Theatre screaming accusatively, "I've been watching you! I've been watching you! It's your fault! You don't know how to conduct!"

The cast was frozen. Nobody breathed. I reached for my jacket, put it on quietly, and with no trace of emotion, but with all the dignity I could summon up, I replied: "Julie, I am too old, and I have done too many things to be talked to this way. I am going home, and you are free to engage anyone else you might prefer."

As I moved toward the steps leading to the stage, the Kanins, Betty and Adolph, Phil Silvers and Neil Hartley all converged on me, urging me to remain. I remember Neil's saying, "This is shocking. I will take it up with David [Merrick]". Betty Comden said, "You knew how it would be with Julie."

I was physically prevented from leaving the theater. I looked back at the auditorium and saw a pathetic Julie Styne standing immobilized in an aisle, his face buried in his hands: he was suffering. Somehow he disappeared from the theater. I returned to my place in the first row, and we continued. I did not see Julie for two days. Then he returned and apologized, and I could only feel pity for him.

In the strenuous weeks that followed, I often admired him, dreaded him, and always, in the end, pitied him. He never did intend the many tantrums that were hurled regularly at everyone. No one was spared.

But the tantrums in production never again struck me directly. At orchestra rehearsals the players in Philadelphia, Boston, and New York were often individually bludgeoned. On one occasion, within five minutes, he unintentionally upset a container of Postum (his) over half the orchestra in one sweeping gesture, a container of hot coffee (mine) over my music and a new white silk shirt, and then a pitcher of cream over his own music. None of this ever slackened the harangue, and I doubt that he was even aware of what had happened.

Once he insisted and continued to insist that an oboe player ("If there is one thing I have, its good ears") was playing incorrect notes when it had previously been established that this one player had no part whatsoever—a copyist's omission.

But daily and continuously the frictions went on among "staff members." Throughout, Phil Silvers behaved angelically and at least tried everything that was given him to do. Nancy Walker was creative, enormously talented, and at last had a proper vehicle. Nancy Dussault and John Reardon proved that they were two of the best singing actors in the theater.

After our opening in Boston, the cast entertained high hopes of being given the day off on the first Sunday. We had worked hard, with enormous daily changes, and we felt that we deserved a small respite. Garson had a different view and called us for noon on the stage of the theater. Backless benches were set in rows, and we sat uncomfortably like pupils in the first grade of a rural school.

Garson began by telling us that Dr. (Tyrone) Guthrie had seen one of our performances the day before and had been full of compliments. This led to a recounting of Garson's work with Max Reinhardt. There was something definitely textual about this: the gospel preacher and his patient flock. This sermonizing on a rarified plane continued uninterrupted until five, when it was time for us to go.

Again we entertained hopes of getting the evening off. But no. We were told in the kindest, but most pontifical, manner that we should go to dinner for two hours and return at seven! (He could keep us until midnight.) There would be no evening off.

At seven, contractually obedient, we were back on our benches. Gar, Ruth, Phil Silvers, and Nancy Walker were seated diagonally opposite us in a huddle, discussing some newly written pages of dialogue. The discussion continued quietly for more than an hour. The stage manager succeeded in interrupting, and after some discussion, Gar confronted us mortals, said that he thought we might as well not wait, and good-night.

After the opening of *Do Re Mi* the stage-managing trio, the cast, and I were exhausted—and far more so than usual. The hammer had ceased pounding, but the bruises were there on the top of the

L. E. (*left*), cigar, Coca-Cola and all, and a most amiable David Merrick at RCA Victor Studios in 1960 for the recording of *Do Re Mi*.

head. We recorded the music on a Sunday, nearly two weeks following the opening, from 10:00 A.M. until 2:30 A.M.! When the show had settled down, the "staff" disappeared on vacations, and again Julie screamed when he learned that I also would rest following the seventh week in New York. The fact remains that from the start of *Do Re Mi* until the Sunday following its opening—a period of thirteen weeks—I had had only one day off! Then, after seven additional but "normal" weeks, I went off first to Greece.

I was in London for a few days prior to my return, and with Michael Redgrave, went to see Ionesco's play *Rhinoceros*. It was directed by Orson Welles and starred Laurence Olivier as the only man who refused to join the animal herd. While the end of the play, with the visible change of the young man's friend into a rhinoceros and the offstage sound of the stampeding human race, was terrifying, Michael and I had another and identical reaction: we wept.

When we left the theater we walked for some time, too moved to speak. Finally, somewhat recovered, we went to supper and tried without success to discover what had so deeply moved us. We agreed that the play seemed to be about the individual versus the mob, or perhaps the artist against the Philistines, but neither of these explanations seemed sufficiently meaningful.

For the next several months at odd moments when trying to sleep, or riding, or daydreaming, *Rhinoceros* haunted me. It had been an unsettling experience, and the cause remained obscure. Finally, an idea occurred to me: might perhaps this be about a man all of whose friends and relatives became Nazis, but he himself had refused? I was not satisfied by the explanation because somehow it seemed too easy; but right or wrong, the play no longer haunted me.

On New Year's Day, Harold and Florence Rome invited me to their apartment for one o'clock dinner. When I arrived, the maid explained that Mr. and Mrs. Rome had gone out to pay a call, that they would be a little late, but would I go into the library where another gentleman was also waiting and make a drink.

I feel very much at home at the Romes, and their "library" is not a place for books but of literally thousands of small pieces of Africana —mostly bobbins. There I faced a miserable-looking little man who rose politely and introduced himself with great difficulty in English as "Mr. Ionesco." He asked if I spoke French, and I decided to let him answer that one for himself.

He looked so unhappy that I was forced to ask the reason and he summed it up in one single English word: "Hangover!" Oh, yes, I had forgotten that last night had been that dangerous one that I prefer not to celebrate. I asked if I could fix him a Bloody Mary, but it was something he had never heard of. I persuaded. I fixed one for each of us, and his disappeared at first taste. Then we had another.

By that time I felt comfortable with Mr. Ionesco, and I asked if I might tell him a strange story about *Rhinoceros*. He seemed eager, and I recounted what had happened to Michael and me. Then I said that I would like to tell him the conclusion I had finally arrived at.

As I finished, Ionesco burst into tears and said, "You are the one person I have communicated with."

The Romes returned, and we had a happy New Year's dinner.

During the fall season, with *Do Re Mi* still carrying on, I wrote incidental music for *There Was a Little Girl*, a play by Dan Taradash, directed by Josh Logan, and starring a very young Jane Fonda. Although I liked the play, it received a poor press in Boston. As a result vast changes were made, and what finally opened on Broadway a few weeks later was in my opinion far less than what we had begun with.

One day also in 1960, my old confrere Marc Blitzstein asked me to conduct at the New York City Center for two weeks a full-scale revival of *The Cradle Will Rock*, which I had originally done. During the intervening twenty-three years, the show had been done several times minus scenery and orchestra, and Lennie Bernstein had performed it with his New York City Symphony in concert form; but never had *Cradle* been done with all of the theater ele-

L. E. at home in 1959 with readied pencils in a brandy snifter. *Photo by Robert Fuhring*

ments working together. We had an excellent cast, which included Tammy Grimes as the Whore, David Atkinson as the Labor Organizer, and among others, Nancy Dussault. The reception was generally favorable, and I felt that the work held up remarkably as a thoroughly original "period" opera. And after waiting nearly a quarter of a century, it gave me great joy to do finally what I had been on the verge of doing so long before.

In this time I also persuaded Goddard Lieberson to let me record Leonard Bernstein's *On the Town*, never previously recorded. I engaged the authors, Betty Comden and Adolph Green; Nancy Walker, who had been in the original cast; and John Reardon, among others. I had some individual piano rehearsals, and as we were nearing the time of recording, my telephone rang one evening. The voice was Lennie's, and I knew the rest. Although he had just completed a performance of the Ninth Symphony with the Philharmonic, he was eager (oh, don't hate me, but it's my baby, and I would so like to do it myself . . . .) to record *On the Town*. What does one say? I received five hundred dollars from Columbia Records, and my name was not even whispered in the notes on the album jacket. *This* is how to succeed at anything without even trying.

During the summer, *Do Re Mi* took a month's holiday and I went to San Juan, Puerto Rico, having been engaged by Barry Yellen, an enterprising young impresario, to conduct what he called a "drama festival": a week each of *Oklahoma!*, *Carousel*, *Guys and Dolls*, and *West Side Story*. I took with me some "key" orchestra personnel, an assistant conductor (Oscar Kosarin), a chorus mistress, some ensemble singers, principals—most of whom changed from show to show— dancers, and so on. We performed in the auditorium of the university, which seats about 1250, the only sizable one on the island.

Among the cast was Helen Gallagher, one of the most distinguished—and perhaps one of the least appreciated—performers in New York. In Puerto Rico she did Ado Annie in *Oklahoma!* while rehearsing Miss Adelaide in *Guys and Dolls*. She was a believable seventeen in the first and an equally convincing forty in the second. One of my Dallas chorus alumni, William Walker, who was beginning to rise at the Metropolitan Opera, did Billy Bigelow. John O'Shaughnessy, from my old RPA days, was stage director.

Two incidents occurred during these four weeks that I think are worth noting. We were in desperate need of a very good rehearsal pianist for the dancers in *West Side Story*. Someone suggested that I might telephone Jesus Maria Sanroma, a concert pianist I had known slightly during my earliest days in New York. Sanroma had been a member of the Boston Symphony and Koussevitzky's musical "secretary," and had often appeared with the symphony as soloist and in recitals, particularly of contemporary music. He retired about the time of Koussevitzky's death and returned to live and teach piano in his native Puerto Rico. Twenty-five years had passed since I had last seen Sanroma, and I could not claim that I had ever known him well. I feared that my "invitation" would be insulting, since, in my own opinion, the role of dance-rehearsal pianist, consisting of endless interruptions and repetitions, is most demeaning and unpleasant. However, since there was a great urgency, I brought myself to call Sanroma, not even certain that he would remember me.

I reached him easily and just as easily did he remember me. With considerable embarrassment I stammered out the purpose of my call. To my amazement and delight, he was quick to accept and even felt honored that I had asked him. He arrived each day accompanied by one or two curious and excited students who came in the role of "page-turners," was happy to do his job, and was never irritated. If I might be indulged: only "big" people behave like big people.

During the second act of a performance of *Oklahoma!*, when I was conducting the scene-change music, I became vaguely aware of a general vibration and rumble beneath me. In a semiconscious state I said to myself, "Oh, those damn subways!" I have said the same thing during hundreds of performances in New York, and it did not occur to me that this was not New York. I then became aware of the audience, which was disappearing up the aisles, and again I said to myself "Those Puerto Ricans have never been to a musical [which was true], and they think it's over."

Perhaps three minutes later the rumble and the vibration ceased and the audience filed back quickly to its seats. (I failed to connect the two in my mind.) Then the audience burst into enthusiastic applause, which I thought absurd.

At the end of the show, I went backstage, where I found hundreds of people trying to kiss my hands, photographers, reporters—all centered on me. I was irked, and I demanded, "Why?"

A timid reporter spoke up.

"Sir, you behaved so wonderfully when the earthquake. . . ."

I did not faint, but it was not because I shouldn't have. Such an idea had never crossed my mind. Next day the newspapers carried front-page accounts and editorials with titles such as "In the Great Tradition."

I was a bloody hero whether I liked it or not. The lady mayor of San Juan, Doña Felisa Rincon de Gautier, called to thank me for saving lives, and when I protested rather testily that I was not aware that it had been an earthquake, she could only ask, "Well, Senor, *had* you known, would you have behaved any differently?"

In spite of my protests and my disclaiming any part of heroism, the mayoress asked me to a party in my honor at the palace that evening after the performance.

The mayoral palace was a pathetic attempt at grandeur. The ample walls were covered with "genuine oil paintings"—all terrible. The furniture looked as though it had been assembled by the International Salvation Army.

Doña Felisa greeted me warmly, but it was hysteria time for me. She wore a high swirling conical hat that would formerly have spelled Carmen Miranda, and when I remarked, "That's quite a hat, Your Honor," she retorted, "You won't believe it, Senor, but I made it myself!"

At 2:00 A.M., after rum and Coca-Cola, rice and beans, roast pig and whatnot, I went to bed happy, clutching a bottle of Alka Seltzer.

20: The BMI
Musical Theatre Workshops

Dʊʀɪɴɢ ᴛʜᴇ ꜰɪꜰᴛᴇᴇɴ ʏᴇᴀʀꜱ after World War II, I conducted twenty-two Broadway shows, wrote incidental music for fourteen plays, conducted fifty record albums, wrote and conducted a considerable amount of music for four major television shows, conducted four other television shows, composed and conducted two little operas, conducted thirty-four shows in summer stock, wrote music for an unproduced show, and published five books. There were many, many other things, but these will give some idea of the feverishness of my activity.

Some of this was boring, and much was frustrating. The people involved in doing a show that is in trouble give much more time and energy because of frantic efforts at resuscitation, constant changing and substituting. Then too, under these conditions, the going is harder. Tempers flare. Everyone accuses everyone else. If the show cannot be made to work, there must be at least *one* person who can be blamed. (Is it the stage doorman?)

Out of the twenty-two Broadway shows I did, eight (or about one-third) were successes. At least half of these achieved what was the look of success, thanks to the genius of David Merrick, because in all honesty many of them were not very good. Three others closed before they reached Broadway. The other eleven were out-and-out flops. After a time and in spite of my receiving two Tony Awards, this kind of frustration became nearly unbearable.

I had been a member of the American Society of Composers, Authors and Publishers (ASCAP) prior to World War II and had received token quarterly royalties that added up to about one hundred dollars annually. I had no complaints about this, because what I was composing was certainly noncommercial. However, when I began composing thirty-minute scores for ninety-minute network telecasts for "Hallmark Hall of Fame" (including songs, choruses, and dances as well as incidental music), I knew that my rating at ASCAP should mirror it. I wrote letters, and each time received replies assuring me that my *next* statement would reflect major network credits. They never did. I tried to find just anyone at ASCAP to complain to, but I could never pinpoint the appropriate person. Letters threatening to resign brought no reply.

Feeling that my complaints were justifiable and that I would never advance, I turned to Broadcast Music, Inc. (BMI), where I easily found responsible and willing ears. I resigned from ASCAP, and against invectives hurled against BMI by some of my closest friends, I threw in my lot with BMI.

Robert Sour, then vice-president with Allan Becker, head of the Musical Theatre Department, quite unwittingly triggered something that was to change my whole future life while utilizing every single element of my past experience.

Early in March of 1961, Bob asked me to discuss musical theater with a group of young composers and lyricists. At the end of a two-hour session one of the approximately fourteen people asked if we might meet again, perhaps two weeks later. I agreed. Between these meetings, I thought a great deal about what we might do. The second meeting was even more enthusiastically shared than the first, and at its conclusion, we agreed to meet regularly each week—provided, I said, we assumed a direction, that we would become, in fact, a workshop.

I proposed to give identical assignments to each team (there were seven or eight writing teams, each consisting of a lyricist and a composer) and each would write the assignment and perform it in "class" so that all of us might discuss its faults and merits. At first there were heated objections to everyone's writing the same assignments, but their objections only strengthened my thinking that everyone would learn a great deal from each other's versions *be-*

cause they would all be working to solve identical problems. Little by little, I evolved a kind of curriculum.

The first assignment was to write a ballad for Blanche Dubois in *A Streetcar Named Desire* at the end of Scene Three, when Blanche has just witnessed the reconciliation between her younger sister, Stella, and Stanley, Stella's husband, following a violent quarrel. Blanche has rushed down an outside stairway, emotionally disturbed, and has run into Mitch, Stanley's friend, whom she had met earlier. I was aware that this assignment was filled with built-in problems, but I felt that encountering these and their solution promised to provide an important lesson.

Some excellent songs were created, and some of the pitfalls claimed victims, for at this point in the play, Blanche entertained no romantic ideas toward Mitch, but some writers composed love ballads.

The second assignment was the composition of a "charm" song—that is, one with an "up" feeling, optimistic lyrics, and rhythmic music. This was to be based on the adolescent Frankie in *A Member of the Wedding*. A comedy song was written for Lola in *Come Back, Little Sheba*, a "musical scene" for the presuicide segment in *Death of a Salesman*, and finally, after much discussion, a scene-by-scene synopsis was created for a projected musical of *The Moon Is Blue* (an impossibility).

This latter idea—the assignment, not the play—seemed very important. I have long felt that our musical theater has thus far produced few librettists. Playwrights often have the notion that providing a musical book is tantamount to slumming. Few people bother even to consider the basic structural differences between a play and a musical book—a fact that largely accounts for the many and costly failures.

It has therefore seemed to me that composers and lyricists should not be at the mercy of writers who may be ill equipped to provide them with workable books, and in order to help them develop a point of view about what does and does not work and why, I evolved the system of having workshop members make skeletal adaptations of plays—especially plays that pose difficult or insurmountable problems. Also, by creating scene-by-scene synopses and defining characters in specific situations, the musical team is in a ext:

ER

position to compose a score that, if good enough, may interest a producer or a writer (furnishing him with some guidelines), and it can, at least, provide the team with an audition piece.

I based the synopsis project on *The Moon Is Blue* because (in my opinion) this lacked a sufficient number of characters for a musical, it needed to have its limited proscenium opened up (the play is in one set, with a prologue and an epilogue in another), and it would require a subplot. In addition, there are at least two "telephone" (unseen) characters who play decided parts, and because the play is thin and dated, there is no limit to what the student-writers can add. It could not turn out well, but working at it must provide an imaginative working experience.

The following season, several of the teams had written full scores to other projects, and—when I thought these good enough—I took them to audition for producers. My feeling was not so much that any of these sketched-out shows might get produced but that producers could become acquainted with the writers' music and lyrics, and the writers might be given trial opportunities to work on show properties already optioned by the producers.

Meanwhile, other writers began to apply for a new workshop. I felt that the "course" should run for two years, and before long, I had two groups going concurrently.

Within the last three years most of the participants have not wanted to leave after two years, and I have continued working with the best of them in a kind of "group therapy" way. We discuss ideas and new shows, listen to their new scores, and so on. There are at present four groups in New York (a librettist's workshop has been added), three in Los Angeles, and two in Toronto. I travel to these latter cities once monthly and hold one class for each group in Toronto and three for each—nine in all—in Los Angeles every month.

In the late spring of every year, I present three showcases in New York and one in Los Angeles. To these we invite producers, directors, writers, agents, music publishers, and television, radio, and recording company executives. The programs, each lasting more than one hour, are performed by topflight professional singers and pianists. I direct some simple staging, and each year some of the best writers are given lucrative publishing contracts which enable them to continue their work without the need of additional jobs. BMI has also supplemented some of these with membership. A number of the shows written in class have been optioned for on- and off-Broadway productions, and some have been produced.

Meanwhile, the "gospel" of the Musical Theatre Workshops, as they are titled, has spread so well that I have at last found it necessary to discontinue regular theater conducting, which for a long time I had found boring and fruitless. The workshops are in every way rewarding and fulfilling.

BMI's patronage has been a model one. No one has ever inquired as to any participant's affiliation. In fact, when it has ever emerged (and of its own accord), we have always found ASCAP members. This fact has never been discussed. No one has at any time tried to sell BMI to them. Nor has anyone from BMI ever requested that I refuse admittance to anyone or that I favor someone whose talents I have found wanting.

Each group in each place averages between twenty and thirty members and as individuals they run the widest possible gamut. Some are late teenagers, others past forty. Many of them are already successful writers in the pop field, already under contract to a publisher and one of the performing-rights societies. Many of them are recorded and published extensively.

Some of them earn their livings writing for television and the movies or as writers of "jingles" and industrial-show scores. Some work in related fields, advertising agencies, record companies, or schools at various levels. There have been cocktail-lounge and nightclub pianists; the owners of the Pan Am Building; janitors; doctors; the author, composer, and lyricist of *You're a Good Man, Charlie Brown*; ministers; a karate teacher; critics; college students and professors; a hypnotist; the composers and lyricists of *Red, White and Maddox, The Contrast, Washington Square*, and *Raisin*; waiters; office workers; and almost everything else.

I enjoy watching their development. I have often been fooled by the slow advance of some who have eventually outdone others who appeared at the start to be farther along than they actually were.

I am stimulated by the enthusiasm most of them have but appalled by the lack of patience that leads some writers of talent to lunge ahead beyond their present capabilities to such devastating disappointment that they have suddenly abandoned what I felt they were capable of achieving.

My work by no means has ever ended with the conclusion of each groups' two or two-and-a-half-hour class. With individual advancement come individual problems and the need for advice. These result in making separate appointments, hearing songs some writers have not wanted to expose in class, and reading scripts and/or synopses. I have never minded these when I believed in the potential of the individuals.

All in all, I would not change any part of the life that these workshops and by now their almost uncountable participants have given back to me. Perhaps their most rewarding aspect is the continuity of relationships with talented human beings. That the theater by its very nature is incapable of providing.

The most recent BMI president, Edward Cramer, and vice-president, Thea Zavin, with the approval of BMI's board of directors, have continued to back the workshops and their aims, as have Ron Anton in Los Angeles and H. B. ("Whitey") Hains in Toronto. Allan Becker, with his capable assistant Norma Grossman, carry on with the enormous behind-scene office work.

What I have written thus far fails to convey the important point that members of the workshops are talented individuals whose styles, backgrounds, and temperaments differ enormously. Their difficulties, success, ambitions, and even their most personal problems are to me as important as anything in the world. In time, they have come to constitute my newest family, and because it is one with which I have so much in common and for which I feel such a deep responsibility, I also feel a great love different from every other kind of love I have known.

Besides the warmth and the joy, there are some hideous frustrations. Several of my most talented writers have composed full scores —some of them as good as anything I know—to successful plays of the past that, in my opinion, they have revitalized. When they have been really first-rate, I have tried to help them secure permission to try to market the property in the hope of securing production. Invariably we have reached the author's agent or estate or a lawyer who has suddenly become judge and music, lyric, and drama critic.

They have usually decided that the score added nothing and was hardly memorable. Of course, this has to have been true, since my writers are unknown and their tunes in no way resemble those of *No, No, Nanette* and *Hello, Dolly!*

This syndrome reminds me sadly of the late Edna Ferber, who steadfastly refused to release musical rights to her novel *Saratoga Trunk* except to well-established theater people. Finally, her project seemed to be in ideal hands. Morton Da Costa adapted the book, and Harold Arlen composed the score, with lyrics by Johnny Mercer. The show limped along for ten weeks—a flop.

Unknowns might have fared no better, and the quality of the artists Miss Ferber threw her lot in with was extremely high. But the point, I think, is that "certified" creative people do not necessarily assure success.

Perhaps it has been my fault. But I have always discouraged the members of my workshops from delving into the complex problems of "rights" to literary properties (novels, stories, plays, and film scenarios) because the odds are too high against their adapting and musicalizing one on a finished level. (Many have already been far superior to most musicals produced in the last ten years on and off Broadway, but this says very little indeed.)

It has been my feeling that composers-lyricists-writers who work seriously at mastering their crafts may learn it fairly well by the time they have written four, five, or six shows. Rodgers and Hart had seven shows produced under amateur auspices before their first professional one.

I have also felt that if a truly fine work emerged, a first-rate interested producer would very likely be able to secure the rights by virtue of his own standing in the theater community. It is still my contention (and I do understand some of the logic behind it) that most authors, agents, and estates that refuse my best writers the opportunity of peddling their works—at least for a limited time—do so because they feel they are not themselves equipped to make the proper judgment and decision and that they just might have an offer for the rights to the same property from Richard Rodgers or Alan Jay Lerner or David Merrick.

What bothers me most is that some adapted authors will not listen to an audition or a tape of a score, nor will they declare un-equivocably at once as Tennessee Williams did in relation to *A Streetcar Named Desire*: "I will never allow anybody to make a musical of this play." Period. Clearly understood and definitely the author's prerogative. But the waiting, the hoping, the vacillation, and then the sloppy nothing when somehow, anyhow, anyplace, a meeting cannot be arranged.

In this situation my own ego asserts itself. Certainly with the record of my activities, my recommendation ought at least help to open a door. Often it has. Too often it has been useless.

Following is a small list of complete shows written in my work-shops that I recommend and endorse. All of these are based on inaccessible properties. In my opinion they are all as "finished" as any musical can be before work is done with the director and changes are made in rehearsal.

Beacon Hill, based on *The Late George Apley*. Novel by John P. Marquand, dramatized by George S. Kaufman (produced successfully 1944). Nothing of importance heard of it in nearly thirty years. Musical book by Barbara Gray, lyrics by Lennoy Ruffin, music by Howlett Smith.

A Thousand Clowns by Herb Gardner (produced 1962). Music and lyrics by Edward Kleban. (Gardner heard this score with Hal Prince, was enthusiastic, and said if he allowed it to be done, he would write the book. This would be after his next play was done. The play opened and closed two years ago.)

Separate Tables by Terence Rattigan (produced New York, 1956). Music and lyrics by Charles Burr. Agent and producer thought them undistinguished. I think they are unusually fine.

Salesman, based on *Death of a Salesman* by Arthur Miller (produced 1949). Adaptation by Barbara Gray, lyrics by Lennoy Ruffin, music by Howlett Smith. (Unheard by anyone!)

Pepper Tree, based on *The Light in the Piazza*, novel by Elizabeth Bishop and its subsequent film treatment. Book by Thomas Royal, lyrics by Ellen Royal, music by John Degatina. Was twice optioned, has been extensively auditioned, but remains unproduced.

On the brighter side there have been three successfully produced shows for children by Annette Leisten and Sheldon Markham based on public-domain material.

There have been original books and lyrics and music by nearly twenty writers. A revue by Charles Burr and Thomas Z. Shepard is under option for production, as are two shows by Edward Kleban.

Kelly Hamilton's *Dance on a Country Grave*, based on Thomas Hardy, was tried out at Brigham Young University and is scheduled for production in London.

Raisin, based on *Raisin in the Sun* by Lorraine Hansberry, with music by Judd Woldin and lyrics by Robert Brittan, enjoyed great success at the Arena Stage in Washington and at its recent opening in Philadelphia. It is now Broadway bound.

Let one important aspect of the workshops be clearly understood: all of the benefits do not accrue from me. When the members have attended meetings for three years or more, they become cohesive: they are a group. Their discussions, criticisms, and praise of each other's work is of enormous value. At these times, I am part participant and part monitor. But the members themselves know that with their fellow participants they have a sounding board for their work, one that is not prejudiced but knowledgeable and truthful. For a writer to earn praise from his fellows is an achievement. To hear the criticism is a matter of unsurpassing importance.

21: Misses

I⸺T IS TRULY amazing that when a mass of large-scale projects can *almost* happen—and in this instance can almost happen to me—that all of them can almost happen at approximately the same time, and that all of them can dissolve finally into nothingness.

It was during the same 1961—a little earlier and a little later—that saw the beginning of my BMI Workshops, while I still conducted *Do Re Mi*, that masses of things were jogging in my direction.

Among the potential shows I became involved with were *Mad Ave.*; *Thirteen Daughters*; a play by Joseph Kramm; *The Spirit of the Chase* (already described); a musical by Earl Robinson and my twice-librettist Lewis Allan (also previously mentioned); *The Aspern Papers*; *Night Life*, a play by Sidney Kingsley; *110 in the Shade*, by Schmidt and Jones, the very talented creators of *The Fantasticks*; *Anyone Can Whistle*, by Arthur Laurents and Stephen Sondheim; a play to be presented by a pair of reputable Hollywood producers; *It's About This Hat*, by Cy Young, a student in the BMI Workshop; and *The Rape of the Fair Country*, by Jack Holmes, another talented student. These make a grand total of twelve shows, only one of which in the end I had anything even slightly to do with.

I declined *Thirteen Daughters* because I thought it was poor. It was.

Mad Ave. paid me a sizable advance and precipitated me into instant auditions for casting without finally having the necessary funds to begin rehearsals. Although it hovered about over quite a period, it never happened.

David Merrick asked me to open *110 in the Shade*, and I was eager to do it, but what seemed to be a larger and more permanent (always more desirable in our lives) project at Carnegie Tech in Pittsburgh put that out of my reach. A young and talented conductor, Don Pippin, began a successful career with this one.

The Carnegie Tech situation was exciting. I was invited to Pittsburgh to meet the heads of the drama and music departments and discuss a curriculum. As I had long wanted to rid myself of continuous Broadway shows, this seemed to provide a sensible "out." (The BMI Workshop was then only a once-a-week affair.) Everyone in Pittsburgh was charming, and we worked out a plan that *seemed* to please everyone. I was to work there each Monday and Tuesday only.

I left Pittsburgh with great optimism. Just before I was to sign the contract (meanwhile I was unable to take on *110 in the Shade*), Sidney Harth, head of the music school, came up with a previously unstipulated and, for me, impossible condition: I would have to remain in residence in Pittsburgh for the entire last month of the season! This would have made my New York projects impossible. I could only reluctantly decline. But it has always been my feeling that since my presence had been sponsored by the drama school, the music-school head was inclined to think that people like me, with the odor of Broadway in my armpits, constitute a threat to their Metropolitan Opera–bound vocal students. (How many of them ever get there in this most unreal of all possible worlds?) For whatever reasons, the new and impossible stipulation rid Carnegie Tech of me.

During the period of this exploration, I spent many a lunch (the tab was always on me) with Joseph Kramm (author of *The Shrike*) about my composing music for his new play, which has still never been produced.

Sidney Kingsley asked me to "set" some period music in his play *Night Life*, but after discussions in some detail, RCA-Reader's Digest needed me to finish an operetta recording project in London, so I was no longer available.

Kermit Bloomgarden asked me to conduct *Anyone Can Whistle*, starring Lee Remick and Angela Lansbury. After hearing Steve Sondheim play his exciting score twice and becoming peripherally involved in a few production problems, Kermit invited me to lunch to explain that Remick and Lansbury, currently completing assignments in Hollywood, were studying voice with conductor Herbert Greene (formerly associated as co-producer with Kermit in *The Music Man*), and the girls, for avowed reasons of greater personal security (they had not sung previously), wanted Herbie to conduct. Kermit offered to make a settlement with me, but like a fool, I simply replied, "Forget it."

I was to direct (not conduct) a new musical by Earl Robinson and Lewis Allan to be produced by a wealthy lady from Chicago. We had countless meetings. I worked hard and long with the authors on rewriting their show (I was paid a retainer). While still with *Do Re Mi*, I flew to Chicago for a weekend to lead a fund-raising audition that was not fruitful. The show was abandoned.

Peggy Webster had me do a little music for *The Aspern Papers*, as adapted by Michael Redgrave, which she was directing. Maurice Evans, Francoise Rosay, and Wendy Hiller were the stars. One of my chores was to help Miss Hiller ("I can't carry a tune") to sing a song, and after a few sessions something respectable was accomplished. David Black, the producer, paid me nothing, nor did he ever thank me for my efforts.

I spent much time with a talented BMI student toward the production of *It's About This Hat* based on Labiche's *The Italian Straw Hat*, a project that I had suggested. My student asked me to stage it. I arranged money-raising auditions, worked hard on the script and score with him, attended many meetings, and at the last minute he asked someone else to stage it; he never told me about this. The show (off-Broadway) played a single performance.

Cheryl Crawford and I took an option on *The Rape of the Fair Country*, by another unusually talented student, Jack Holmes. I had brought it to Cheryl after having taken Jack to David Merrick, who loved the score and lyrics but hated the book, which was concerned with the formation of unions in nineteenth-century Welsh coal mines. We went to Lawrence Shubert Lawrence, Herman Levin, Hillard

Elkins, and many, many others before Cheryl and I finally decided to produce it in partnership. Then I took Jack to Columbia Pictures, Columbia Records, RCA Victor, and other potential backers. Everyone liked the score.

Cheryl and I spent two years and about eight thousand dollars of our own money on developing the project and finally gave up, feeling that the book was unworkable.

Of the twelve shows with which I was somehow involved, six never happened at all, five were abysmal failures, and one enjoyed a *succès d'estime*, which, translated, means it had a short run.

Throughout this period, which was running over with frustration and time-wasting nonsense, productions were by no means the only causes of gloom.

Two different playwrights came to me for advice and help in transforming original material into libretto form. One—a lady—was a stranger to me, but I liked her material and worked hard to help. Nothing. The other—a man I knew well—came to me dozens of times with a collaborator, and we worked but never arrived anywhere.

I took an idea for a musical given me by T. Edward Hambleton of the Phoenix Theatre to one of America's best playwrights. He thought the idea was perfect and agreed gleefully to work on it immediately. He was then incommunicado, but at length sent me a complete script—mimeographed and all! To my horror, I found it impossible. I tried to tell him item by item what I thought needed fixing, but criticism simply did not interest him. He knew, or so he thought. Instead, he rewrote the whole libretto, and when it was finished, he again sent me a mimeographed copy. It was no better than the first and the project came to an end.

The ambitious husband of a then-celebrated young English singer-dancer-actress tried during many months to involve me in the development of a sketchy idea he had for creating a show for both himself and his wife. I did not like the idea, and he kept changing it. I did not like him (loved her), and I warned that what he had in mind would not work. The idea and the once-adored wife-actress both seem to have disappeared several years ago after suffering a disaster at a European festival.

A semi-star comedian I had known well for many years came to me for help in creating a one-man show for himself. We talked many afternoons because I was fond of him and knew that he needed help, but his idea was too nebulous as a basis for anything, and after considerable time-wasting, the actor gave up.

A now somewhat successful author, Noel Behn (a stranger to me), approached me to join Sandy Meisner to help establish the American Musical Theatre Academy, which would fill a great gap in musical-theater education. Students would be taught acting, speech, movement, singing, and singing styles. I was excited by the idea.

I later discovered that once Behn knew of my enthusiasm, he flew to Hollywood to tell Sandy about plans that already included me but about which Sandy formerly had known nothing. Sandy agreed. Then Behn approached Hanya Holm, the choreographer, and with this triumvirate Behn set up the school in a building that had been a hospital during the Civil War. (Today it is a parking lot.)

Sandy, Hanya, and I spent many days interviewing applicants, and with a sense of artistic seriousness, we declined to accept a majority of them. The result was a small but select enrollment, which plunged the school into ever-increasing debt.

A second year only compounded the first season's financial difficulties, and it was Sandy's idea that we call in Philip Burton (he had adopted and reared Richard) to take over the school's management. This was done with Behn's blessing.

The school was reorganized under the new name, American Musical and Dramatic Academy (AMDA), and we began again.

This time, however, Philip, a too-practical Welshman, took many paying students, used several of Sandy's and my past students or assistants as instructors, and nearly put the school on a paying basis. Sandy, Hanya, and I withdrew. While I was there, I had some excellent students, including Elly Stone (*Jacques Brel Is Alive and Well and Living in Paris*); Ethel Smith (once famous only as an organist); Tina Louise, a beautiful, talented newcomer (she had been in *Li'l Abner*); Paula Truman, once of the *Grand Street Follies*, now seriously wanting to be brought up-to-date; Paul Sorvino of *That Championship Season*; and quite a few others.

During all this turbulence, *Do Re Mi* kept me alive, and *I Can Get It for You Wholesale*—another Merrick "special"—was waiting in the wings.

22: Onward and Upward
with the Arts

Fᴿᴏᴹ 1962 ᴛᴏ 1967 I was to do what I thought were my last five Broadway shows and for an extraordinary reason I declined two others.

The first that I did was *I Can Get It for You Wholesale*, the last of my eight Merrick shows, composed by my friend Harold Rome, based on Jerome Weidman's novel, staged by Arthur Laurents, and choreographed by Herb Ross. Lillian Roth was the star. But that is not the whole story, for we found an extraordinary girl—"the least likely to succeed," it might have said in her high school annual—Barbra Streisand. This show marked her Broadway debut.

Being unused to theater ways, she was a highly undisciplined performer. She had one solo, "Miss Marmelstein," and it took quite a while and a lot of doing for her to understand that the direction lavished on her by all of us was intended to produce a precise performance.

Her face is by now legend. Her hair was even more careless and unruly than she. During rehearsals she had no money, and for unknown reasons she did not live at her parents' home in Brooklyn, so she slept in a friend's office on West Forty-second Street. Her clothes were poor, and I remember that when she was finally able to rent an apartment, she wanted to take home a dilapidated wicker chair from the rehearsal theater.

It would be folly to claim that everyone had patience with her. No one did, because she *appeared* to be uncooperative and her lack of punctuality left everything to be desired. However, all of us who worked with her recognized her great potential (how great, no one could have guessed) and protected her from David Merrick, who for one reason or another (chiefly physical appearance is my guess) wanted to fire her.

When *I Can Get It for You Wholesale* opened in New York, Barbra stopped the show cold with her one song. It was a triumph out of a movie scenario. Night after night it was the same. She became the talk of the town. Her agent, Marty Erlichman, who worked hard for her, must have been possessed of very special vision.

Once Barbra, Elliott Gould (the young leading man whom she subsequently married), and Marty invited me to see Barbra after a *Wholesale* performance at the Blue Angel, a "smart" nightclub. I was not only thrilled by what she did but amazed to discover that she actually had a unique kind of beauty.

When *I Can Get It for You Wholesale* settled down for its run of three hundred performances, most of the "brass" left on vacations. One night Barbra asked my permission to do "Miss Marmelstein" in "her own way." I was irritated, since she merely stopped the show with it nightly! I refused. Night after night she persisted. Finally, I was so irritated that I said I did not care *what* she did. At that performance, she not only failed to stop the show for the first time but got no applause whatsoever: the audience was confused and was not even certain that the song had ended.

After the show she said her performance "wasn't right," but next night I would see. The next night she got the same nonresults. And the next and the next. Finally, we had several rehearsals (at her request) and were able to recreate partially what had been lost, but she never again succeeded in stopping the show.

During this time I recorded the scores of two short movies, one each by Laurence Rosenthal and Henry Cowell; gave a number of lectures around the country; continued with my workshops; and embarked on a monumental recording project for the Reader's Digest with RCA Victor.

This project was to consist of nine LP's (eighteen sides) that had to be cast, meticulously organized, and recorded in twenty-nine sessions! This gigantic album consisted of truncated versions of eighteen operettas.

We used the Met Opera's Anna Moffo in many of the casts and a number of other well-known singers but sorely needed another lyric-coloratura soprano to share the principal burden. We set up an audition in Webster Hall, where the recordings piloted by Chuck Gerhardt would take place. The glass-enclosed engineers' booth was covered with a drape so that we would not know the auditionees by name or recognize them. One by one as they sang through a microphone, a floor manager announced them by number only.

At one point we heard a distinguished female voice and requested that she sing a second song. All of us were thoroughly delighted, and we raced out of the booth to meet the singer, who turned out to be Jeanette Scovotti, formerly from my Gilbert and Sullivan and *Li'l Abner* choruses. We engaged her, and in a short time she was at the New York City Opera, then the Met, and now at the very avant-garde Hamburg State Opera.

Anna Moffo, who is beautiful and charming, was easy to work with; her only problem was her insecurity. (Anyone else?)

Later on I went to London (referred to earlier) for several weeks to record six more sides. How could anything in London pose any problem?

In the next season I was called in hurriedly to try to straighten out and open (in two days) *The Beast in Me*, based on a book by James Thurber and with charming music by Don Elliott. I was able to "clean it up" considerably, but it lasted only until the end of the week. During this brief association, I worked with an excellent pianist, new to me, named Judd Woldin, who subsequently entered my workshop and met a lyricist there with whom he was able to work (Bob Brittan); together they created a distinguished score for Lorraine Hansberry's play, *A Raisin in the Sun*, which has often been scheduled for Broadway production, but now has opened at Washington's Arena Stage, and will come to Broadway.

At the New York City Center I did a revival of *Wonderful Town*, starring Nancy Walker, and enjoyed a great surprise on opening night —one of those rare chemical affairs—when Leonard Bernstein, seated in the third row, led the audience to cheer the overture!

I recorded for Columbia *The King and I* and the hitherto unrecorded *Lady in the Dark*, both produced by another of my talented workshop composers, Tom Shepard.

In the summer, I went for three weeks to the Carter Barron Amphitheatre in Washington, D. C., to conduct revivals of *Brigadoon*, with dear Sálly Ann Howes, and *Flower Drum Song*. During one week of rehearsal, the extraordinary Ethel Merman performed nightly in that huge place to audiences of about five hundred! It's strange, but not entirely unknown here in theater circles, that many New York stars are unheard of just about everywhere else.

In the fall I became involved with the musical version of *What Makes Sammy Run?* with libretto by the Schulberg brothers and songs by Ervin Drake, starring Steve Lawrence, Sally Ann Howes, Robert Alda, and Bernice Massi.

This show represented another of the reasons why I wanted "out" of the Broadway theater, where too often too many people are too positive about everything without having had any experience in this most difficult and complex of all fields. The producer Joe Cates—a very nice man—had never produced a musical. (Presently he is dynamically successful as a film producer.) Budd Schulberg had written an excellent novel—a form as closely related to a musical libretto as chocolate candy to Camembert cheese. The composer was a pop-song writer, and Steve Lawrence a successful pop singer and, as it happened, a very talented actor who had never appeared in a show. Arthur Storch, who is doubtless a good "serious" stage director, was doing his first musical and was to be replaced. It was almost totally a case of the blind leading the blind.

Abe Burrows helped to salvage quite a lot from an unworkable libretto. Drake came up with two hit pop songs that, together with Steve Lawrence's strong personality and loyal public, allowed the show to go on for a time.

During a rehearsal in Philadelphia, I was standing with Abe Burrows between the first row and the orchestra rail. Abe as usual was wearing his Professor Higgins checkered hat, and we were chatting amiably while a scene was being played. A song came along, the pianist took it up, and Sally Ann began to sing. Abe turned to me.

"Now begins unreality," he said with a chuckle. I never forgot it because it describes so well the status of the song in a musical: unreal, yet songs at their best convey superreality like Shakespeare's soliloquies.

Before *What Makes Sammy Run?* was quite ended (1964), I became involved in yet another problem show, *Bajour*, by Ernest Kinoy, with music and lyrics by Walter Marks, directed by Lawrence Kasha (first such Broadway assignment, but an old friend as stage manager of *Li'l Abner*), starring Chita Rivera and Nancy Dussault. Ed Padula was producer, and Peter Gennaro, choreographer.

I thought this one would work. The missing pieces in the book were, I felt, discoverable, but another problem reared its head and proper work on the book was never done.

One of the principal flaws was that two females starred, but the roles of their male opposites were nearly nonexistent. Then there was a personal element that became serious. At the final run-through before leaving on the pre-Broadway tour, we had the usual invited "gypsy" audience. Nancy Dussault fractured them. She had only to crook her pinkie and they screamed, and her singing was first-rate.

Chita Rivera was *supposed* to be the prime star. Her material made her less endearing, and her reception was incomparably less than Nancy's. Much of the out-of-town effort was spent toward improving Chita's role. It never did really happen.

One of my worst experiences in the theater was trying to work with the choreographer Peter Gennaro. He is as articulate as a hippopotamus. His reputation for being difficult about orchestrations is more famous than he is. Everything went well until he arrived in Boston and came to hear the orchestrations for his ballet for the first time. I had rehearsed them carefully and thought they were effective. When I finished the first (the company sitting around), Peter asked, "Shall I scream now or later?"

I observed that I thought he had no reason to scream at all and suggested that he refrain. What was so disturbing?

Well, he didn't know. It just didn't sound like love. (This was true. It sounded like a Chopin polonaise.) What kind of love should it sound like? ("I don't know.") Should it be two-piccolo love, two-trombone love, two-violin love, two-drum love, or what? ("I don't know.") Well, I said, I would never recommend spending all the money it would cost to reorchestrate so much music until he could become more articulate.

In the end, bits and pieces were redone. Peter was never happy, but then many people just never are.

It was a time of disasters large and small.

I was engaged to go to Boston to rehearse and bring to New York a revue, *La Grosse Valise*, which had been a big hit in Paris. It was a concoction by Robert Dhery (*La Plume de Ma Tante*), who was on hand with his wife, Colette, who had choreographed it; Gerard Calvi, who composed the music; Victor Spinetti, who had been so admirable in *Oh, What a Lovely War!*; and an English actor whose name I have blessedly forgotten and refuse here and now to look up. The latter's claim to fame was his performance as the Second Grave-digger in you know what. Harold Rome was present to adapt the French lyrics, and Joe Fields adapted the book.

The first trouble was that there was too little book for Ol' Massa Fields to do much adapting. I have never seen a script like it. There was little dialogue but page after page of stage directions.

Then how do you tell a noncomic or a noncreative actor how to be inventive, which is to say, in this case, how to be funny? Does anybody think that anyone told Charlie Chaplin, W. C. Fields, or Harold Lloyd how to make people laugh?

If there are lines to be spoken, then there is a way to speak them less (or more) effectively. But with few lines to carry the message, where are you? (Who directs Marcel Marceau?)

I am told that the original French star was a great mime. Our Gravedigger was none at all—in either English or French.

The company from Paris (mostly dancers), and especially Robert and Colette Dhery, were enigmatic. Joe Kipness was the co-producer, and when he and the rest of us battle-axes from the big city asked why no one seemed to be rehearsing, Robert would shrug his shoulders. When Colette was quizzed about her dancers, she said they were tired. All of it had the unbelievable quality of a pastel nightmare.

But in time there actually were a few hours of rehearsal here and there and some new songs by Calvi-Rome. Daily the Gravedigger drew farther and farther away from anything like humor. Daily Joe Fields, Harold, and I went to Joe Kipness, who is blustering and lovable, and begged him to find a real comic for the leading role.

Daily Kipness, in his good-natured way, said, well, we would wait and see. And then we would play gin.

Joe Kipness, Harold, Joe Fields, Calvi, and Phil Adler, the good-hearted business manager, and I lived at the Ritz-Carlton on the same high floor. Phil's wife Polly (not the one who had a house) had brought an electric percolator and an electric toaster from New York and always had something to eat for just anyone at any hour. Joe Kipness's pretty wife, Janie, kept Polly company when we were at the theater.

One late afternoon, not long before the dinner break, while we were working in the theater, all the lights went out. We sat still in unrelieved blackness for a while thinking that something in the theater had gone wrong and would presently be righted. The French dancers began singing delicate folk songs and languorous popular French songs in the dark, and the atmosphere became warm and congenial so suddenly that it was quite touching.

After perhaps twenty minutes, it was decided that we would go to dinner and return at eight. With the aid of lighters and matches we were able to grope our way into the street.

There was quiet and excitement. Young men (I later learned that they were boys from Harvard who had been commandeered for this emergency job so that police were free in case of robbery, etc.) were standing at street intersections waving white handkerchiefs in the auto lights. They were directing traffic well. There was order and obedience, a show of intelligence and strength, and above it all, quiet and a sense of seriousness. Emergency.

The two Joes, Harold, Calvi, Phil, and I picked our way back to the hotel, still not fully apprised of what had happened. In the lobby of the Ritz-Carlton there were many candles, and one burned on each of the marble stairs leading to the dining room on the mezzanine.

We waited for a moment in the lobby while Phil called up Polly on the eighteenth floor. (Elevators were of course not operating.) Polly felt hideously guilty because she believed her electric percolator had short-circuited the current and caused the blackout. She and Janie had disconnected it and hidden it under the bed.

All of us from the theater went to the dining room, and after having been served cocktails and dinner by candlelight, the captain informed us that the food was not up to standard and that there would be no charge!

After dinner we heard on a transistor radio about the extent of the blackout, that it affected the entire upper Eastern seaboard and would not be repaired until the following day. Candles in hand, we walked slowly to the eighteenth floor, often laughing, I think nervously.

In my room it was spooky. The toilet would not flush. Nothing could be seen out of the windows but the headlights of autos. There was nothing to be done. It was the most helpless feeling I have ever known.

Well, the blackout is now history and so in a moment will be *La Grosse Valise*. Rehearsals were resumed next day. Victor Spinetti, a charming chap, evidently caught the lethargic disease from the French dancers. He came to rehearsals at any hour that suited him. He was reprimanded, but nothing did any good.

A day or so before the Boston opening, Victor was given a new song which he rehearsed—more or less—and we did it a few times with orchestra. At the first performance, when he was on the stage alone, I began conducting it "umpa-pa, umpa-pa," and Victor began to sing it. After only a phrase or two he simply sauntered offstage nonchalantly and left us umpa-ing. I was mystified and furious.

In the intermission I flew to the stage manager for an explanation, and his reply was, "Oh, him hurt ums itty bitty finger and came offstage for a Bandaid."

Wow-ee!

But the real catastrophe happened the next morning in the Boston papers, where the show received mixed reviews, but our Second Gravedigger was praised highly for his extraordinary performance!

All was lost. Joe, Harold, and I saw Kipness, and he was jubilant. Nothing now would be done to change anything, and we were certain there would be no show.

The two weeks we played Boston were poorly attended, but the ever-hopeful Joe was counting on Broadway.

We played several previews in New York. The audiences always left noisily in droves during the first act. The night before we opened, Joe came backstage and wept.

We opened and closed.

This really is a very old story, and one that I will never comprehend. Why did the Boston critics like that actor? How could Joe Kipness be so blind to what was going on? Why did Robert Dhery not care? (He was prevented by Joe Kipness from returning to Paris before we left Boston.) Why were the dancers so tired? (That was new.) Why was the gifted Victor Spinetti suddenly so unprofessional? Didn't anybody care?

In that same year (1965) I was engaged by the vigorous Don Kirschner, head of Screen Gems (Columbia Pictures) as executive director of Musical Theatre Development. Don wanted me to work with his contract writers on creating musical shows. I auditioned many talented people who were turning out successful pop songs and television and movie themes. With several of them I began work on shows, but in the end nothing ever progressed far enough: the people were either too busy with assignments that brought them immediate money or they lost interest. In spite of this and fewer and fewer calls from Screen Gems, my contract was to be renewed annually for four years!

I recall an occasion brought on by the press stories of this job when Albert Marre, the director, called me. (I had known Alby in *Shangri-La*.) He wanted to read me the script of a new musical and have his wife Joan Diener sing me the score. I hate being read to, but Alby insisted and I acquiesced.

Afterward, I reported to Kirschner that although I had not liked the score or the book, I thought it would be a great success and advised his investing the remaining necessary fifty thousand dollars in the production. Somehow, it was not done. The show was *Man of La Mancha*!

Meanwhile, I needed another show as my principal source of income, and Joe Layton asked me to conduct *Drat! The Cat!* I agreed to do it, and it was decided that I would go to the producer's office the following Monday (this was a Friday) to sign the contract. Then a most unexpected thing occurred.

23: The Strange Case
of the Old Lady

WHEN I FIRST CAME to New York in 1929, I met Miss Evelyn Leo, a lady in her late fifties, the friend of my teacher, and a cousin of a gracious Cincinnati lady who had been kind to me. Throughout my early years I saw Miss Leo every month or so. When she invited me to lunch in her apartment it invariably consisted of two sardines on a piece of toast, half a tomato, and coffee. I had usually brought her a nosegay (my Southern upbringing) but between her indignation at the nickel raise in bus fare, the paucity of her lunches, and her painfully plain—almost threadbare—wardrobe, I concluded that she might enjoy a chicken from the corner rotisserie more than a bouquet of flowers—provided, of course, the former did not offend her.

I screwed up my courage and brought a chicken for the first time, and far from being offended Miss Leo was jubilant and telephoned me several times the following week to tell me how long the chicken was lasting.

Once or twice I took her out to lunch, and this also delighted her. During our sporadic conversations, I gathered that she had had an extremely wealthy father, had been brought up in great style in a house on Fifth Avenue, had had private tutors, had gone to Europe often (especially early in the present century), and had had a few friends, including the girls who subsequently became Mrs. Felix Warburg, Mrs. Max Warburg, Mrs. Joseph Cullman, Mrs. Schiff, and so on: the crème de la crème of *Our Crowd*.

Evelyn Leo in Hamburg, Germany, in 1903. She was then about twenty-eight. Beautiful and positive.

With a stock-market crash her father lost his wealth and, I believe, died. Miss Leo was forced to earn a living and support her mother (who incidentally lived to be ninety-nine). Evelyn (as she had long ago asked me to call her) became "social secretary" to her girlhood friends. Each winter she generally spent two months with Mrs. Felix Warburg at her home in Palm Beach and often visited her in later years at her home in Westchester.

My relationship with Evelyn grew because of two physical catastrophes that she suffered. Around 1947 she had a serious heart attack. She was about seventy but had always been active. Although I did not feel close to her, I was aware that most of her friends had, by then, died, and that those who remained had mostly been alienated by her (she was not generally well liked). I thought how impossible it must be to want to recover if you felt that nobody cared.

I therefore went by the hospital daily to see her. She was appreciative, and when she had miraculously survived, I found myself visiting her in her apartment more often than formerly. Perhaps ten years later she broke her hip and was hospitalized for six weeks. Again I went to see her daily, and again our relationship became even closer.

When she had recovered, her doctors insisted that she go into a nursing home, where she could be looked after. First she went to an elegant one on Park Avenue, got along with no one and after a couple of months, through the untiring efforts of Anita Warburg (a daughter of Mrs. Max Warburg), she was transferred to a place run by a French countess. She hated everything about it, and then through the efforts of another deceased friend's daughter, Mrs. Henry Moses, she was admitted to the new Jewish "home" on West 106th Street, where the cost was enormous and the food and attendants were almost as bad as Evelyn said they were.

During these years I brought her food, since she complained so bitterly about what was served, and I visited an hour with her each Sunday. As she was extremely anti-Semitic (though she herself was Jewish), she especially liked me to bring her ham. Between my weekly visits, she seldom had callers and never any regular ones. She had all of her meals served in her room because she could not bear the sight of "those old people" in the little dining rooms that operated on each floor.

She had undergone a cataract operation on one eye and refused to have anything done about the other. She wore a hearing aid that seldom functioned properly, and on two occasions I discovered the cause: she was reusing old batteries that she could never bear to discard. She could walk only laboriously and with the aid of a "walker" and got along hideously with her nurses, who constantly refused to wait on her. As a consequence, she had new nurses every few days and constantly complained about this. It never occurred to her that the difficulties with the nurses could have had anything to do with herself.

Although she could not read for long at a time, whenever she could, she did. She studied Italian, read serious books, poetry, the *Reader's Digest*, and the New York *Post*.

I was always nervous about her financial status, about which I knew nothing, but I had long ago decided that when she was no longer able to go on paying I would ask the wealthy sons and daughters of her old friends to help her. I felt confident that they would.

By now it was April of 1965. She was ninety-two. I went for my usual Sunday afternoon visit. She was always eager for news: what had happened to me *this* week. I told her that I would sign a contract to conduct *Drat! The Cat!* the next day. She looked down her nose at me and said, "Lehman, you're a fool," to which I replied, "So what's new?" This infuriated her. She said I was terribly tired (I was). She reminded me that I wanted to write a book (I did). Why didn't I go away somewhere all summer and work on the book if I wished, but in any case get away from New York.

I said truthfully that I probably could afford to do this, but if I did, I would return with no money and no pending job. I closed this part of the conversation with, "You must not tell me what I can do. I must do what I think is possible."

The following morning about nine, my telephone rang. A very pleasant-voiced man said he was Walter Beer, Miss Evelyn Leo's attorney. (I never knew that she had an attorney.) It was most important that I come to his office as soon as possible. I told him of my noon appointment. No, he said, I must come before that. I was irked and observed that Miss Leo must mind her own business. Mr. Beer was quietly persistent, and at length I agreed grudgingly to come to his office as soon as I could.

On arrival, I was quickly ushered into Mr. Beer's sanctum and found a charming gentleman whose connection with Evelyn had obviously been through his parents. I was warmly welcomed, and Mr. Beer observed, "I want to look at the one man who has melted Evelyn Leo's heart!"

I found this astonishing. It was quickly followed by a question: "Would you be willing to agree to go anywhere you might like to go, to work on your book or not, but to guarantee that you would not return to New York in less than three months?"

A quizzical L. E. about 1967.
Photo by UPI

I bristled. I said all of the things I had said already to Evelyn and resented her having brought her lawyer into it.

Wally (now, after some years) smiled and said, "But you *can* afford to go if you will agree to stop work and go away. Miss Leo wants me to give you thirty thousand dollars!"

My first reaction was anger.

"Miss Leo couldn't possibly afford to give *anybody* thirty thousand dollars." My additional feeling was that as her lawyer Mr. Beer ought to prevent her trying.

Wally only smiled. He assured me that she *could* afford it and hoped I would agree.

I telephoned my lawyer Arnold Weissberger and asked him to tell the *Drat! The Cat!* people that I could not do the show. From Beer's office I went directly to see Evelyn. I found a tight-lipped empress enthroned in a wheelchair. I tried to tell her how surprised I was, and I reminded her that I knew she had never spent a penny in her life.

"I have never denied myself anything because there was never anything that I really wanted," she said.

I burst into tears. She explained that she only wanted to try to save my life, and she wanted me to leave for wherever I wished to go as soon as possible. Then it was that I also understood that she was not only giving me a large sum of money—unique in her life—but she was also depriving herself of my weekly visits.

I think it was three weeks later that I left for the small island of Tobago after a three-day visit with my mother in Mississippi. I needed to rest. I wanted to work on my book. The opportunity for both was now amply provided.

Tobago is beautiful and the handful of people I was quick to meet were hospitable and unusual. They included, as social arbiter, Lady Dorothy de Verteuil, active, in her late eighties, once married to D'Oyly Carte; Mr. and Mrs. James Rosenwald, who lived on an opulent plantation; Dr. and Mrs. Hilton Clarke; and Mr. and Mrs. Jean de Hollain, who occupied a lovely house and provided eggs for Mr. and Mrs. Chris Grunland, who ran Blue Haven Hotel, where I stayed. Besides these there were Mr. and Mrs. Robert Johnson, he a retired government official. (They had brought a Japanese house with them from the East.) At nearly every party given by any of these, the others were present.

After about three weeks of resting and writing, I was becoming restless. I received a call from Barry Yellen, the boyish young man who had brought me to Puerto Rico for his "drama festival." This time he was asking me to come to Rome to conduct recordings of scores to feature-length films for children, which he was producing. The timing was perfect from my point of view, since I could leave after six weeks of this work-on-my-book exile; fly to Portugal, where I had never been; spend a week in Spain; and arrive in Rome in time to work. I accepted with alacrity.

On my arrival in Rome, I found a small note written in a crinkly hand from Evelyn. I had promised myself when I left her that I would write to her daily. I had abided by this, most often with a postcard, occasionally with a long, descriptive letter. My enthusiasm from Spain had produced a very long letter. In Rome I found her little note, which said:

My dear [she never used my name],

I have been through Spain many times but never enjoyed any trip
as much as this one.

Love, E. L. [never a full signature]

I had a fine time in Rome with the Italian orchestra I worked with
for about eight days. As I spoke no Italian, I was provided with an
interpreter, but I realized that he lacked a sense of humor. I therefore requested him to say nothing to the orchestra unless I asked
him to.

On the first day the orchestra manager came to fetch me from my
dressing room to begin. He made a flowery speech prior to introducing me to the orchestra, after which there was bored applause.
I had had no idea until that moment as to what to do. First I said
exaggeratedly badly, "Bon gi-or-no," which produced stifled laughter.
Then I said what every orchestra-player has dreamed any conductor
would (but seldom if ever) say: "Mea culpa!"

This produced screams and hearty applause. I knew I was in.

We worked hard and got on well.

While I was in Rome, Johnny and Virginia Becker, who lived in a
palazzo, asked if they might give a party in my honor. Seven was the
hour, and so I arrived punctually, only to find myself to be the very
first. Within half an hour some fifty had assembled in a large stone-
floor hall where waiters were squirming their way about, carrying
large trays of martinis (unnumbered but increasingly lethal), and I
was delighted when at about a quarter to nine a bell was rung. Alas,
all the guests were herded into another large room, which turned
out to be a puppet theater. For an hour a rather good show went on;
that is, the parts I could see clearly through the martini haze.
(Ginny Becker operated puppets and this was her "recital.")

The show ended at about ten, and we returned to the first hall,
where a small table now stood in the center holding a block of hard
cheese, a butcher knife, and many slices of bread. I, along with the
others, hastened to have a morsel and the waiters swooped down
once again with trays of martinis.

As the clock drew on toward eleven, I realized with alarm that a
seven o'clock invitation in Rome is not what I might have thought it
was. This, my dear, was a *cocktail* party, and the guest of honor was
d-r-u-n-k.

I made profuse excuses about being tired, and I am certain nobody minded my swaying away. Somehow I managed the terracotta staircase, found a welcome cab, and was off to just anyplace where minestrone was served.

On my return to New York a few weeks later, I went directly to see Evelyn, who was more excited by my visit than I had ever known her to be about anything. We talked at length. I brought her many small gifts and souvenirs and finally I said that "our" book was well under way and that I wanted to dedicate it to her.

Her shocking reply was, "No!"

I argued, and eventually understood that her reasons were deeply Victorian: she did not want anyone to know about "us." (What was there to know?) However, ultimately, she agreed that, if I wished, I could inscribe it "To E. L.," which I did. (She often remarked about my initials being the reverse of hers.)

My weekly visits took on two other aspects. First, I now *owed* them to her (an uncomfortable feeling), and at last I saw what everyone else had always comprehended: for Evelyn, I was husband, lover, and son—all in one.

As she grew older, she became more direct about this. She suffered a great deal, complained more and more about everything, and was deeply concerned about outliving her money.

She died at the end of 1971, at ninety-eight. Withal, she had lived with dignity: She was a lady. I believe she always had known me very well—perhaps better than I knew myself. She knew that I was extravagant, but she accepted this as an integral part of me and never criticized it. For herself such a trait was unthinkable.

After her death Anita Warburg and another devoted old friend, Jessica Feingold, went through her things and delivered all of her letters and papers to me. I examined them cursorily and destroyed all but one letter. It was written (dateless, but around the turn of the century) when she was a very beautiful young girl on a visit to Venice. The stationery is the (Hotel) Bauer Grünwald's and is addressed to her:

Honored Madam—
    For two hours I followed you this morning from the Italian Bank for one glance of your *beaux yeux* but alas! not one did you vouch-

safe. But it matters not—one peep at you from behind the awnings of Saint Mark's was something. Permit me to thank you for your unconscious kindness and believe me, hoping you will accept this little token of my wistful esteem—

Your Unknown Admirer

24: Some Endings

I SPENT THE SUMMER OF 1966 in New York. In June, Jules Dassin, whom I had known twenty-five years earlier, called me. He was to write and direct a musical based on his charming film *Never on Sunday*. I invited him to dinner, where I cautioned him that in my opinion, this translation from film to stage would be very difficult and urged him to think carefully about it before starting. I advised the making of a subplot because of the single-mindedness of the only plot in the film and the creation of some suspense, and most of all I thought the subplot on the stage was necessary because, in the film, Melina Mercouri (his wife) was in nearly every frame. She could not physically (I thought) be in every scene, and the use of a subplot would not only be a relief for Melina but also for the audience.

Julie said he thought this was all very interesting and promised to think about it. (He did nothing about it and Melina *was* in nearly every scene).

Soon after this meeting, Kermit Bloomgarden, the nominal producer, called me to audition a leading young Greek actor who had never before sung. Nikos Kourkolos was brought here to audition during his filming of a picture in Greece. We met one afternoon in the Lunt-Fontanne Theatre.

Nikos, a beautiful man in his early thirties, sported a heavy,

309

rather unattractive beard, but even that failed to obscure his essential handsomeness. He was without accompanist and, indeed, had difficulty recalling any song. At length he began. There was no voice, no projection, no anything vocal.

After this attempt, I went on stage and spoke with him. I explained an old projection story: think of trying to communicate with someone in a room in which someone else you do not want to awaken is asleep. Do not sing louder, just project by very clear articulation and greater tongue and teeth energy. The second song revealed a voice audible, pleasant, and promising. I advised everyone to use Nikos but to bring him back long before December rehearsals and send him to a voice teacher. Everyone agreed.

During this summer I went to Mississippi each month because my mother, who now lived alone in her house, her sisters having died five years before, was in rapidly failing health. Three devoted Negro women stayed with her in eight-hour shifts. My aunt and cousins did everything to make her feel less alone, but I was all that really mattered to her then.

My mother's compulsion to do, to go, was still apparent in those failing days. Her daytime maid, Lucille King, would take her riding in her car nearly every morning. Often they went to the supermarket for exactly what, neither could say; but the expedition allowed Mama to be outside, to speak to people—nearly everyone—to see what was going on. Lucille and Mama frequently went to Woolworth's, partly because parking places were easily found behind the store and partly because anything Mama decided to buy—just to be doing something—was inexpensive. There were many of these visits and long before the end came, Mama knew all of the salesgirls' names and they knew hers. Just before her last birthday, less than two weeks before she died, she and Lucille went on their nearly daily expedition to Woolworth's. The girls knew of her approaching birthday and presented her with a much-decorated cake with "Happy Birthday to Mrs. Engle" (*sic*) written in icing on the top. It was certainly one of Mama's happiest moments.

When I arrived on my August visit, my cousins who met me at the airport told me that my mother had deteriorated rapidly and not to be shocked. One of them added, "I believe she is only waiting to see you this one more time."

At home I could scarcely believe what I saw. She could not walk and could only speak with great difficulty. Her night maid had put her to bed, and she obviously could not resist sleep.

Next morning she was carried into the living room (she was small and weighed very little), and we talked for two hours, more happily than ever before. The doctor, Max Berman, examined her and said she might live on for a couple of years or go at any moment. I had prayed that she would not live. She was eighty-six and lonely, and I had a horror of her vegetating alone with only hired attendants.

After our first visit together, the maid put her to bed and awakened her at five and at eight to give her nourishment, which she declined. She did not then know me. Early the following morning, the maid awakened me. It was obvious that Mama was dying, but she was in no pain and unconscious. Quietly she ceased to be.

I ordered the funeral for the following morning, and in an effort to escape well-intentioned friends of hers who would come to console me, I left quickly for Miami, where I spent five days; I returned to Jackson to settle my mother's affairs and, with the aid of my cousins, went through, and disposed of, all of her personal effects, most of which were press clippings about me.

Although I felt the sting at the time, the real effect was not to become strong for almost a year.

There is an inescapable and unpleasant result of the swiftness of air travel which the seasoned traveler is all too familiar with: the abrupt change of time that demands a vast bodily adjustment—one often requiring many days.

The flight leaving New York at noon arrives in London at 6:00 P.M. New York time, but in London, clocks indicate 11:00 P.M. By the time one has cleared customs, passport, and immigration authorities and made the trip from the airport to hotel, it is likely to be 1:00 A.M.

In spite of some travel fatigue and the many small adjustments to be made, it is impossible to consider sleep: the body accustomed to New York time is still operating on it, and although it is clearly 1:00 A.M. in London, the traveler, still living in the past, feels that it is 8:00 P.M. and finds sleep an impossibility.

The same journey made by ship in four or five days creates no such problem since the ship's clock is put ahead one hour each night and the change is made so gradually as to pass unnoticed.

This assertive difference in time when flying versus the unassertive one on shipboard is analagous to events in our lives.

Most of us live with our families. At first it is the one we were born into. Later, most people marry and become surrounded additionally with a life-partner, children, in-laws, and inherited friends. Going away to schools and making careers add more people to the surrounding environment.

When we stay fixed in space with people, we notice few changes in them unless or until some dramatic crisis creates a sudden change, calling attention to itself. The day-to-day encounter, like the journey aboard ship, makes the effects of time largely invisible except in the case of the children who grow, needing larger clothing, more sophisticated schoolbooks, dental work, tuition, and so on. This we clearly observe, but the change is not swift.

However, in my own case—which is by no means unique—I left home for school when I was sixteen. Each summer of the first five years I returned home for the entire summer. As time and I progressed, although these visits were continued annually or sometimes semi-annually, especially when plane travel became commonplace, each was increasingly shorter until a visit often consisted of only a weekend.

What I came home to was certainly not a house, because it was a new one and a stranger to me, but to my parents, my two maiden aunts, Tatsie and Flo; Uncle Isy; Aunt Gussie; and my cousins —always like my sisters—Beatrice, Phyllis, and Celeste. My few friends were also usually there. Lula Greer always drove over from Port Gibson, as she too, though unrelated, was a part of the family.

Even the town I left became a city that bore scarcely any relationship to what I had known during sixteen impressionable years.

On my first homecoming—by train, of course—all of them had been at the depot to meet me. Papa stood proudly in shirt-sleeves nervously puffing on a large cigar. Mama was anxious to see me but somehow more avid to snare every passing acquaintance to talk *about* me. Tatsie and Aunt Flo—next to Papa—seemed the most truly eager. Uncle Isy, I always felt, was enduring a pleasant duty, while Aunt Gussie and the girls were in holiday mood.

Beatrice, Phyllis, and Celeste about 1960.

This was the tableau I remember at the train. It was invariably there, and the people in it never seemed to mind the cindery smoke puffing out of the engine, the wildly clanging bell, the whistles, the sudden noisy gusts of steam, and the invariably humid heat. Since I never thought about it seriously, I accepted it as unchangeable.

On perhaps my second summer visit, Tatsie was so caught up in expectation that she took an earlier train to Canton, a small village perhaps thirty miles from Jackson and arrived in time to board *my* train and be with me alone during the last fifteen minutes of my trip.

When flying became commonplace, the scene shifted to an airport and later to a newer one. As I saw my family about twice a year, it was I who saw the sharp changes, the aging, the many signs of growing older, and of course, they saw the changes in me. The first exchanges after the round of kisses had to do with my having gained weight, lost more hair, or how well I looked.

But years passed and brought changes that could have been expected except that somehow their inevitability was only grudgingly reconciled with the shifting tableau. First it was my father who was hospitalized with painful cancer. Then we would rush from the airport to the hospital. In a couple of years he was no longer even there. Then Uncle Isy had a lingering illness and also died. Tatsie and Aunt Flo died quickly and easily within a single year. My mother was next, and finally Aunt Gussie, who had erroneously assumed for years that she had always been seriously ill.

The tableau became my cousins—singly, or two or three, with or without their husbands. They were always genuinely happy to see me, but what had been was now sorely missed.

With the change of time, I swooped down from the sky to a new place, but I was always still back in another time, perhaps not wishing to change, certainly unable to. And to me, the original tableau is as alive today as it was so many years ago, and it will not change. Time-change is what we fight when we travel. And as we live and grow older.

In the fall of 1966, I continued with New York workshops and Columbia Pictures-Screen Gems; gave lectures here and there around the country; and led six seminars at the New Dramatists. By summer I was to begin work on my last show. Or so I had planned.

By October, Nikos, minus his beard, arrived back in America. We had friends in common in Athens, and he treated me at once like an old friend. Although his voice lessons were being paid for, he himself (with a wife and baby in Greece) was receiving only twenty-five dollars a day, which had to provide a hotel room, food, transportation, laundry, and all! I invited him frequently to meals, theater, and such, and took him to agents who might get him extracurricular work. *No* jobs ever materialized.

Then Julie, Melina, and Manos Hadjidakis, the composer, arrived in New York. We had more meetings than any pharaoh ever dreamed of while building a pyramid. And at all of them everybody, in every department, was asked to be present. The wasted time was prodigious.

Hadjidakis is a very fat man who looks much older than he is. A number of upper front teeth are missing and the others are a "bright canary yellow." He speaks more English than he admits and usually tries to hide behind his French. He is enormously talented and shy.

I was invited often to Julie and Melina's apartment, where a Greek servant fixed marvelous dishes. There was music, gaiety, dancing, and singing. Melina was all Greek except for figure and wardrobe, which were Paris. She was chic, knowing, charming, petulant—a gracious hostess, sometimes a child but more often the mother of everyone else.

Julie always had Hadjidakis play his latest song, and I found all of them very pretty, but I was disturbed by their similarity, gentleness, prettiness, nontheatricality, and their lack of real endings. I spoke of this frankly and was finally able to include into the score of *Illya Darling*, as it came to be called, Hadjidakis's old hit song "Never on Sunday." It turned out to be the only successful song in the whole show.

Everyone was kept busier with the preparation of this show than with anything I had ever done before. We interviewed many bazouki (the Greek mandolin) players. Few read any music, and all were arrogant since they had well-paying cafe jobs, which they were reluctant to leave for the pre-Broadway tour of *Illya Darling*.

Julie had two production ideas which were quite impracticable: he wanted Melina (near the start of the show) to dive into the orchestra pit followed by a number of men! (It was to be the Aegean Sea.) Everyone protested. It was dangerous. Also the pit would have to be cleared. Thirty or forty minutes would be required to install and connect music stands, place chairs, distribute music, and seat the players before there would be any playing. Julie was very slow to believe this, and indeed he never quite abandoned the idea.

The other idea was to "fly" four bazouki players on a platform festooned with flowers. Their music would comprise the overture. There were several versions of this, and in the end they were mildly effective.

I made simple vocal arrangements as requested by Hadjidakis, who approved them all. They were taught to the male chorus (singers and dancers), but Julie wanted only unison or two-part singing. There were arguments and much wasted time. One day it was one way; another day, another.

Everyone connected with this production was doing musical theater for the first or (in Julie's case) second time. Much money was wasted. Almost from the start of rehearsals, we worked overtime an hour a day. After the opening in Philadelphia we never rehearsed *without* the scenery, which meant paying a full stage crew—an unheard of extravagance in the theater because of its prohibitive cost.

Julie engaged Joe Darion (*Man of La Mancha*) as lyricist against much advice to the contrary; he then became so dissatisfied that he spoke of sending for a Greek poet who spoke English!

Schedules were seldom made for next day until after the cast had been dismissed. The stage managers spent many late hours telephoning everyone.

Ralph Burns (orchestrator) was nearly frantic at not getting songs early enough to orchestrate. Theoni Aldridge (costume designer) said there would be *no* costumes if precise personnel were not selected for each scene and measured at once. (Julie shifted personnel in nearly every ensemble number almost daily.)

I complained that it was impossible to train a chorus with shifting personnel, shifting arrangements, missing lyrics, and unfinished songs. (Even the *finished* songs sounded unfinished.)

There were meetings all the time. I never knew who to take orders from since Hadjidakis (composer) and Dassin (director) were always at odds with one another and each gave conflicting orders.

From time to time all the principals except Orson Bean suffered from laryngitis.

After rehearsing two and a half weeks, the ensemble still did not know what to do, what notes to sing, or which lyrics were being used. Dassin nightly promised me more rehearsal time, but the next day, plans were changed and I usually ended up with none.

As I had predicted, there was too much Melina, although her charm was obvious. The part of the romantic leading male (Nikos) was too unimportant and there was—as we found—no second act.

Hadjidakis wanted me to conduct everything slowly, while Dassin wanted it fast. They argued and, as always, left me with no clear direction.

My orchestra rehearsals began January 9 in Philadelphia. (We had begun stage-rehearsing December 5.) As I had no interference, everything went smoothly. While this was under way, the late Jean Rosenthal, the very talented lighting designer, was setting her cues in the theater. However, when Dassin arrived in Philadelphia he categorically and petulantly declared, without seeing what Jeannie had spent several days working out, that he would do his own lighting.

We opened January 16. Nothing was good. The only musical

number the audience bought was "Never on Sunday." It stopped the show, and we did an encore.

About the middle of our Philadelphia engagement James Felton of the *Philadelphia Bulletin* asked me for an interview, which appeared prominently in his paper on the Sunday of our departure for Toronto. The headlines of the article were, RETIRING FROM RAT RACE: NO MORE PIT STOPS FOR *ILLYA* CONDUCTOR?

In the piece I was quoted as saying:

"I've had it," says Lehman Engel, music director of 160 Broadway shows. At 56, he's still moving forward, but he doesn't plan on swinging a baton anymore after *Illya Darling* runs its course. He's musical director of the show, which ended its tryout run here yesterday, and is headed for New York via Toronto and Detroit.

"It takes too much time, and I have better things to do than to run bad shows," he explained in his hotel suite the other night, taking a hard look at Broadway with soft eyes.

Then I spoke of my book (*The American Musical Theater: A Consideration*), which was by then in the editing stage. In connection with this, I was further quoted:

"A good show will work when all of its elements are equally good— libretto, characters, music, lyrics, choreography. *Oklahoma!* and *West Side Story* are good because they work on every level. And they'll go on being good shows. That's the difference between a hit that might run on Broadway for a year or two and the shows that will become staples.

"What we need is a theater of feeling. Who can identify with the grotesque, middle-aged women who star in some of the big shows today? It's hard to feel much for a one-eyed prostitute in Turkey."

This latter remark was taken personally, but I was not to learn about it for a few days.

Rehearsals in Toronto in the enormous O'Keefe Centre went along fairly well, but Manos's presence slowed things down. He wanted many, many changes and because of his inarticulateness and his language problems, rehearsals often nearly came to a standstill.

We opened on Wednesday and got very bad reviews. Two days later Kermit Bloomgarden called me into his suite. He told me he thought I had been stupid in giving the Philadelphia interview, that Julie and Melina were upset because of my reference to "grotesque, middle-aged women." (I know that I had intended it only as a reference to a growing trend in the American Musical Theatre.) However, I could certainly understand their feeling. (Had I done it intentionally?)

Kermit said that since I was unhappy, they would release me at once. I agreed that I was extremely unhappy, but inasmuch as I had put in so much work I was not willing to quit: my contract however could be bought. Kermit made me an offer, and we finally reached a settlement. I was asked *not* to conduct that evening. My assistant took over.

I stayed in my hotel room that evening, as there was no flight to New York. William Littler of the *Toronto Sun* came to interview me and wrote a piece that appeared the following Monday. Again I had—but sincerely unintentionally—offended. The headlines read: BORED CONDUCTOR OF *ILLYA* QUITS, IS REPLACED BY WOMAN.

During the following six weeks, I had letters and phone calls from many of the show's people, but none from Nikos, whom I had settled with an agent (who got him a film contract) and none from my assistant, who had replaced me.

At the New York opening *Illya Darling* got a poor press, but Melina contrived to draw audiences for a number of months. All that I foresaw that could be wrong with it was wrong. I was tired of playing Cassandra and felt the time had finally come when I expected never again to become involved in a Broadway production.

In April, I was off to Europe.

25: Odds and Ends

LATE IN THE FALL of 1967 my book *The American Musical Theater* (derived from both my workshops and my years in the theater) was released.* It is the first—and to date the only—analytical book on the subject, but I was unhappy with the finished product. First of all, it is an outsize coffee-table book, profusely illustrated. (I never saw an illustration prior to publication!) The pictures often appear in groups of pages that occur just anywhere—often bisecting a sentence. Second, *because* of the pictures, the book, which ought to reach students, is priced at $12.50. Then, too, the general appearance is misleading, since it looks like a picture book instead of the serious one that it is.

Originally I was to record some illustrative music that would accompany the book, but because the book's cost (because of the extensive decoration) had soared, two records were "assembled" from existing theater songs in the Columbia catalog. Tepid serendipity.

The launching of the book was a well-kept secret until a publicist friend of mine, Leonard Gerber, reached many of his contacts on magazines and papers.

The publication led to my meeting the then-president of Macmillan, Jeremiah Kaplan, who enjoys a formidable reputation. I have my mother to thank for that because she had always preached that

* New York: CBS Heritage Collection, 1967.

"if you want things done, go to the top." Jerry Kaplan and I have enjoyed a warm personal relationship. I had then begun another book—a study of basic differences between plays and librettos for which I felt there was a certain need, since a majority of contemporary failures can be attributed to faulty librettos. Nobody seems to have thought seriously about it. I showed what I had written up to that point (about ninety pages) to Jerry Kaplan, and he encouraged me to go ahead even though he was critical of the way I was then doing it.

Early in the new year (1968) a letter from the State Department in Washington asked my interest and availability in going to Turkey (Ankara—Dullsville!) late in November to rehearse and open a production of *Porgy and Bess* at the Turkish State Opera. The impresario had my recording and was eager to have me conduct.

I went to Washington: I would leave late in November for nine weeks, and as this included my normal Christmas vacation from my workshops, I accepted.

Meanwhile, Glenn Jordan engaged me to conduct the first five weeks of the twenty-fifth anniversary season of the St. Louis Municipal Opera in the summer, immediately after which I was to speak at the Salzburg Seminar in American Studies. I had also published a seventh volume in my *Renaissance to Baroque* series, recorded music for a Greek film made by, and with, Theo Roubanis, formerly a student of mine and more recently married to Lady Sarah Spencer-Churchill.

By mid-April, with my showcases to finish in May, I also worked several times a week helping to prepare Douglas Fairbanks, Jr., for the role of Higgins in *My Fair Lady*, which was to open the St. Louis season, and studied my other two shows, *The Pajama Game* and *Annie Get Your Gun*.

Before leaving for St. Louis, I was approached by Bernard Grossman, head of the Consular Law Society, who wanted the Austrian government to give me a citation at a banquet in June. The basis for this was my book, in which I had written that the American musical theater had descended from Viennese operetta. The presentation occurred at the Harvard Club as an embarrassing parenthesis in an otherwise busy evening. The Austrian cultural attaché presented me with a lovely picture book, *Imago Austriae*, in which there is pasted:

To MR. LEHMAN ENGEL in appreciation of his research on the American Musical and the Vienna Operetta and his contribution to the mutual understanding between the people of the United States of America and Austria.
New York, June 5, 1968. Austrian Institute,
Gottfried Heindl, Director.

St. Louis in summer is an inferno. I had once seen the Muni Opera (as it is called) when my parents took me as a child to St. Louis. The vast amphitheater seats more than ten thousand, and the organization is well run.

I took with me, as assistant, Gordon Harrell, a young Texan who plays piano well, prepares choruses superbly, and is always silently anticipating the next problem. I have many relatives in St. Louis—a brother of my father's, his wife and children, a first cousin, and more distant ones. All of them were attentive without ever intruding. Despite the exhausting difficulties of the St. Louis operations, things went smoothly and my five weeks passed before I realized I had started.

Immediately afterward, I went to Salzburg. I had never before been in Germany or Austria because I had felt uncomfortable about being among ex-Nazis, but I experienced no problems.

I flew to Frankfurt, changed planes for Munich, and went to Salzburg by a train which I nearly missed because I was unable to find a porter to help with my usually absurd amount of luggage. I boarded at the very last minute, panting and sweating and hungry and thirsty.

I found myself in a compartment with a plain and agreeable middle-aged German couple. I searched everywhere for water or anything to drink or eat, only to find nothing. Conversation with the couple was limited since I do not speak German, but a quick reference in memory to the songs of Schubert and Schumann netted a few useful words.

Although they were embarrassed to eat in my presence, the couple finally opened their lunch box. They offered to share it with me but I was so thirsty that I did not salivate sufficiently for them even to notice. Stupid! I remembered suddenly that I always carry a flask of vodka in my briefcase. When I produced *this* I was in a bargaining position, but—alas!—all that remained of their lunch was an apple, which I did accept while they drank my vodka.

At the Salzburg station I found a most welcome Harold Clurman with a young man from the American Institute waiting to meet me. They whisked me off to Leopoldskronschloss, which sent me into a tailspin. I am not exactly accustomed to seeing palaces, much less sleeping in them.

The Leopoldskronschloss is baroque and lovely. It is said to have been built by a cardinal for his mistress. *The Sound of Music* was filmed there—vast lily pond, swans, and all.

I was fed and watered in a nearby cafe and began to revive a bit. My suite at the *Schloss* was on an upper floor (fifth, I believe), and a modern elevator simplified the otherwise long climb. Although it was rather poor, it was adequate for three days. The most extraordinary part about all our quarters was that while the dining room, library, classrooms, and several other rooms on the second and third floors were elegantly baroque, with vast crystal chandeliers, mirrors, and murals, our living quarters resembled maids' rooms, which they probably had been in the Great Days.

After a bit of personal tidying up, I was introduced to "students" from all over Europe, and finally attended a faculty cocktail party in honor of my arrival. Besides the previously mentioned Harold Clurman, there was Robert Anderson (author of *Tea and Sympathy*) and his charming actress wife, Teresa Wright; Mr. and Mrs. Donald Oenslager (he is the scene designer); and Mr. and Mrs. Paul Baker of Dallas, where Mr. Baker is head of the Dallas Theatre Center. Then there were the officer-hosts and their wives, and by then I had met them all.

Dinner in the great dining room was a simple affair belying the surroundings, with faculty and students interspersed (no permanent seat assignments), little service, and quite edible food. Afterward, we strolled along the porches and by the pond, and I retired early.

At four in the morning I was awakened by the trumpeting of the sun rising behind a mountain. Time change, too. I was wide awake, hungry, and nervous about the six lectures ahead. I arose, showered, shaved, and dressed, and then tiptoed down the several flights of stone steps and on to the ground floor, where I listened for any sign of life in the kitchen. All was silence.

My next thought was to call a taxi. Near the great door I found a cab card and dialed the number. Unfortunately, there was a great deal I did not know about dialing at the *Schloss* because after a ring, a sleepy voice answered: it was Donald Oenslager's! I did not reply.

Eventually, I discovered the clue to unlocking the massive front door, and I went out into the glorious mist of sunrise. The streets were empty. Although I did not know in which direction to walk, I took off. I passed many cafes, but all of them were closed.

After walking perhaps ten blocks to no avail, I sadly retraced my steps; and then, when I was almost back at the *Schloss*, I saw a woman raise the shades of her grocery store. I ran inside, bought a piece of yesterday's strudel, a container of milk (she had no coffee), and three plums. Across the street I saw a little park, sat down on a bench, and enjoyed the feast. When I returned to the *Schloss*, breakfast was being announced. I entered the dining room and ate again.

After my first lecture, which began at nine and was attended by faculty and students, Harold Clurman invited us to his quarters for cocktails before lunch. Everyone seemed pleased, and I was relieved. However, remembering the events of the early morning hours, I winced when I suddenly heard Don say, "Some S.O.B. rang my phone before five this morning and then didn't even speak!"

I was tempted not to speak again but characteristically (meaning that I always speak), I confessed.

Don laughed, and I *think* he forgave me.

In two days more, it was all over. I had made plans with Walter and Kaasi Slezak, who drove from their home in Switzerland to meet me. We spent another day in Salzburg, but at a hotel. The Slezaks took me to see Mozart's house. I was of course delighted, but I was having a physical reaction to the hard work in St. Louis and the heat there; the swift trip to Salzburg, together with the time change which I had tried to ignore; plus six lectures in three days. In Mozart's house I was easing up for the first time. I began experiencing ugly moments when I thought I was going to faint. I knew that I must be looking pale. Finally, I decided to return to my hotel only a couple of blocks away. I explained to Walter and Kaasi and made a great effort to cause no alarm; I could easily find my hotel.

I weaved my way down the semicrowded staircases, reached the street, and followed the river to the bridge that led to the hotel. I slept for several hours and then telephoned the Slezaks. It was then that I learned that they had been so concerned about me that they had followed behind until I was safely inside the hotel. Then they waited for this telephoned assurance.

The following day, Walter drove us to his hometown, Vienna, where I had never been before. When we arrived, Walter, who had driven for so long, was still filled with the enthusiasm of a little boy; he took me to Sacher's for a splendid dinner, and afterward to a beer garden behind Beethoven's house. Strung across the garden was an impressive grape arbor, but the music provided by a small table-to-table ensemble was just as terrible as it would have been in the United States.

My old friend Alberto Fiorella (from my Dallas days) met me in Vienna, and we continued sightseeing where the departing Slezaks had left off. We went on to Munich and then to Yugoslavia, arriving at Dubrovnik at midnight. Nobody looked at our passports or our luggage. (Iron curtain?) Dubrovnik was as charming as I had remembered it from an earlier visit.

We then went on to the beautiful island of St. Stephan. This small, nearly circular island is connected to the mainland by a narrow causeway. The entire area is walled. Inside, and straining as if to see, there are a large number of ancient white stone cottages with red tile roofs, one or two stories high, which are said to have been the homes of fishermen nearly a thousand years ago. The houses are arranged in no order or direction—a cubistic jumble—and today they are the "rooms" of the hotel that occupies the entire island. The cottages are reached by winding cobblestone paths that circle, climb, and fall away, and at irregular intervals run past little trees, flowers, and vines.

When Alberto and I decided to retire to our separate houses, we said goodnight, and I climbed the stairs to my second floor. (Alberto was just around the corner.) As I opened the door I was frightened at seeing a bat circling the interior of the room! I yelled for Alberto, who came running, and we were both at a loss to know what to do.

Finally, we went to the commissar-manager for help. She was a lady with red hair who closely resembled Ljuba Welitch as Salome. How to speak to her? English? No. German? *Ja!* Then I recalled: "Eine fledermaus!"

She summoned a porter, who returned with us, broom in hand, but the bat had flown away. Having seen too many movies, I slept with my hands around my throat.

A day later we went on to Athens. Both of us were tired, and so we went out very little during the hot days. Alberto returned to New York, and I proceeded to Istanbul.

I had told the State Department that I would be in Istanbul, hoping that they would arrange a meeting for me with Aydan Gün, impresario of the Turkish State Opera, in order to discuss *Porgy*, which I was to conduct in the winter. At Istanbul, I was disappointed at finding no message at the hotel. Finally, on my last day I telephoned the American consulate, where I spoke with a charming Turkish lady who knew about everything. She was certain that Washington had failed to tell anyone of my presence and said she would call the cultural attaché at our embassy in Ankara, who would surely then call me.

Perhaps five minutes later my telephone rang and a voice out of the past addressed me as "Lehman." He was Alvis Tinnin, a Negro tenor who had sung in the chorus of *Call Me Mister* and was now cultural attaché! It was a happy reunion. He told me that Mr. Gün was summering at a seaside resort near Izmir, that he would call Gün, and arrange to have Mrs. Ölçer, the lady with whom I had spoken, fly with me to Izmir, and then proceed by car to meet Mr. Gün.

Izmir was hot and beautiful. A State Department driver took us from Izmir on a dusty two-hour trip to the coast, where we encountered Mr. Gün at what, by our standards, would have been considered a shabby hotel. We sat in the shade behind the hotel, where a card table had been quickly rustled up, and drank beer. The conversation with Mrs. Ölçer as interpreter was in every way agreeable. I was assured that the chorus and cast would know the entire score by the time of my arrival late in November (it was now August) and that I would be the artistic director.

The following day Mrs. Ölçer returned to Istanbul, and I rode with a driver-guide to the glorious ruins at Ephesus, lunched on a high hill at the house said to have belonged to the Virgin Mary, and stopped to pick and eat the most wonderful ripe figs I had ever had. (Mississippi—home—was always with me.)

It was during these two trips to Europe that I came to full realization of the meaning of my mother's death three years before. She had always written to me wherever I went, and she was so fearful that her letters—unimportant in themselves—would not reach me that I never arrived anywhere without finding at least one awaiting me. I never checked into a hotel without missing what had been regular, inevitable, and often most foolish.

Also I had always bought my mother many small gifts at every place I visited, and I found myself subconsciously still looking for them. Sometimes I almost began to price such things and in midsentence withdrew my question.

I had also always written her a number of letters, and this need (now on my part) was somewhat met by the flow of mail I sent to my aunt and cousins in Mississippi and to Miss Leo in New York.

Little by little, I came to the dramatic realization that in the whole world there was no one who really cared about the little things that I always sent or wrote my mother—the things that had thrilled her, such as press clippings about me, even mere mentions of my name, the details of my work, the precise state of my health, what I bought, what was given me, and so on. This realization came slowly but at last totally. Although it was true that I found myself missing this reaction, which never failed to be expressed in her next letter, at last I understood. This caring had been nonexistent except between us, and when my mother died, this was finished. When I was able to comprehend this change, I was perhaps less of a little boy. Soon I did not miss it, even though I shall never be wholly able to forget it.

In the fall I resumed my New York workshops and inaugurated two in Los Angeles. I shuttled across the country each month until November 22, when I took off for Ankara.

26: *Porgy* in Ankara

Turkey's weather late in November largely parallels New York's. Ankara is a government city that holds no interest beyond the tiny Hittite Museum. There is a fine hotel belonging to a Swiss concern with a charming housekeeper named Mme Couvoisier. Everything is ersatz, since nothing is imported.

Work on *Porgy* was difficult, especially with the orchestra, because of atrocious discipline. The players talked incessantly and their attendance—particularly among my five cellists—was appalling. I learned that as the opera was state-supported, no one could be fired, and so the bad boys of the cello section took it upon themselves to be ill many, many times.

The principals were easy to work with, especially after I discovered their Achilles' heel: after all *they* were renowned artists! I understood, was tactful, and had little difficulty.

The most difficult part of the nine-week joust was with Mr. Gün— the impresario, stage director, and husband of our Bess—who, in my dealings with him, was devious, undependable, and as perfect and godlike in his own eyes as he was short of stature. His wife was a rather sweet lady with an easily forgettable voice.

It was in his capacity as stage director that I had most problems. As he understood no English, he was prone to jump to wrong conclusions largely because of faulty translations. For example, there is a musically complicated crap game in which isolated nomenclature such as "boxcars," "crapped out," "nine to make nine," "Little Joe," and others were translated literally and therefore were meaningless to him.

Bess entered waving hello to the other ladies, who actually are meant to snub her. He thought the rag song "A Red-Headed Woman" was about the Virgin Mary! The "Buzzard Song" was an enigma since the bird of the title was understood to be an owl. Maria, a kindly lady, was acting like Clytemnestra. So it went.

I opposed—but to no effect—the set designs because the houses were like traditional Negro huts and not, as intended, "a former mansion of the aristocracy." I opposed the use of black makeup and kinky wigs, but I might as well have saved my voice.

Through many fights, many walk-outs, and resignations on my part (my cousin Phyllis, traveling with our old family friend Lula Greer, was present at one major fight and resignation), *Porgy and Bess* finally opened January 11, 1969. I was greeted with warm applause at my entrance for each of the three acts (a custom *not* practiced generally in Turkey) and at the close. The press was ecstatic.

After the premiere the cast and I were plagued with flu and several performances had to be canceled.

I will quote from a diary I kept:

January 23. I have continued to have fever, a bad cold and a deep dry cough. Not wanting to become involved with strange doctors in a strange land, I have stayed in my hotel except for the four performances during nearly two weeks, and tonight is to be my final one. How strange it is to feel sentimental about completing a job I have found so unpleasant. But I do. The weather is very cold but I will wrap up warmly and tomorrow night I will be in New York!

Everything at the Opera House appeared to be as usual. The Little Man (valet) dressed me. Various members of the orchestra stopped by to shake hands silently. One player asked Hassan, the interpreter, a strange question, which he relayed to me: "What time are you leaving your hotel tomorrow?"

"Eight-thirty."

When I entered the pit, I was surprised by the silence. (My last performance and no applause.) I mounted the podium and was adjusting my glasses when I realized that the orchestra was standing. The concertmaster pointed a finger at the audience, which I regarded sheepishly over my shoulder. They too were standing! It does not say anything about this sort of thing in the rule book, and so, improvising, I wheeled around making a gesture with semicircularly raised arms, turned back to the orchestra, and motioned them to be seated. Then I heard the audience sit. Whew!

Act One went by with the usual unpredictable irregularities, but it went by. When I came out for Act Two and for Act Three, the audience applauded and cheered. The orchestra refused to share this with me when I gestured them to rise.

After the performance, when Bess brought me to the stage, there was no general lineup as there always had been. Instead Mrs. Gün shoved me gently forward, alone, and I was caught between the stage personnel, who stood well behind me, and the orchestra

In Ankara, Turkey (1969), at the Turkish State Opera, with the cast of *Porgy and Bess.* I objected, in vain, to the black faces and kinky wigs.

and the standing cheering audience. Nothing was possible for me except tears. When the curtains closed for the last time, the male principals kissed me on both cheeks. The absence of the women made me realize that perhaps I must approach them. They stood about waiting, and one by one I kissed them.

Returning to my dressing room, drenched as usual, I was in the process of being shoveled into dry clothes when there was a knock at the door. In marched the five resident maestros, silent and ceremonious. Each took my hands and kissed both about the knuckles, and all departed as silently as they had come.

When I was dressed, the Little Man packed together all of my wet clothes and we set off up several drafty flights of stairs to the stage door, which is preceded by a circular lobby. When I entered it, there was quiet steady applause from members of the chorus and orchestra, who lined the walls. Bowing and once again tearful, I beat a hasty retreat to the outside where a good part of the audience was waiting about in the cold and *they* too took up the applause.

I stepped quickly into Dr. Tinnin's embassy car with a single wave to the people, and off we went to my hotel.

As I was hanging up my wet clothes, I remembered the question about my departure time and began to wonder whether there would be more people the following morning. As I needed to leave for the airport at 8:30, I descended to the main floor as early as possible.

Coming out of the elevator, I found a smiling group in the lobby, and there was more of what I had been through the night before. This time there were also little gifts. As quickly as I could politely withdraw, I left with Dr. Tinnin and Hassan for the airport. The day—rare in Ankara at this time of the year—was crystal clear. A bright red sun decorating a deep blue sky saw me off.

27: Some Interludes

THE YEAR 1969 began with *Porgy* in Ankara and ended with *Scarlett* in Tokyo. Between these two distant poles, I did much work.

I spent the first of what were to be several annual weekends at the Cincinnati College-Conservatory to coach classes in potential musical-theater performers, and I spoke. While I was there, I was greatly impressed with a young lady student who sang a diverse program of "modern" songs with considerable style and in a unique voice—somewhat hoarse, raucous, and nasal, and at the same time electric and winning. As she was presently coming to New York, I called my old friend and agent Gus Schirmer and sent the girl, Pamela Myers, to sing for him. Afterward *he* became excited and put her under contract. Soon television guest appearances and a summer theater tour, which provided her with invaluable experience, culminated in her being cast in the role of Marta in Steve Sondheim's *Company*. She had a single song "Another Hundred People," and through it she became a very special potential star on Broadway.

My season, which had been resumed late in January, climaxed in my three annual spring showcases in New York and one in Los Angeles. The performers included Helen Gallagher, Nancy Dussault, David Cryer, Patrick Fox, Bernadette Peters, Jonelle Allan, Clifton Davis, Warren Galjour, Rosetta Le Noir, Sid Marshall, Patti Karr, Barbara Williams, and Brooks Morton, who all worked hard, were paid small honorariums, and gave glowing performances. (I became more and more apprehensive about the "traditional" items I had included. Side by side with more progressive works, they paled miserably.)

Summer made its appearance on schedule. I wound up the BMI Workshops for the season, gave a lecture at Wagner College, conducted a pair of concerts with the Boston Pops, and a revival of *The Consul* at the Temple University Festival at Ambler, Pennsylvania.

The Boston concerts were sold out and I thought that, considering my one rehearsal, they went well. It was ferociously hot in Symphony Hall, built long before air-conditioning. On stage, we suffered miserably under the bright lights. I inherited in my dressing room an elderly black valet. Before the first concert he offered me cold beer, but I explained that I always drank vodka at these times. Quietly he supplied the ice but remarked rather wonderingly, "Mr. Fiedler, he like bourbon."

The Consul in Ambler was not good. I had two student casts to rehearse simultaneously. The orchestra consisted of incipient virtuosi who did not play easily in ensemble. Unfortunately, as these people were active in countless simultaneous conflicting summer-school activities, many individuals arrived late at rehearsals, left early, or were absent altogether. The performances were neither good nor well attended.

I was suddenly struck by the almost incredible role played in my life—and, as I thought about it, in everyone's—by friends. I had never since my first job, thirty-five years earlier, *asked* for a job. However, in thinking back over even the most recent events in my life, I became aware that much of what I did was promoted by friends. (I doubt that they would have been devoted had they not respected me but. . . .) Marvin Schofer, a member of my very first workshop was now in the publicity department of the Boston Symphony. I feel certain that he instigated that engagement. Dr. Tinnin, the black former chorus singer in *Call Me Mister* twenty-two years before, certainly at least encouraged Mr. Gün to apply to the State Department for me to do *Porgy*. My engagement at the Temple University Festival, in spite of my prior connection with *The Consul* and whatever reputation I had gathered, came through David Kanter, who

Margaret (Peggy) Webster in Tobago, W. I., in 1970. She was at work on her last book.

had been assistant stage manager for *Call Me Mister* and, later, stage manager for *The Consul*.

I could go on and on with similar relationships, but I think I have made my point. I think it is an important one because it affects everyone's activities for good or ill but much too often goes unrecognized and disregarded.

In August I went off to Tobago with Peggy Webster for a real rest, which provided us alternately with time for doing nothing and even more time for working—each of us—on a new book. The climate was ideal, and our being together at lunch and dinner—occasionally meeting by accident on the beach—was ideal. We were insurance against boredom, and neither of us ever interfered with the other's working or resting.

Fall came too soon. Workshops were resumed in New York, Los Angeles, and Toronto, but this time I added two monthly days to Nashville! I do not quite know how I managed them.

Nashville, in the end, did not work out, but I continued my efforts for two seasons. At my first several sessions when I talked, the room was packed with professional writers. As soon as I made assignments, which as usual required creating and performing songs for criticisms, the room emptied out except for four who stayed on for the two years I continued.

With Brooks Atkinson at a Sigma Alpha Mu banquet in 1969. Brooks presented me with the fraternity's "Man of the Year" award. *Photo by Bob Golby*

I held a class on each of my two evenings at Peabody College—a result of BMI's offer through Frances Preston, the beautiful local vice-president, to the head of Peabody's music department.

On one of my trips to Nashville a young man came to audition for my BMI class. He was personable, and unlike the other Nashvillians, spoke rather elegantly. He sat down with his guitar (very usual) and sang one of his songs. I felt that this was *really* distinguished, and I asked for another. It was equally exciting. I called Frances Preston to hear him and she was impressed. I said I would be pleased to have him in the class, and we left it at that.

A month later when I returned there was a message that he regretted being out of town but hoped to come next time. The demand for him grew quickly and reached giant proportions. He never reappeared.

He was Kris Kristoferson.

At the beginning of December, Sigma Alpha Mu, my college fraternity, gave a banquet in my honor and presented me, through Brooks Atkinson, with their annual "Man of the Year" award. Before the middle of the month, I was off to Tokyo to conduct the world premiere of *Scarlett*.

28: *Scarlett* in Tokyo, and Other Travels

THE MUSICALIZATION OF *Gone with the Wind* was created for Tokyo, where the nonmusical stage version had been produced successfully three years before. The director-choreographer Joe Layton had been a dancing Brazilian naval officer in *Wonderful Town*. Harold Rome was the composer-lyricist. Trudi Rittman, who has created musical frames for nearly every composer in the American musical theater, was the musical integrator; David Baker, the rehearsal pianist; and Meyer Kupferman, avant-garde composer, the orchestrator. David Hayes designed the scenery, and Pat Campbell, the costumes. With myself as conductor, the American staff for the Tokyo production was complete.

Joe was the first to arrive about nine weeks ahead of the opening. Trudi, Meyer, and David followed soon afterward, then Harold with Florence; and I—the last—came three weeks before the opening, having seen the songs but not the elaborate musical "treatments" of them provided by Trudi.

This production was different from all others. The differences took two forms. The songs were imbedded in an almost endless musical texture that became underscoring for dialogue between sung phrases and music for dancing and pantomime. Second, the dramatic scenes were generally acted down in front (in "one"), while frequently behind these there was continuous ballet. Then too, while most music was played by the live orchestra of thirty-five,

In Tokyo in 1970 during rehearsals for *Scarlett*—subsequently retitled *Gone with the Wind*. *Left to right*: Harold Rome, who wrote the music and lyrics, his wife Florence, and I.

some was prerecorded and heard phantomlike. Three times the live and recorded music were played simultaneously and contrapuntally, producing a nightmare effect. Layton seldom allowed a song to end, an effect appropriate for Tokyo audiences, who applaud infrequently except at the end of the show, but frustrating for Western audiences deprived of self-expression and given no clear idea of the songs themselves.

The cast was interesting. The Scarlett, Miss Jinguji, had been the principal "male" actor in the all-female Takarazuka Theatre until she married. Resignation was then obligatory. She is an electric actress in her mid-thirties, thin, tragic but with an unending sense of humor, and a face that must remind anyone my age of Louise Fazenda. The Rhett broke his leg ten days before opening and was replaced by Kinya Kitaoji, a popular young singer who learned everything with amazing speed. The Ashley, Jiro Tamiya, is well known in Japanese movies as a villain and could scarcely have been more romantic than in *Scarlett*. Melanie was a famous young Occidental-looking singing actress; nearly all small parts were cast with performers famous among Japanese audiences.

As there are no unions in the Japanese theater, the director could use as much time as he wished. The orchestra—also nonunion—was less docile: substitutes appeared frequently and decisions were sometimes made to rehearse or not to rehearse without my knowing definitely until rehearsal time.

The Imperial Theatre (with a capacity of eighteen hundred), where we opened, is modern, with a vast all-movable stage that ascends, descends, revolves, and whatnot. It is built into one side of a modern office building that has a large rehearsal room on the ninth floor. As in nearly all office buildings in Tokyo, the ground floor and the one below are jammed with many small restaurants: Chinese, Japanese, French, Indian, chicken, fish, and sandwich restaurants and many of each kind. At rehearsal intermissions, all personnel poured into these eating places and somehow finished in about twenty minutes. There were also neatly wrapped wooden boxes of food that could be taken away. Most popular was the box filled with circular mounds of cold white rice wrapped in seaweed. This, with hot green tea brought from home in thermos jugs, was never absent from rehearsals. Seedless tangerines were ever-present. There were also boxes containing a single five-layer sandwich.

There was at least one physical and one moral difference between Japanese and American rehearsals. The physical one is that the chairs and tables looked as though they were made for children, since Japanese legs are short. Likewise drinking-water fountains and wash basins are so low that even not-very-tall Occidentals like myself had to bend considerably in order to use them.

The moral difference is reflected everywhere. I often saw a wallet or a "mound" of money (bills and change) lying around loosely on a table at rehearsals. Sometimes pieces of jewelry and watches. These were left by actors or dancers who did not want them jingling in pockets or falling out on the floor. Sometimes these were forgotten and left overnight when cleaning personnel tidied things up. Never were they missing! (In New York, stage managers warn casts against leaving money lying about.)

Near the end of the rehearsal period we spent two days at a "gymnasium," in reality an enormous indoor stadium. The temperature hovered around freezing, and we rehearsed in overcoats eight hours daily. As the floor was "special" (most floors in Japan in one way or another are) we had to deposit our shoes outside and don thin cold slippers.

To my alarm, I found (always secrets) that there was to be a matinee *every single day*, including Sunday! I let out a war whoop and bequeathed all of them to my assistant Fukumori, who was in any case taking over after my departure. But the poor cast and the poor orchestra! Matinees began at 12:30 and ended at 4:45. Evening performances began at 5:30 and, with one half-hour intermission, lasted until 9:45. I understood that no one was paid extra for this. Most performances were sold out.

Poor Fukumori did matinees and then sat beside me at night to nudge me (sometimes the nudges were pugilistic) when word cues came along. But eventually, poor Lehman. We opened on Friday. From the following Monday through Thursday, I prerecorded the orchestra from 11:00 P.M. until 5:00 A.M. for two LP records at the Victor Company, where everything was bedlam. Orchestral parts were missing or full of errors. Players (mostly *not* from the theater orchestra) strolled in and out to eat, repark cars, go to the toilet, or make phone calls.

During my four weeks in Tokyo, I was seldom away from Florence and Harold Rome. We went to dinner almost nightly, and of course, Harold stayed through all of the long nights of recording. I saw little of Tokyo, which seemed to be an unplanned wilderness of small structures except for the modern downtown area, which after its destruction in World War II had been rebuilt to resemble an American city.

When the records had been done, I set off by car for Hakone and stopped en route to see the impressive bronze Buddha at Kamakura. Hakone in the cold mountain climate is architecturally everything Westerners think of as Japanese. I journeyed by the most perfect train I have ever ridden to Kyoto (the name is an anagram of "Tokyo"), saw Fujiyama clearly during most of the trip, spent a few hours in Nara feeding very "pushy" wet-nosed deer, and finally boarded a plane at Osaka for Hong Kong.

There I enjoyed the unique hospitality of the Peninsula Hotel, overlooking the busy harbor; was fascinated by the mixture of rickshaws and autos to be found everywhere, and then left for Bangkok, certainly the most colorful city in the world, filled with strangely shaped multihued temples.

Although my energy was running low, I continued on to New

ABOVE: Dame Edith Evans with L. E. in London (1972), after lunch with
Anna and Arnold Weissberger, and Milton Goldman. *Photo by Arnold
Weissberger* BELOW: L. E. in London on the Victoria Embankment, the
Thames flowing by.

Delhi, where I observed indolence and poverty, and little to recommend the city. Being tired I canceled previously planned Indian excursions and after only two days decided to return to New York.

In the first-class section of the JAL plane there was only one other passenger—an elderly gentleman, and I felt it second nature to say, "Good evening," to him.

I received no response.

When the Japanese stewardess came on call from him, he ordered beer in English with a thick German accent. I loathed him. In my imagination, he was a leftover Nazi, and he had seen at once that I was Jewish. I remembered what Sartre had written: "Hell is other people." He sure was.

After a stop in Teheran, the plane took off for Cairo. There was a clear full-moon night, and I prayed that the Israelis were sleeping. Two buses waited on the airfield: one for first-class passengers, the other for economy class. We would spend about an hour in the airport. First off the plane, I boarded the bus and stood near the entrance. The German passenger followed and stood next to me.

"Have you ever been to Cairo?" he asked.

"Yes," was my complete answer.

After considerable silence I felt strained, and so I observed, "It's chilly for this time of year." (Inane and true.)

"No, no, it's cold for this time of year," he fairly yelled at me. (Deaf!) Then he invited me to join him for a coffee.

Sartre was not quite right: Hell is yourself.

Then Rome, Frankfurt, London, and finally, after twenty-six hours, New York.

What a long night's journey into day!

29: Work and Wandering

In JANUARY, I resumed my workshops in New York, Los Angeles, and Toronto, and was elected to membership in the Player's Club. When summer came and there was an intermission, I was at work on the book I had shown Jerry Kaplan, called *Words with Music*, and I went off to Guadeloupe for a rest and for writing and then, after several weeks, on to Europe—more travel with more writing.

Having once been into Germany unmolested, I was interested—if only once—in attending the Wagner festival in Bayreuth. Accordingly, I obtained a schedule of operas, prices, and the modus operandi. Looking at a map it seemed to me that Bayreuth was not too far from my dear friends Walter and Kaasi Slezak. Counting back from this proposed visit, I chose *Götterdämmerung*, *Tristan*, and *Meistersinger* to hear-see at the festival.

I received a welcome letter from the Slezaks at once, and a day later, a circular from the festival, returning my check with the information that everything had long since been sold out. As I seldom believe in impossibilities, I wrote to Walter, and by return mail, he informed me that he had spoken to Frau Winifred Wagner on the phone and she had invited me to sit in the "Family Loge" for these three performances!

In all my life I had never before stayed in a hotel so poor as the one they assigned me in Bayreuth. The managers were pleasant, and the food was not bad, but my room was an attic affair, narrow and lacking in all conveniences. Toilets and bathrooms were in the hall.

Evening clothes were in order even though the operas commenced at 4:00 P.M., when the summer sun was still bright.

The lady concierge advised me to hire a cab to pick me up daily at the hotel and then again at the Festspielhaus after the performance.

When I arrived for *Götterdämmerung*, it was still early. People were standing outside on the grass in small groups. As I had also been told by the concierge to go into the dining pavilion behind the Festspielhaus *before* the opera to book a place and to give my orders for each of the two intermissions, I made those arrangements.

The theater—lifeless on the outside and built of fading red brick—has a balcony overlooking the grounds where a group of brass-players blew fanfares to summon the strolling audience inside.

The Family Loge turned out to be the royal box (despite its plainness) since it occupied the center position. There are fixed seats on concrete steps, with two rows of four seats each at the front and then a little aisle and two rows of two seats each rising above.

Frau Wagner was on hand as hostess and assignee of seats. She is a very tall, lean, regal lady with an Edwardian hairdo. She speaks fluent English (she was English-born) and had been married to Richard and Cosima's son, Siegfried, who had died many decades ago.

Frau Wagner was charming, solicitous, and firm. She assigned me a seat in the second row next to her.

The lights went out promptly at four. All noise and conversation ceased abruptly. As the orchestra pit and conductor were hidden totally from view, there was no applause when the conductor entered. The acoustics were superb.

The production I saw was "modern." Only the most necessary props were employed. The lighting in everything was a notch above total darkness.

The audience was breathless: it did not cough or rustle programs or talk. Only after the last note of Act One had died away (about two and a half hours later) was there applause. As this happened, Frau Wagner leaned over and said to me, "It's too damned slow," and sprang out of the loge, disappearing as on a broomstick.

I went into the pavilion, where everything was meticulously organized. Each person was shown to his seat, where his food or dessert or cocktail had already been served and paid for and tipped for in advance.

On being summoned by fanfares, everyone fled back again into the theater. As soon as the second act began, I knew that Frau Wagner had berated the conductor, since everything was a notch too fast. On the whole, I found the production and performance superb, and it was a special pleasure to be in a musical theater in which the audience refrained from applauding the scenery.

The second night was *Tristan* and an occasion, since Birgit Nilsson and Wolfgang Windgassen were singing and Karl Böhm was conducting. On arrival in the Family Loge, I found Frau Wagner again receiving, this time in a close-fit dress of gold lamé, which proceeded in a straight line from her neck to her toes. Dozens of small gold buttons followed one another from top to bottom.

Some of the people from the previous night were there again, and there were also newcomers. Frau Wagner placed everyone (this time I sat in the back of the loge), and just before the lights went out, it was clear that the tall old lady had held out no seat for herself. Quite nimbly she plopped to the floor, causing each male "guest" to rise and insist on her taking *his* seat. Her command had probably been sounded often: "Let's have no fuss [pronounced "foss"]. I'm used to sitting on the floor. Please take your seats."

The following morning I went to a florist and (as Walter Slezak had advised) sent six dozen roses to Frau Wagner with an elaborate note of gratitude.

I also recalled Walter's telling me that both the cast and production of *Meistersinger*, which I would hear that final night, were poor, and I also recalled Frau Wagner's saying after *Tristan* that she might not see me again as tomorrow was one of her granddaughter's birthdays ("barthdays") and she would be at a little party. In anticipation of displeasure—I told my driver to look for me about half an hour before the end of the opera.

On arrival at the loge, I found Frau Wagner present only to thank me for the roses and my generous note, and after she had bubbled over with gratitude and platitude, she left.

What Walter had said about that *Meistersinger* cast and production was a vast understatement. During the intermission I began telling the others in the box that I would have to leave early in order to make a plane—this so that in the event Frau Wagner returned or heard about my premature departure she would not be offended.

Before the third act, a heavy rain accompanied by lightning and thunder began. This could be heard even above the Wagnerian din. In the orchestral interlude between the two scenes of the final act, I tiptoed up the few creaky steps of the loge, opened and closed the door noiselessly, and breathed a sigh of relief. Down the marble staircase I went on tiptoe and along the corridor on the main floor, where I encountered puzzled glances from ushers and coat-room attendants. I arrived at the outer door, and through the heavy rain I could see my driver switch on his lights and approach. As I closed the door behind me, preparing to run to the cab, the door was abruptly reopened by an English-speaking usherette. In the most sympathetic voice imaginable she asked, "Could I get you a doctor, sir?"

I answered her question and dashed out through the rain.

On one of my trips to Los Angeles during the following spring, I received a call from Julius Rudel, the very able director of the New York City Opera and music director of the nearly completed Kennedy Center for the Performing Arts in Washington. They anticipated reviving Kurt Weill's *Lost in the Stars* and wanted me to conduct it. Although I wanted to do this, my major concern was time. When? We would rehearse for three weeks in New York, beginning in December, and play four weeks in Washington in January.

This suited me ideally. Rehearsals would fit in with my Christmas break (the workshops are then on holiday), and I could commute between Washington and New York for classes after the January opening. William Warfield, whom I had helped to cast in the *Call Me Mister* road company years ago, would star. Julius explained that money was scarce, and he asked me to cooperate. I did.

By fall, Diana (Mrs. Herman) Shumlin had been engaged as co-producer with Roger L. Stevens, the director of the center. As Stevens had a chance to book David Merrick's musical *Sugar* for four weeks prior to Broadway (a potential financial coup) he simply set back the *Lost in the Stars* date by one month. My life was then going to be a muddle.

Warfield also had a contract to do *Porgy* in Vienna, and this new date was to allow him to play so short a time in Washington that Stevens made a settlement with him, and he was replaced by Brock Peters.

The stage director was Gene Frankel, who had never piloted a musical and was himself thoroughly unmusical. I engaged my lady pianist and assistant conductor, and we spent several periods with Frankel going over the score. He seemed to like none of it and asked for cuts constantly.

When we went into rehearsal, there was artistic chaos. Frankel's idea was to transform *Lost in the Stars* into a South African show. (This kind of idea is as incorrect as trying to make Puccini's *Girl of the Golden West* into an American opera simply because it is set in California about 1849.) Toward achievement of his goal Frankel brought in a bongo drummer, a black lad from Brooklyn, who was an amateur and not a union member. The boy could not see without his glasses, which Frankel did not want him to wear on the stage. The drumming was louder than the orchestra, seldom with it, and as wrong for Weill's orchestrations as possible.

At a run-through in New York, Julius Rudel made it clear to Frankel that the drummer was to be eliminated. This in no way deterred Frankel. There were also masks, and neither masks nor drums play any part in South African life. That did not seem to matter.

The irritations grew. After an opening in Washington that drew mostly favorable reviews, Julius Rudel came again and issued *orders* to Frankel about the drum. Frankel agreed and then next day changed his mind. Lenya Weill came to see me and was distraught. Meanwhile, Diana Shumlin discharged Frankel a number of times, but Stevens always immediately reinstated him. Other directors were interviewed, but it was becoming late for a change. A tour to Boston and Toronto had been arranged, and a Broadway opening was the new goal.

It became increasingly clear that Frankel would operate as he pleased. Dancers and dancing were introduced to the accompaniment of even more drumming.

In Boston, while there were some good reviews, the powerful Kevin Kelly roasted the show, and we played to near-empty houses. I myself sat in the first row in the audience in order to be able to conduct. Oliver Smith's set—as requested and approved by Frankel —was an abstract affair that extended a lip out over the center of the orchestra pit. In Washington I had had to stand to the right of it. In Boston it was necessary for me to sit in the first row in the auditorium where I had to conduct the stage (the all-important chorus) with my right arm *above* the set floor and my left for the orchestra *below* it, *between* the bottom of the set and the orchestra railing!

On the last day in Boston—just before Toronto—Stevens sent for me. His manner was pleasant. He thanked me for my work, for having been responsible for Mrs. Henry Moses donating seventy thousand dollars, and so on. He was certain that Julius Rudel and I knew more about music than he or Frankel (I was not about to argue), but as I was unhappy, he would release me: Frankel needed to have complete freedom.

I said that I would not *quit*, but that if he wished, he could fire me—shades of *Illya Darling*. In that way he would be required to pay my salary for the run of the show. He chuckled in agreement, and we shook hands.

I learned later that a prominent Washington critic had attended a performance with Stevens after we had run about three weeks and liked the music much better than he had on the opening night (at this latter time, my assistant was conducting because I had gone for a week to classes in Los Angeles). We all knew that we had had an excellent dress rehearsal and that *everything* was "down" on opening night. (Stevens, too, remembered this clearly.)

Nightly I went to Brock Peters's dressing room during intermission and at the end of the show, and almost invariably it was necessary to point out a bar of music in his soliloquy that he habitually bypassed. This never seemed to cause any friction. Actually, on most of these occasions we usually commiserated about the latest atrocities committed by Frankel. Peters *seemed* as much upset about them as I.

Perhaps it is clearer now to the reader why I no longer want to be in the musical theater. When thinking becomes so muddled that a

Eudora Welty about 1960.

In 1971 the Cincinnati College-Conservatory of Music presented me with an honorary doctorate in music. *Left to right*: Dean Jack Watson, director of the College-Conservatory; L. E.; and Dr. Walter Langsam, president of the University of Cincinnati. *Photo by Heizer Photographers, Inc.*

director actually *believes* he can make a Broadway musical African by superimposing unscored bongo drums, projecting pictures of masks, and introducing rituals none of which are indigenous to the show itself or to South Africa and when such muddled thinking can even go unrecognized by the critics as spurious, something is very wrong.

This is not the theater that—164 shows ago—I was initiated into. It always had its uncertainties and its know-nothings, but today these characteristics are noisier and more abundant than ever before. Thank you. But no thanks.

Words with Music came out in the spring to great reviews, including a glowing one in the *New York Times* by my old friend Eudora Welty, an entire page in the *Los Angeles Times* by Dan Sullivan, and wonderful ones almost everywhere else.

I then finished another book, *Getting Started in the Theater.*

After successful showcases here and in Los Angeles, I conducted three pop concerts with the Pittsburgh Symphony at the Temple University Festival near Philadelphia, with Comden and Green as soloists at the first, Peter Nero at the second, and Ferrante and Teicher at the last. Then I went to Europe, where I saw many old friends in London, visited Jim Wise in Tourrettes (Helen had blessedly passed away after long suffering), spent two weeks touring Sicily, and then went to Malta, the château country in France, Paris, London, and home.

In 1971 I was given an honorary doctorate in music at a special "exercise" by my alma mater, the Cincinnati College-Conservatory (now a truly important musical institution) and in the late spring, in Jackson, on the occasion of the induction of Millsaps College's new president, Dr. Edward Collins, he presented me with the degree of Doctor of Humane Letters. Also, the Hartford Conservatory of Music through Robert Brawley gave me an honorary citation.

Epilogue

Last night I dined alone at Le Perigord, a quite nice French restaurant in my neighborhood. Cocktails finished and dinner served, I stared ahead across the crowded room. My vision was not altogether clear. Faces were blurred. My attention focused on a couple who sat on a banquette along the opposite wall. I thought, "Oh, there is Zorina Lieberson . . . and the young man with her is—oh, of course, Gower Champion." Perfectly natural: two dancers.

Then I began to interpret with my mind. Zorina, or Brigitta (which is her real name), is in Santa Fe with Goddard, her husband. More important, I began to see, if only fuzzily, that the couple I half saw were very young. They might indeed have been Brigitta and Gower twenty-odd years ago, but not today.

That is one aspect of life at sixty-two. I often see someone perhaps a little indistinctly at theater or opera or walking along an avenue, and I *almost* greet him when I stop short on realizing that I am wrong. This misjudgment is neither unhappy nor otherwise, but it is one of the things I must attribute to my own aging.

There are also the annoyances attributable to one's ego when telephoning a producer's office or the florist shop where you have been a customer for twenty-five years and hearing a strange New Voice on the phone who asks you to spell your name and then pronounces it badly. You ask to speak to the producer, and New Voice asks if *she* can help you! Apoplexy time in Dixie. And New Voice florist asks your address and whether or not you have an account.

349

Of course this is what the inevitable passage of time does, but you have to reason with yourself that the new situation is normal and unavoidable, that the petty annoyances and brief inconveniences are certainly not directed at you personally. The friendly voice you knew has retired or died.

Recently I went to Haiti for a twelve-day rest between periods of frantic activity. I was not happy there alone and with suddenly nothing to occupy me. A recent—and oh, so rare a thing at this period of my life—an *affaire d'amour*, on which I had lavished great hopes, had ended. I ended it because I detected ever so faintly (but to me, definitely) a sincere effort to please me without the feeling behind it which would have told me that we shared equally the emotions that I felt, needed, and dared to hope for; there was a forty-year difference in our ages. I was depressed, not only because of this particular experience but because what came into focus in my mind was that I must stop expecting such things, must know in advance that never—never again—would they possibly become what I wanted them to be and what I had fortunately experienced in reality several times in my life. Something had ended. Every part of it.

In Haiti, I waited, watching a turbulent sky, for a long time. It was still and hot. I saw the dark-blue clouds advancing ever so slowly and then the heavy rain, like a scrim, fell in the valley below. I waited as though for the end of the world and feared only that it would not come. Then the trees began to blow about, directionless and frantic. A bewildered black butterfly pursued a senseless course. Everywhere, lizards slithered hastily about over the trunks of trees. The birds—smarter—had fled from the skies.

Finally the rain came, and with it thunder and lightning such as I had never before heard or seen. And somehow I was happier. I was not alone in suffering. Nature, who is to be blamed for so much, was also at violent odds with itself. And I was glad.

God gives us the miracle of our bodies and the greater miracle of our souls that inhabit them. But at that moment of glorious giving we are also cursed. Our bodies grow older and find the going increasingly more difficult while our souls with their desires and needs —alive and consistent from the beginning of consciousness—never change. We go along becoming gradually altered in the way we look but still thirsting for whatever it always has been that we have desperately wanted. And we are crushed between the what we seem to have become and the who we really are and always have been. It is perhaps the most painful of all dichotomies, the most predictable, the most illusive, and the most difficult one to face—and face it we must—as an inevitable reality. How to do it? Yet do it we must. And alone. We are given no choice.

Even as the rain continued its relentless pounding, the thunder became more distant and the near-blackness of the sky gradually turned into a pinkish gray. Somehow—at least this time—it would not be the end of the world.

The seasons and the years seem to pass so very swiftly now, and although I work a great deal all the time—even on vacations—there seems to be insufficient opportunity to accomplish even half of what I set my sights on. This desire to work, accompanied by profound interest in what I am doing, has become a glorious part of my life. What a marvellous difference the passage of time makes! Throughout all these long years—until I was about forty-five—I dreaded being alone. If an evening came round and I had no invitation to do something or to go somewhere, or had bought no tickets to attend almost anything, I became surfeited with an almost everwhelming sense of rejection. What to do? Nobody liked me. And thousands of those specters sat with me uninvited, making my life miserable.

What a change now, when I cherish an evening alone, fight for a weekend involving no people—not even my closest friends. To be alone to read, to work, not to have to dress—morning to night—to gorge myself on quiet (sometimes even hectic) reading, writing, digging myself out of the debris under which the preceding week has buried me.

Sometimes when I go out I meet someone I recognize at once as belonging to the genus I've always found attractive. For a moment, I feel excitement and then I reject what by now is only a reminder of the past—not really an impulse: I have been here before. I no longer need or want what seems to present itself as a possibility.

Many lifelong friends drop away like leaves from an old cherished book—forever lost. Monty Clift, Harry Cumpson, Peggy Webster, Mary Morris, Evelyn Leo. And so many more. This happens only to

those of us who outlive the others. We think of things we did or
said together. We check the impulse to remember something we
mustn't forget to tell them.

My mother alone somehow lingers on today. When crossing
crowded streets, I still hear her admonition, "Be careful"; but I
walk on, now and for a long time past on my own. When I undress
at night, she still tells me to hang up my clothes ("How would you
feel if the doctor had to come during the night?"). Sometimes I
obey. Sometimes I tune her out like the radio. But her voice still
penetrates the millions of miles and the long decades when she
found me an unwilling if helplessly obedient listener.

I have found this somehow most meaningful in Peggy Webster's
case. Our friendship was always strong and our working-together
constant. Yet there seemed never to have been any pressing need to
communicate with her daily when she was in New York or with any
regularity when we were separated by great distances. I saw her
three times in London the summer before her death and dined with
her alone in New York two nights before the large party Alfred
Knopf gave her on the formal release of her last book. It was a good
party and a befittingly glamorous one, although I among only a few
others knew that she was barely maneuvering her way through it
because of great physical suffering. When I kissed her good-bye at
that party, I knew (and I prayed) that it was for the very last time.
The end came in London only about two weeks later, but meanwhile
she had written me several brief letters from the hospital. I do not
fully understand our great friendship—a unique miracle—and I find
it quite difficult to cope with the fact of her death.

I do not recall feeling any transition in my life from being the
youngest student or conductor or the youngest many other things to
the strange point where I knew without the need of any specific
signposts that I am now on the other side of youth. When I conducted
in Turkey only three years ago, an adorable little girl came running
to me at a dinner table, her arms outstretched, speaking rapidly in
Turkish, which I do not understand. I picked her up, and she embraced me. Her parents and other guests were hysterical with
laughter. I asked what she was saying, and her father rather em-
barrassedly said, "She is calling you Grandpapa!"

This somehow does not seem strange to me.

On the other hand, when I remember things that happened long ago or even in my childhood, I reexperience the emotions I felt when they happened. They are not dulled by the passage of time. In that sense, when I reexperience them, I feel as young as I felt at the time: the excitement before a performance when, seated in a theater, I would see a ripple flow across the closed curtain and was filled with intense anticipation that I was about to see something thrilling. Or the awe I experienced when I stood surrounded by hallowed silence in my grandmother's weed-ridden garden long after she had left it. (I was a child.) The mysterious enchantment I felt (as in Wyeth's painting) at the sight of a lace curtain blown about by a gentle breeze. (This has been always.)

These and many others are small and very personal things I knew and comprehended as a child, and when I am reminded of them now—in that moment I am again a child. The experiences are not changed nor are they diluted by time. Love that ever was also goes on unchanged.

As a man who has spent half a century in the theater, done every kind of thing and seen so much, I now find myself, as teacher and writer, in a dilemma. Truly I do not know whether I have the right to say of something supposedly new that I am bored because I have seen or heard it long ago and in a more authentic form. Or whether it is the right of today's people to believe that they themselves have created it and it must be so, for their audience appears to be seeing or hearing something for the first time. My own behavior at such times is indeed the puzzle that now too often confronts me.

What is indeed right about this? Should I shatter illusions or go along with them? I cannot tell.

It is also wonderful after so many years in the New York theater to walk in the tatty theater district an hour before performance and shake hands with musicians, stagehands, actors, and doormen and find them greeting me like an old friend. When will I come back? they ask. Who knows?

I find today that I retain a residue of poetry and of Shakespeare— not as much music. Someone makes a remark, and I hear it continuing in my mind, sometimes giving voice to it—a phrase, a line, a stanza touched off by a word or an idea in an ordinary conversation: cummings, Eliot, Rossetti, Whitman, Emily Dickinson, Tennyson, Milton, Keats, and many more. And *Alice in Wonderland* and a great part of Shakespeare. I think these things that I learned so long ago or remembered without trying to must circulate inside me perpetually like my blood. They are seldom very far away from my consciousness, and effortlessly, I feel enriched and refreshed.

When I was beginning in New York, I was occasionally invited to parties at many of which there were celebrated composers, painters, poets, and other artists. I met them, and they greeted me quite properly without conferring upon me any particular identity.

Many years have passed. There have been a great many parties and a great many distinguished people; only yesterday I went through a driving rain to attend one given by Arnold Weissberger and Milton Goldman in honor of Mrs. Sean O'Casey. I was very tired, and the sizable living room was crowded. Suddenly I was seized by an extraordinary realization: a great part of my early life was in that single room. Nobody was as closely related to so many of the people—not even the hosts, whose invitations had brought them there—as I! And my reunion with them—unlike the distinguished people at parties forty years ago—brought warmth and joy and sometimes tears.

Mrs. O'Casey, the guest of honor (a little lost, I thought), is of course Sean's widow, and although we had never before met, she knew me from her husband's accounts following the opening of *Within the Gates*, my first show, in 1934.

Seated just behind the stalwart Mrs. O'Casey was Martha— Martha Graham in black lace, her beautiful mask now a bit askew. "We must get together when you return from Los Angeles next week," she said.

Mr. and Mrs. Donald Stralem were cordial as always. It was in their apartment, where—surrounded by friends as wealthy as they, Betty Comden and Adolph Green, with Saul Chaplin at the piano— they raised much of the money for *Bonanza Bound*, which I conducted. (It closed in Philadelphia.)

I was embraced by Virgil Thomson, now much stouter than when

I last saw him (how long ago?), and white, jolly, and hard of hearing. We must get together. He was with his old friend Maurice Grosser, the painter of simple, enchanting pictures. Now a bit grayer, he is still a little boy.

Jane Pickens Langley, whom I had used in *The Beggar's Opera*; Gusty Weissberger Schenker, Orson's one-time secretary; her mother, dear old Anna Weissberger, who brought Orson chicken soup (now still smiling but a little vague); Leah Salisbury, the play agent, looking handsomely older (I last saw her with Harry and Elsa Moses back in the early thirties when they were producing *Grand Hotel*); and next to her, Herman Shumlin (who had directed *Grand Hotel*) with his pretty wife, Diana. Next was Kermit Bloomgarden. I had written music for *Heavenly Express* in 1940—his first production, which was to be followed by so much of Lillian Hellman and Arthur Miller.

I was kissed by lovely Sylvia Miles, whom I had not seen. I first knew her during *Fanny*, when she was the wife of Gerald Price, the "Admiral." And Maureen Stapleton, one of our finest actresses and warm and affectionate. (I was suddenly reminded of the bad day with Monty on the bare stage of the Phoenix.) And beautiful Arlene Dahl, who had performed with me in Dallas two decades ago. And Tammy Grimes, who had been in Marc's *Cradle* when it was finally done fully. And Jean Dalrymple, who had used me on several occasions to conduct at the City Center, and Arnold Weissberger himself, who in his beginning had worked in the law office of my old friend Arthur Strasser when we founded the Arrow Music Press in the thirties. It was Arnold who had done the actual legal work of organization.

There were others, all gracious, whom I had known only slightly, the Leonard Lyonses, Mrs. Stravinsky, Emily Genauer, Geraldine Fitzgerald, Angela Lansbury, Peggy Wood, Tom Prideaux, Alexis Smith, and more.

A young man was introduced to me by Leah Salisbury, a talented director (she said) from the Long Wharf Theater at New Haven. His name is Arvin Brown. He was flattered, and when I said I would like to see their productions but found no late train returning to New York, he said he would have me driven back if I would call him.

He was I—forty years ago. What a lifetime—and so much of it there in a single room.

No one reading this must understand from what I write that I am unhappy about the inevitability of growing older. If I had the choice, I would not under any circumstances be fifteen or twenty-five or forty again. I went through these precarious times and came through with everything I could hope to gain from them—chiefly, some understanding of myself and my relationship to the world I live in. And some respect, some success, although not the kind of success I had dreamed of in the garden. The fact that this is so proves to me that no other way was possible for me.

Now I can hope passionately to write or compose or teach and, like Scheherazade, leave myself always with something more to say and to do tomorrow. Perhaps in this way I will stay around a little longer to do and say it. When this can no longer be, as inevitably it will not be, I will hope I remember that for me, in spite of everything to the contrary, it has indeed been a bright day. I have been blessed with the love of friends, the sometimes chameleonlike magical love, here and there, of those few who for the moment have been more than friends—and in the end less—and the family love that not nearly everybody else has enjoyed. And not least of all, the work, the desire to work, the ability and the need—nearly always knowing what it was that I wanted to do even when I was not able to do it.

My life includes today, as well as all the measured years that began with my birth. While all of it has contributed to making me who and what I really am, it was probably the profound experiences in my grandmother's garden and the fond lingering memory of them that truly created and sustained me throughout what has seemed to me, by turns, to be only a single day and very often an eternity.

Index